PRAISE FOR *Love* AFTER MARRIAGE

D1313029

Barry and Lori have keys to bring healing, breakthrough, and restoration in marriages. Their vulnerability and transparency are disarming, while the truth that they walk in cuts right to the core. They have a message of a powerful God who is capable of redeeming all situations and relationships, regardless of the history. The Lord is breathing on LAM (Love After Marriage) and we continue to hear testimony after testimony of the amazing fruits of their ministry.

Eric and Candace Johnson
Senior Leaders of Bethel Church, Redding, California
Author of *Momentum: What God Starts Never Ends*

Barry and Lori Byrne's impact on marriages is undeniable. God has raised them up in this critical hour where it seems that all hope has been lost for marriages. Everywhere we turn it seems as though another marriage has failed, and yet I believe God is restoring hope for marriage. Within this book is a refreshing and redemptive approach to love and commitment that will strengthen your own relationship with your spouse and release grace for your family. Barry and Lori's ministry is powerful not only because of the truths they teach but also because their lives are the very message. I thank God for Barry and Lori, and I know my marriage is stronger and healthier because of them.

Banning Liebscher
Director of Jesus Culture

Barry and Lori are some of the foremost marriage leaders of our day. The dramatic change in the lives of people they work with is consistently miraculous. These two create a level of intimacy, transparency and vulnerability between couples who have been married for years that is surprising to even those who thought they had a good marriage. I highly recommend their book and anything else you can get your hands on by these two gifted leaders.

Danny and Sheri Silk
Senior Management Team, Bethel Church, Redding, California
Founders, Loving On Purpose Educational Services

Barry and Lori Byrne have had an exceptionally positive impact on our culture here at Bethel Church. We have watched God use them to restore literally hundreds of marriages over the last several years. Their ministry is really unique. Their transparency is disarming, their passion is inspiring, and their own relationship is a powerful message to anyone who is living in a dysfunctional or boring relationship. *Love After Marriage* is more than a book; it's a training manual for everyone longing for an extraordinary love affair with their spouse and it is a marriage manifesto for couples that are interested in strengthening their relationship with one another. We highly recommend this book to everyone; whether you're considering marriage for the first time or you have been married for many years, this book will rock you!

Kris and Kathy Vallotton
Senior Associate Leaders, Bethel Church, Redding, California

Love
AFTER
MARRIAGE

*A Journey Into Deeper
Spiritual, Emotional and
Sexual Oneness*

BARRY & LORI BYRNE

Chosen

a division of Baker Publishing Group
Minneapolis, Minnesota

© 2012 by Barry and Lori Byrne

Published by Chosen Books
11400 Hampshire Avenue South
Bloomington, Minnesota 55438
www.chosenbooks.com

Chosen Books is a division of
Baker Publishing Group, Grand Rapids, Michigan

Chosen Books edition published 2015
ISBN 978-0-8007-2474-0

Previously published by Regal Books.

Printed in the United States of America

Library of Congress Catalog Number: 2015930784

Scripture quotations are from the New American Standard Bible,
© 1960, 1962, 1963, 1968, 1971, 1972, 1973, 1975, 1977, 1995
by The Lockman Foundation. Used by permission.

15   16   17   18   19   20   21   7   6   5   4   3   2   1

There is a movement happening in marriages. God is reclaiming what has been lost and redeeming what has deteriorated the family system, as we know it. When there is a generation of passionate husbands and wives, inevitably there will also be true fathers and mothers. And when there are mothers and fathers instilling an identity of love, acceptance and vision to a generation of children, the tares of destruction from the enemy will become the spoils of victory for the family of God. We dedicate this book to the restoration of marriages around the world.

CONTENTS

ACKNOWLEDGMENTS

We are grateful to:

Our Lord Jesus Christ, for Your abundant love and grace in our marriage and family. Thank You for letting us partner with You and for initiating this ministry through a dream.

Our four sons: Caleb, Jeremy, Justin and Brendon. You are the delight of our lives, and we are so proud of who you are and all you are becoming.

Barry's parents, Paul and Josephine Byrne, who modeled love and commitment in marriage so well.

Lori's parents, John and Grace Tebay, who laid a foundation of life and love in marriage. You have poured so much of God's love and truth into our lives, our marriage and our sons.

Our pastors, Bill and Beni Johnson. You constantly spur us on in our journey of intimacy with the Holy Spirit and continually equip and challenge us in the most amazing ways.

Danny Silk—you believed in us, stretched us and saw the vision for LAM long before we did.

Kris Vallotton—you have always been such an encouragement to us. Thank you for recommending us to the staff at Regal.

Dozens of friends who have diligently prayed for us during the writing of this book and who also pray regularly for the LAM ministry.

Our son Brendon, and Justin and Jessica Collins, for your indispensible contribution to this book by joining in the editing process. We couldn't have done it without you!

The hundreds of couples who have completed LAM workshops and who are carrying on the ministry in their marriages, their families and their churches.

FOREWORD

By Bill and Beni Johnson

Healthy marriages are living testimonies that reveal the nature and heart of God. When done correctly, marriages influence culture, help set values and priorities for generations, and create an awareness of the One to whom we will give an account of our lives. But when done incorrectly, they pervert and distort a nation's concept of God. They turn its focus to self-preservation, all while legitimizing things that were intolerable only a generation earlier.

The power of marriage is found in the beauty of unity in the midst of celebrated diversity. Two are only better than one if they are united; when they are divided, two are actually less than one. That is how this life was designed. Perhaps with that equation, we can see how a society falls so quickly into barrenness and loss. It's tough to survive when we go from *two to less than one* over and over again.

Barry and Lori Byrne have recognized the heart of God for marriages and families. In turn, they have put their lives out in front for everyone to see so that they might be a help to others. Their honesty and transparency are disarming and inviting, yet sobering. Theirs is a "no holds barred" approach to getting people well. And it works.

Love After Marriage has been born out of their journey for health in their own lives. The discoveries recorded in this book are sure to have a powerful impact on relationships for many years to come. This book is both inspiring and raw in all the right ways.

Good books provide insights to inform and stories to inspire. But great books, like *Love After Marriage*, give one more element that makes them potentially transformational in nature: tools. Simple tools, born out of wisdom, can help nudge the otherwise helpless couple into a time of life-changing discovery. This book takes the participant on a journey of discovering God, His goodness, His practical passion for us and all our relationships, His wisdom and the role we get to play. It is self-discovery in the right sense, without the shame or the "me first" attitude that nauseates us all. It is eye opening in an exhilarating way. It is an invitation to live—to really live!

These tools will successfully equip anyone who is willing to pursue healthy relationships. While the focus is on marriage, many of the tools will actually equip people for all the relational aspects of life. We must first be well, and then we must be the ones who bring a message of hope to the dying marriages all around us. We've been given the task of bringing tools to those who just don't know how to do it right.

Beni and I are amazed by the wisdom that God has given to Barry and Lori. Their Love After Marriage materials have been extremely effective in bringing wholeness and healing to couples—actually, more than we have ever seen with any other materials or events. The impact on our own church family has been phenomenal. We have seen the results that come out of *who they are* and *what they do*. It is amazing, a pastor's dream, really. People get well—really, really well.

Some who pick up this book may be thinking, *There is no hope in my situation*. This book could be a lifesaver, literally, for you and others who have been buried in an impossible marriage. The stories of couples who have come with irreparable brokenness and then opened up and received healing are an inspiration of hope. Read this book, and you will find help. And then, as a couple, partner with the Holy Spirit to see how life and hope can come to every area of your marriage.

If you are just getting started in life and want the right tools to have a fulfilled and healthy marriage, this book will help launch you into all that God has made available to you. It could save you years of heartache and set you on the greatest journey of your life.

Beni and I are happy to recommend this book. We are equally happy to commend to you Barry and Lori Byrne. They live this message, impart it, and have paid a price to make it available to us all.

Bill and Beni Johnson
Senior Pastors, Bethel Church, Redding, California

INTRODUCTION

We wrote this book because we want your marriage to be empowered directly by God through the voice of His Spirit. Listening for His voice and following it will make *all the difference* on your journey toward spiritual, emotional and physical oneness in your marriage.

Perhaps you feel that you and your spouse have a good marriage, but there are areas that need to be strengthened. You would like to go deeper and further in spiritual oneness, or emotional and physical intimacy. Or it may be that you are feeling discouragement about your relationship, thinking, *Marital happiness is for everyone else, but not for us. We've tried everything! Our issues are impossible to change. There is just too much history and hurt to risk hoping again.*

We want you to hear us clearly and unmistakably say: It does not matter what your experience has been. No matter what is in your history or your family line; whatever you've had or not had in life; whatever limitations, whatever amount of betrayal or violation you have experienced, we have discovered from our 32 years of marriage and through ministry to thousands of married couples that there is a way through every one of these obstacles!

Your spouse cannot make up for all of the pain and lack in your life, but Jesus can. He has placed within you a strategy to overcome everything that Satan has used to harm you. The question is, are you willing to continue to seek and believe for His redemption in your life and your marriage until you receive all you need?

The LORD says, in Isaiah 45:2, "I will go before you and make the rough places smooth; I will shatter the doors of bronze and cut through their iron bars." This describes who our God is. He breaks through the obstacles that are impossible for us. He will bring your breakthrough if you are willing to fully partner with Him. It does not matter how long you have been stuck or how bad your marriage has been, our God will do the impossible on your behalf.

Whatever your desire for your marriage, the Lord wants you to have breakthrough, and He will take your marriage to a higher level. He is inviting you right now to trust Him in this life-changing opportunity to lay hold of a marriage that is beyond what you can imagine!

Hearing God's Voice

Marriages get revolutionized as couples hear the Holy Spirit speak and follow Him. God wants to be intimately involved in your marriage. He is waiting for you to welcome Him in and listen to Him. His voice comes in many different ways, so you must learn how to listen from your spirit. By hearing His voice, you gain divine empowering for your relationship.

Hearing and obeying God's voice have greatly multiplied His presence and power in our marriage. After 20 years of following the Lord as adults, we encountered Him in an unexpected way that opened our spiritual ears to hear specific words about our lives as never before. Hearing His voice launched us into completely new realms of wisdom and revelation to know God and to flourish as one flesh.

We must know God's words from the Bible; that is our foundation for the truth. However, Jesus told us that His Holy Spirit, the Spirit of truth, would show us future things and He would reveal Jesus and the Father to us (see John 16:13-15).

As Christians, we talk about how important it is to hear God's voice, yet Lori and I have found that many couples are unable to hear Him for their marriages. As a consequence, these couples miss out on life-giving, supernatural aid available to them. Luke 1:37 says, "For nothing will be impossible with God." The Greek literally translates as "no *word* will be impossible with God." That means, whatever God says, He will make a way for it to happen. This makes hearing His voice so important, because once He speaks, all of heaven will support His words. Our job is to listen for His voice, hold on to what the Holy Spirit speaks and believe it.

We do not want you to be limited to our knowledge, experience and teachings. You will have many opportunities throughout this book to listen for God's words regarding you and your marriage. If you are not familiar with listening to His voice, you will have plenty of opportunity to practice and learn. We are excited for you to develop this intimate connection with the Lord.

It's Up to You

To get the most out of this book, you will need to do more than read through it together. If you diligently do the activities and homework, you will undoubtedly have some good, intimate experiences together, even if they come through some intense times of communication. But if you go beyond doing the exercises in this book and practice them regularly in your daily life, you can have a completely changed marriage! We have witnessed this numerous times.

We recommend that you set aside ample time each week to read through *only one chapter and complete the activities.* Through the remainder of the week, set aside time to do your homework. Take as much time as you need; depending on your specific needs, you may want to spend more time on some chapters than on others. Invite the Holy Spirit into all that you do and make praying together a regular part of your communication. Focus on understanding each other and becoming proficient at intimate, loving relationship—spiritually, emotionally and physically.

We bless you to receive all of the advancements, surprises and miracles the Father wants to give you as you fully participate in this marriage adventure with Him.

With love and affection,
Barry and Lori Byrne

PREFACE

Barry and I were lying in the back of a large, open, flatbed truck. In the dream, we were naked and making love. The truck was on my parent's street, in front of their house! I looked down the street and noticed that there were men on ladders, on both sides of the street, trimming trees.

Oh no! I thought. *They're coming this way, and soon they'll be able to see us!* With an added sense of urgency, I exclaimed, "We'd better hurry up!"

Watchfully keeping my eye on the gardeners, I realized that they weren't trimming normal trees. One of the trees they were working on was turned completely upside down so that its roots were exposed, pointing skyward. They were using chainsaws to cut off its roots. A few other workers were thinning out the branches of another tree and shaping the next, and on and on.

They were doing something different to every tree.

Then I woke up . . .

The Invitation

When I awakened from the dream, I pivoted in bed to look at the alarm clock: 5:30 A.M. What was I to make of this strange dream? Making love in front of *everyone* . . . what could that possibly mean? That didn't sound normal.

Barry was already up. He grinned at me, and I could tell he knew by the look on my face that I had a real God dream to share. Barry and I love sharing our dreams with each other. Usually, if one of us doesn't have the interpretation, the other will. I told him the dream and waited expectantly, hoping he knew what it meant. As he spoke his thoughts, I became ecstatic with the hope that this dream really was from God.

"I know exactly what it means. This dream is about the marriage ministry we've been asking the Lord about."

Barry went on to explain his thoughts. He believed it was an invitation to start a marriage ministry! Our lovemaking in the dream symbolized the fact that this marriage ministry would reach into the deepest depths of a couple's love and intimacy. God was inviting us to use our lives to bring His love to other married couples in an incredibly vulnerable and intimate way.

The trees represented the marriages we would help. Some marriages would require root work; others would need to understand each other more deeply; some would necessitate reconciliation; and still others would be desperate for helpful tools. Every marriage would cry out for something different, just as each tree needed restoration in its own way.

We realized that God would provide exactly what each couple needed, but we, and the couples, would need to be flexible to allow the Holy Spirit to bring His plans for restoration. He had plans and strategies to enable every marriage not only to survive but also to flourish!

It is interesting that Barry and I were not personally trimming the trees. We did not understand that aspect until later, but the workers trimming the trees represented the participants who would be in our workshops where every couple is placed in one of many small groups. During the course of the workshop, each group becomes an exceptionally intimate spiritual family. As a result, much healing occurs through couples ministering to each other.

When I exclaimed that we must hurry, it was an expression of the Lord's urgency and readiness to heal marriages, regardless of how hopeless they feel. It was a promise that couples that are ready to be completely honest and seek His answers for their marriage would see dramatic change.

The fact that this all took place on my parent's street was also significant. God has blessed my parent's marriage relationship. They truly love each other; but equally important is the fact that after 57 years of marriage, they continue to like and enjoy each other. They minister powerfully together, and at 75 and 79, they *still* enjoy their sexual relationship. By setting the dream on their street, God was informing us that this ministry would be built on the foundation my parents laid. The foundation represented the effort they poured into their own marriage, as well as what they have invested into hundreds of marriages throughout their ministry as faithful pastors. Fortunately, we have had a good model from which to learn.

As soon as the interpretation was out of Barry's mouth, the Lord began a download of ideas revealing what this marriage ministry would look like. We could barely write fast enough to keep up with all that He was giving us. When we had finished writing, we were so excited that we danced all around our bedroom. From the revelation in the dream, we knew that we were to create a marriage ministry based on what we have learned through our own lives—our history, our failures, our successes . . . and even our sex life, gulp! We knew that the dream was an answer to our prayer, providing us with more passion and strategies to implement His plan.

A few months later, Barry received the name of our ministry—Love After Marriage (LAM for short)—in another dream. Once again, God was directing us through a dream. We would never want to venture into any ministry without knowing that God was directing us. In *Matthew Henry's Commentary on the Whole Bible*, he states, "Divine direction is one of the best evidences of divine favor."[1] What an indescribable gift to be able to partner with the Lord when He gives us divine direction!

God's Confirmation

"What can we do about marriages in the Body of Christ?" was the ongoing question we had been discussing with Danny Silk, our Family Life Pastor at Bethel Church, in Redding, California.

At Bethel, we see the Holy Spirit moving in ways we had only dreamed about before. God is doing miraculous healings on a daily basis—not just through the leaders, but also through members and students of the School of Supernatural Ministry. Many people are experiencing great personal breakthrough by way of the inner healing ministries; and the gift of prophecy operates in most everyone. Inspired teachings are the norm. However, even with this supernatural activity, too many marriages were still struggling and not reflecting the same supernatural influence evidenced in so many other areas.

We wanted to help. Barry has been a marriage and family therapist outside and inside the Church for 30 years. On many occasions, we have counseled together, and I have years of pastoral experience using various inner healing methods. We could have done what we knew how to do and created a marriage ministry for Bethel Church. But we needed something else—a key for restoration of marriages that would go beyond counseling. We needed something that would attract God's presence and power. Without the God-factor, we knew it could end up being a lot of hard work with little return.

Marriage is a favorite target for the enemy's attacks. We hear from Christians and churches all over the world that marriages are suffering. Many are failing. Our enemy takes particular delight in destroying the very relationship Jesus used to describe His relationship to the Church—He as the bridegroom, and the Church as His bride.

When we started Love After Marriage, we assumed it would be "front line" work. Because the attack on marriages is strong and universal, we realized we needed prayer coverage. We approached a friend who is a powerful intercessor and asked if she would consider covering our ministry with prayer.

Surprisingly, she replied, "Oh, that is why . . ." She told us that the prior week, the Lord had given her visions of us in her home. Before we approached her, she prayed, "Lord, why are Barry and Lori in my house?"

The Lord told her, "I am doing something in Barry and Lori's love that will go all over the world, and I want you to pray for them."

She had already begun praying for us even before we asked! God was clearly moving, and He wanted to get our attention to confirm our decision.

This precious, obedient lady shared with us one more thing the Lord told her:

> The impact of the ministry would go far beyond simply teaching to imparting and passing on what He has given to us. He wanted us to give away every good thing He has taught us on our journey toward oneness and intimacy.

Even better news is that God wanted us to pray, release and impart to *you*. Over and over again, we have watched God impart abundant grace for intimacy to couples that are willing to receive it. Many eager, searching couples have already gone through the LAM workshops and come out with a level of spiritual, emotional and sexual intimacy they had never experienced before.

We do not want this book to be only informational. Like our workshops, we want it to be *an interactive experience between spouses*. We want you, as an individual and as a couple, to hear and receive directly from the Holy Spirit. Jesus is so excited that you are giving yourselves to each other and to Him as you work through this book that He will be "running out" to meet you. Your marriage and your oneness have been a priority on His heart for a long time. As you listen to Him and obey the things He's asking of you, you will be astounded at the ways He will move heaven to meet you.

Are you ready for that? We want to begin by praying and releasing to you all that He wants to give you as you read through this book together.

Our Prayer for You

Dear [insert your names here],

We call your spirits to come into a prominent place above
your body and soul. We bless you to trust the Holy Spirit to lead you into
all truth. We bless you with an unrelenting desire to know the truth that
will set you free—truth about your heavenly Father, about yourselves and
about your marriage. We release and impart to you an atmosphere
of safety, vulnerability and openness as you read this book together.
May the Spirit of God lead your spirits into a place of peace, rest and
transparency, with nothing to hide and nothing to fear.

Jesus, You know this precious couple; You knew every detail of their
lives while You were weaving them in their mothers' wombs. We ask that
you would begin releasing hope and expectation. Position them for the
breakthrough they need.

In the name of Jesus, we bless you to receive and hold on to
everything the Lord has for you in this journey of increasing intimacy
and oneness! Amen.

Note
1. Matthew Henry, *Matthew Henry's Commentary on the Whole Bible* (Peabody, MA: Hendrickson, 1996), Exodus 33:12.

Love
After
Marriage

1

GOD IS FOR YOUR MARRIAGE

"Tell her now," the Holy Spirit said to Bill. Sara and Bill were alone, eating dinner together on the first day of their Love After Marriage workshop. Bill knew without a doubt what he had just heard. He also knew this workshop operated in an atmosphere of complete openness and vulnerability. Although he was scared, he was even more determined to open up and share with Sara what the Holy Spirit had asked of him. But he hadn't expected to hear so clearly that *now* was the time to confess his affair with another woman. He knew in his spirit it was God speaking, and he was ready to do whatever the Holy Spirit asked of him.

Pushing through overwhelming waves of shame and guilt, Bill placed his trust in the voice of the Lord and proceeded to pour out the truth to Sara. Though it was not a full-on sexual affair, there was an ongoing emotional affair coupled with inappropriate physical contact.

Sara was devastated. She'd had a sneaking suspicion there was another woman, but she had never let herself believe that Bill was actually stepping over the line. She felt as though her life was crashing down around her. Stabbing feelings of shock, sadness, anger and betrayal swirled in her head like a dizzying tornado, leaving brokenness and chaos in its path.

At the end of the day, Bill and Sara told us about the tornado that had just ripped through their relationship. Bill said that he had already ended the illicit relationship and was only maintaining a "professional friendship" with the woman. We confronted him regarding the deception of maintaining this "professional" relationship and led him through a prayer of repentance. All the while, Sara was sobbing uncontrollably.

It was at this point, while Barry and I were ministering, that I looked Sara straight in the eye and boldly said, "If you think that all of this is only his fault, and you have no part in it, you will miss out on all that the Holy Spirit wants to do for your marriage this week." I couldn't believe what had just come out of my mouth! How could I have said something so direct and seemingly uncaring? Sara had just heard news so devastating that it felt as though her whole world was crashing in. Before I could back-pedal, she immediately stopped crying, quieted herself and gently nodded her head yes several times. I knew she had fully "gotten" what the Lord had me speak to her. We spent a few more minutes praying for them and then sent them home.

Throughout the following days and nights, the Lord came to this precious woman and spoke to her repeatedly, giving her understanding and perspective. She had recently received ministry to get free from a controlling, manipulative and critical spirit, which had been prevalent in her life for a long time. Now this darkness was again crouching at her door, desperate to find a home in her. She stood firm, giving it no foothold. When she recognized these old patterns returning, she repented immediately and asked her husband's forgiveness.

The Lord revealed, in a very loving, non-condemning way, that she and her husband had never really had a good emotional connection. She understood that this lack of connection made another woman an attractive alternative to the deadness of their marriage relationship. Although Sara had seen her husband as an emotionally unavailable workaholic, and he had acted out a violation of their marriage covenant, she still needed to understand how they both had contributed to the broken state of their marriage and how they both needed to be part of the restoration.

During this sensitive time, they also disclosed their painful information to their small group in the workshop. The environment of truthful, loving acceptance proved to be a healing balm and greatly aided in their restoration process. The prayer and prophetic ministry they received from the small group became a current of God's love and truth to give them hope for their future.

A couple of days later, they arrived for the morning session looking hopeful and excited. Sara was actually beaming! She eagerly raised her hand when we asked if anyone had a testimony about what God was doing in his or her marriage relationship. She stood in front of all of the workshop participants and revealed how deeply her husband had hurt her. Then she told how the Lord had graciously met her and revealed what she needed in order to be filled with hope for her destitute marriage. She was truly a walking transformation!

We were completely taken aback by this new woman standing in front of us. Her countenance exuded life and expectation. Throughout the week, as Sara and Bill listened to the teaching, the Holy Spirit spoke to them over and over again, bringing truth and love to each area of difficulty in their relationship. They continued talking, repenting and reconciling, while receiving ministry and prayer from their small group.

At the end of the five-day workshop, they stood together and declared before the entire group what great things God had done for them in just one short week. Bill was so touched that he wept for joy as he talked to the group. Sara was literally jumping around like a pogo stick, ecstatic about the emotional connection she and Bill were experiencing. They ended the week with great expectations for their marriage and a deeper spiritual and emotional oneness than they had ever experienced in their 31 years of marriage. God had pulled them out of the rubble and placed them on a rock of love and hope.

That was two years ago. Bill and Sara were overjoyed in all that God was doing in their lives, but what they didn't realize at that time was how God was equipping them and positioning them to minister to others in their retirement. Today, they are strengthening marriages as part of a leadership team in their church. In addition, God is leading them to develop a ministry to missionaries. Just a few days ago, a longtime friend commented to Sara, "There is such a difference in you two; you're a different couple. Now you're working together as one, as a team! It is easy to see there is so much more peace in both of you."

We love Bill and Sara's story because it shows the miraculous way that God has decided to show up in marriages. Even when faced with the utter despair of discovering a spouse's unfaithfulness, God used their situation to begin a process that transformed their marriage. In our Love After Marriage (LAM) workshops, God has always met any couple that cries out for His help, proving that nothing is impossible for Him! No situation is too far gone—no marriage is too devoid of hope—that God can't bring it back again!

With God Nothing Is Impossible

What is the state of your marriage? God created the marriage relationship. His passion is to make *every* marriage a living example of His amazing love flowing between two people in lifelong covenant. During the past three years, we have been privileged to witness hundreds of couples receive the breakthrough they were so desperately seeking. Here are just a few examples of obstacles God's love has surmounted. See if any of these sound familiar to you:

One woman told us that she did not love her husband; she was not attracted to him and was afraid that she had married the wrong person.

A couple wanted more for their marriage but didn't know how to go about getting it.

A man, addicted to porn from a young age, felt such despair, shame and hopelessness that he could find no peace with God or intimacy with his wife.

An exceptionally beautiful woman saw herself as fat and ugly every time she looked in the mirror.

A woman tormented by fear at a very young age turned to control and manipulation. This brought separation and rejection from the ones she loved.

A man reported that he had "lost his manhood" and was unable to perform sexually.

A woman felt emotionally disconnected from her husband. In her own words, she "went somewhere and was not able to remain present" every time they made love, every time she began to connect with God in an intimate way, and every time she heard truth.

A woman could not give herself to her husband sexually because of a rape that occurred in her teens.

A pastor told us on the third day of a five-day workshop that he'd been having an affair and hadn't told his wife.

One couple had never experienced emotional intimacy nor enjoyed sexual intimacy in more than 20 years of marriage.

A man had been sexually abused as a young boy. This had significantly hindered his sexual relationship with his wife, and he couldn't even allow her to lay her head against his chest.

A young woman, controlled by fear, had alarming heart palpitations every time she made love to her husband; the doctors said there was nothing wrong with her heart.

A wife had just ended an affair and felt hopeless that she would ever work things out with her husband.

A couple could not communicate or connect. As a result, they lived with ongoing frustration, pain and hopelessness.

A man experienced excruciating physical pain whenever he made love to his wife.

A woman hated her body and was afraid to be naked in front of her husband.

A couple on the verge of divorce had already separated due to persistent marital conflict, and they were living separately when they came to the workshop.

A young man who was completely shut down emotionally saw how it was hurting his wife but didn't know how to change or get free.

A couple came to LAM just to learn how to minister to other couples and discovered that God had greater things in store for their own marriage.

A husband and wife had a very good spiritual connection but couldn't connect at all sexually.

Each of these examples represents one or more marriages the Lord has touched, healed and miraculously restored! In later chapters we will tell you the outcome of some of these and many more stories of how the Lord brought His supernatural breakthrough and healing to couples. As we have watched the results of the LAM ministry, we have become utterly con-vinced that the Lord wants to change, restore and strengthen *every* marriage. Now He has asked us to put LAM in book form to bring transformation to your marriage! Because of all that He has done, it is with great expectancy and hope that we eagerly wait to hear about the things He will do in your marriage relationship. If God has done it once, He will do it again!

The Power of the Testimony

Our pastor, Bill Johnson, calls that "the power of the testimony"! Throughout this book we will share numerous stories and testimonies, because they *can release hope in you*. In Bill's book *When Heaven Invades Earth,* he tells an amazing story that demonstrates how the power of the testimony works. A little boy who suffered from clubfeet received prayer at a meeting. He had sores on the top of his feet because they would rub on the carpet when he tried to walk. After receiving prayer, this three-year-old boy was able to place his feet flat on the floor! Previously he had been unable to run, but now he began running around in a circle exclaiming, "I can run!"

Later, Bill Johnson shared this story when he was teaching on the power of the testimony at Bethel Church. A family in the audience that was visit-ing from another state had a two-year-old girl whose feet turned inward at a 45-degree angle, causing her to trip over them when she ran. When the mother heard the testimony of the little boy's clubfeet being healed, she said in her heart, *I'll take that for my daughter!* At the end of the service, she picked up her daughter from the nursery and found that her daughter's feet were perfectly straight![1]

We have watched the power of the testimony work to bring all types of healing—relational, physical, emotional, sexual and spiritual—as people believe for God's goodness to manifest in their own situations. We will release the power of testimony throughout this book. So, as you are reading together, step out in faith and believe God for what you need. The Lord is so moved by faith. It is His joy and desire to give good gifts to His children. He longs to give you His Spirit and the Kingdom so that your life and your marriage will reflect Him.

Working with the Holy Spirit

Paul tells us in Romans 8:26 that the Holy Spirit helps our weaknesses. As a young woman, I remember my dad preaching on this passage. The word "helps" is the Greek word *sunantilambanomai* ("to take hold of with another"), which creates the word picture of two people on either end of a log. Picture this: On one end of the log is the Holy Spirit, and you are on the other end. In order to break up the logjam and get your breakthrough as you go through this book, there will be a part of the log the Holy Spirit will carry for you; but there will also be a significant part that you must carry. Our mighty God will bring huge logjam breaks and wonderful miracles as you pursue Him for your marriage. But equally as important will be the things *you* must walk out as you partner with the Holy Spirit.

Hearing from the Holy Spirit

What does it look like to partner with the Holy Spirit? To start with, you must hear His voice. This is one of our greatest desires in writing this book and putting on the Love After Marriage workshops. We want couples to hear the Holy Spirit's voice regarding everything in their lives, especially for their marriages. He not only wants to speak to you, but He will also direct and lead you into all truth. Through this next activity, we'd like to give you an opportunity to hear from the Holy Spirit Himself about your marriage.

ACTIVITY

Put on some instrumental contemplative music (in future pages, we will call this "soaking music," where you listen and *soak in* all that the Lord speaks to you). Get comfortable. Have a pen and paper ready to write. Later, you can record your answers at the end of this chapter.

We bless your spirits to be in a prominent place over your souls and your bodies. We bless you to hear and receive all that the Holy Spirit reveals to you. Remember, He will lead you into all truth, and when you ask Him for bread, He will not give you a stone.

Okay, let's begin. Start your soaking music. One of you will need to read the following aloud and direct the time.

1. Close your eyes (so that you won't be distracted) and ask the Holy Spirit to help you remember a time in your life when you strongly sensed or felt His presence. This might have been a moment when He answered a prayer, gave you a dream, spoke

to your heart or met you powerfully during a time of worship. Maybe you just woke up one morning and felt Him near, giving you hope and joy. Whatever comes to your mind, ask Him to bring you back to that moment and experience it again. As you remember, allow your spirit to rise up with thankfulness to Him. Stay in this place of thankfulness for a few minutes. Now, let's move to number two.

2. Ask Jesus to be with you right now in this moment just as He was in the memory He just gave you. When you both sense His presence, go on to number three.

3. Ask Jesus, "What do You want to say to me or show me about my marriage?" Take as much time as you need to listen—it may be a few seconds or several minutes. Write down on a piece of paper what you hear.[2]

4. Share with each other what you just heard from the Lord. Spend time thanking God and praying together concerning the things He just showed you.

SIDE NOTE: If you have trouble praying out loud together and would like to overcome this, try the following four steps. Remember, God doesn't need you to pray with eloquent or lofty words. He just wants you to talk to Him about what is in your heart, like you would with a trusted friend who deeply loves you.

5. Each of you pray together silently, holding hands. Ask Jesus to help you talk to Him together out loud.

6. Take turns speaking out one sentence, telling the Lord what you are thankful for in your marriage. Start with His name: "Jesus, thank You for . . ." Do this three more times each.

7. Now take turns speaking out one sentence, asking the Lord for something you want for your marriage: "Jesus . . ."

8. Now go back and see if you can share and pray about what God showed you earlier. After you tell each other, take turns speaking a sentence, thanking the Lord for what He showed you, and just talk to Him about it. Start with His name, "Jesus, thank You for showing me . . ."

Sometimes your breakthrough to praying out loud may be as simple as just starting to do it. It may feel clumsy or unfamiliar, but as you resolve to do this and push yourselves, praying together will become a powerful offensive weapon. Your united prayers are ascending to the throne and accomplishing much!

We've found that many couples have trouble praying together and especially praying out loud. If you decide right now that you're going to pray out loud for the rest of this book, you will certainly gain some victory in this area. We are standing with you and praying for you as well.

HOMEWORK

Three times this week spend some time praying together. We like to walk and pray together in the mornings; but if walking doesn't work, figure out what will be the best for the two of you. This needs to become part of your lifestyle, so ask the Lord to show you how praying together can fit into your regular schedule.

Notes

(You will have a notes page at the end of each chapter to record thoughts, questions or revelation that come as you work through the chapters together.)

_____

_____

_____

_____

_____

_____

_____

_____

_____

_____

_____

_____

_____

Notes

1. Bill Johnson, *When Heaven Invades Earth* (Shippensburg, PA: Destiny Image Publishers, Inc., 2003).
2. We learned this activity from Dr. Karl Lehman. He calls it the "Immanuel Approach." For more information, see www.kclehman.com.

2

NOTHING HIDDEN

*Truthfulness and honesty need to be some of the highest values in my life.
If I am not honest with myself, I won't be able to be honest with others.
If I am not truthful with others, I will also end up deceiving myself.*

It was during a morning chapel service in high school that these thoughts
came to me (Barry), and I had no idea at the time how far-reaching their impact would be. I didn't recognize God's voice at the time, but looking back, I
know that He was speaking to me. Not only were these words burned deeply
into my heart so that I never forgot them, but they also became a guiding
force in my life. Granted, there have been moments when I have not been
100 percent honest, but truthfulness is a core value for me. As a result, I am
known for being very straightforward and, at times, too blunt.

In my desire to understand *truth,* I looked deeper into its biblical meaning. In the New Testament, the original word for "truth" is derived from two
Greek words meaning "not hidden" or "not secret." It seems clear that the
biblical idea of truth goes much further than merely not lying. If I am going
to relate to my wife in *truth*, I will not hide or conceal any information that
would affect or impact her. Unfortunately, many in our society, including
Christians, believe that we should hide things that may make a person feel
uncomfortable or create conflict. This idea sounds good, but it compromises
a basic characteristic of the Godhead. God is truth, and we are to become
more and more like Him as we are conformed to the image of His Son.

Hiding or altering important facts and feelings creates more relational
problems than it will ever solve. How does this play out in a marriage? If I
am reporting an event to my wife, the truth will lead me to be as accurate
as I can be so that she will experience the same thing that I experienced. I
will not exaggerate or understate things for my own purposes.

In 1963, a neighboring family invited me to go see the movie *Beach Party*. It showed girls in bikinis, which bordered on pornography in the minds of some people at the time. As a boy of 10, I cared little about girls in bikinis and thought the movie itself was really fun. After I got home that night, my mom and older sister questioned me about what movie I had seen. When I said, *"Beach Party,"* my mom commented, "It wasn't very good, was it?" I knew by her tone that she did not approve of the movie, so I instinctively replied, "No." The truth was, I really liked the movie, and in my 10-year-old mind it was not immoral to me. Unfortunately, I lacked the inner strength to say what I felt, and instead I chose to answer what I knew would make me acceptable in my mother's eyes.

As a couple, if you respond to your spouse out of fear in an attempt to avoid disapproval, you will create an environment that stifles your ability to know and truly see each other. But when you risk being honest, despite potential conflict, you set the stage for a safe and enjoyable relationship.

There can also be a temptation to avoid the complete truth by editing inward thoughts and feelings so that you are perceived in a particular way. For example, if I am asked whether I like someone that I find irritating, I may be tempted to offer what I believe is the "right" Christian response by saying, "Yeah, he's okay." I edited my stronger feelings of irritation and emphasized a minor feeling that he is okay.

A more honest response might be, "I am really working to get along with him, but there's something in his personality that rubs me the wrong way." We need to find a way to accurately and kindly represent our inner thoughts and feelings in all of life so that we will not be tempted to varnish the truth when it counts the most.

Truth and Love

Truth is never intentionally vague or elusive. However, we must remember to tell the truth in a loving way. Not only is this a challenge, but it is also an art that must be practiced and developed over time. Simply put, we are not born with wisdom and tact. Unfortunately, we often learn to tell half-truths rather than risk speaking the truth in love (see Eph. 4:15). When deciding how to proceed, remember that a "cold" or "hard" version of the truth is usually cruel, destructive and void of love. Often, people who pride themselves on being "brutally honest" are really protecting themselves from feeling. They focus solely on facts in an attempt to stifle emotions. Conversely, a humanistic love, which centers on another person's feelings regardless of truth, can be equally destructive. Neither brutal honesty nor protecting another's feelings at the cost of the truth represents God accurately, because He *is* truth AND He *is* love.

While we were conducting a three-day Love After Marriage workshop in Switzerland, we witnessed once more the powerful effect of speaking the truth in love. During our first session, we challenged the couples, as we always do, to open up to each other and talk about any significant hidden areas that had never been shared. The pastor of the church commented to us, "This is not normal for Swiss people. We are usually very reserved and closed."

The next morning, a 60-year-old woman asked if she could give a testimony in front of the group. She explained how she and her husband had been married for more than 30 years, and the previous day they had talked about things that had been hidden since before their marriage. She revealed the painful secret that she was sexually abused when she was a young girl. By sharing this with her husband, she exposed a lifelong secret that had constantly accused her inner thoughts and brought her shame. She concluded her testimony by saying, "Last night my husband and I made love. It was the first time in my life that sex was a beautiful thing rather than a dirty, ugly experience."

Because she faced her fears and confronted her hidden areas of shame, their marriage was catapulted to a new level of intimacy overnight. The lie of sex being shameful was gone! Her openness resulted in a freedom that permeated their entire relationship, even reaching into their sex life. She was finally able to enjoy the God-ordained beauty of their sexual union, *and* she was free to stand with confidence and share her intimate story of God's liberation, in front of a culture that loves to be private!

Now let's think about this; how could talking openly with her husband create such dramatic results? How could 50 years of shame and false guilt be washed away in one day simply by speaking openly with her husband? We find the answer in Ephesians 4:15: "But speaking the truth in love, we are to grow up in all aspects into Him who is the head, even Christ." When this couple chose to be truthful in a loving way, the shame and false guilt could not remain. This openness allowed the character and nature of Christ Himself to be released into the deepest parts of their marriage.

Being truthful in love is essential to our maturing and becoming Christlike. It is important to remember that not everyone will experience overnight changes as this woman did; but whether the change is quick or slow, being loving and truthful will make a marital relationship free, just as Christ intended. It made this couple's relationship what Christ wanted it to be: a place of love, freedom and enjoyment.

A Package Deal

A godly, loving marriage requires the qualities of openness, transparency and vulnerability combined with the presence of the Holy Spirit. Lori and I have worked to build our marriage and family on this foundation; these concepts and values permeate all of our teaching in Love After Marriage workshops. I'd like to share with you a few of the benefits that any couple can experience when living a truthful and loving lifestyle.

Freedom
There is nothing so freeing as living with nothing to hide.
While Lori and I were dating, it took us about one month to conclude that we really liked each other. Lori placed a high value on virginity and had faithfully guarded her sexual purity. So, after a couple of months, I decided that it was important to reveal to her that I'd had a sexual relationship with one of my girlfriends. I believed she needed to know since it was of such importance to her. I also needed to know if she could still accept me after learning this painful detail about my past.

By this time I *REALLY* liked her, so I felt very anxious as I made my confession. I knew this information had a lot of potential to negatively affect our relationship. I breathed a massive sigh of relief when I discovered that my past was not a problem for her. Not only was I relieved, but also Lori's response dramatically raised the level of respect and appreciation I had for her. She chose to focus on who I was, and not what I had done in my past. Had I hidden this information until after marriage, it would have laid a foundation for suspicion about my truthfulness and trustworthiness for many years to come.

> And you will know the truth, and the truth will make you free (John 8:32).

As a young married couple, Lori and I were learning to hear the voice of the Holy Spirit. We soon realized that the Holy Spirit wanted to speak to us about day-to-day details and, at times, reveal things that we knew nothing about.

One day, during Lori's quiet time, the Lord spoke to her concerning a young man named Matthew, an employee in the grocery store where she shopped. Lori began having "thoughts" that this young man was struggling with shame and infidelity. She knew nothing about him except that his wife had recently given birth to their first child, a little boy. It took Lori a couple of months of prayer and seeking to receive confirmation that it was truly the Lord speaking, and to find wisdom for a way to raise this topic with Matthew in a manner that would be loving and kind. At this time in her life, Lori was not accustomed to hearing from the Lord so clearly, so it was with much trepidation and uncertainty that she finally approached Matthew at the grocery store.

"Do you ever talk to God?" Lori began.

"No! God would never want to talk to me!" was his reply.

"Well, I talk to God, and sometimes He talks to me. Sometimes I get it right, and sometimes I don't."

"Why, did God tell you something about me?" Matthew asked, with apparent concern in his voice.

Lori took a deep breath and launched out. "I feel like God said that you are ashamed. God wants to forgive you and He wants to wipe your slate clean. I felt God say that you have had an affair in the past; you're not in one now, but you are contemplating it again."   .

"Who has been talking to you? How did you know that about me?" he said in utter shock and disbelief.

Matthew denied the infidelity but admitted to a methamphetamine addiction and to deep, longstanding feelings of shame. We later discovered that he also had a strong sexual addiction that had led him into situations and behaviors that confirmed what the Lord had spoken to Lori.

We began to meet with Matthew and developed a close relationship with him and his wife. When he gave his life to the Lord, things began to change. While we were helping Matthew and his wife become a family again, the Lord gave us His heart toward Matthew and led us to invite him to live with us, and our four boys.

During the next year, Matthew dealt with his drug addiction and became drug free for the first time since he was 14 years old! In his second year as a Christian, Matthew dealt with the stronghold of his sexual addiction. At the time, he was attending an early morning men's discipleship group in our home. One morning, he came to the group and excitedly announced to the men, "I'm a free man! I told my wife everything that I've been hiding from her! I have nothing left to hide!"

In a state of hard-to-suppress excitement, he said, "If someone had told me a year ago how freeing it would be to tell the complete truth, I would never have believed it!" Matthew discovered the freedom that comes from abiding in Jesus' truth and living it. Matthew and his wife were able to experience more closeness and freedom than ever before. To this day, he is still like a son to us.

Trust in Marriage

Truthfulness is a foundation for trust in any relationship, but especially in the covenant relationship of marriage. When you vow to take your spouse " 'til death do us part," you give him or her great power to influence you. This means you have the power to deeply hurt each other. At the same time, this covenant relationship has the power to bring a deeper experience of joy and love than any relationship outside of the covenant.

The primary way you affect each other is through your words and actions. If you don't say what you mean, or you don't follow through, your spouse will not be able to trust you. Each time you fail to do what you say, you betray your spouse's trust. Each time you misrepresent the truth, you invite doubt and suspicion into the marriage. Words that should bring clarity and confidence will become a source of confusion. Once married, everything you do and say will in some way affect your spouse—for good or for bad.

Before meeting Lori, I dated a young woman I considered marrying; however, there was something nagging me that I couldn't quite put my finger on, and it kept me from proposing to her. Near the end of our relationship, an issue arose that revealed that she had been misleading me by speaking half-truths. I felt completely deflated and betrayed. I risked everything by being open and honest with her, yet she could not honor me with the same vulnerability. Astonished, I declared, "You lied to me!" She confidently asserted that she had never *lied* to me.

It was at that moment I realized that her standard for the truth was different from mine. To her, concealing information was not lying, and so it was acceptable. In my eyes, her misleading me was far from okay. It fell short of my definition of truth and the words the Lord had spoken to my heart—"*Truthfulness and honesty need to be of the highest value in my life.*" My standard for truthfulness had to remain my highest priority. Knowing Julia's standard of truth made it clear to me why I had felt so confused and why it never felt safe for me to fully trust her. That relationship would never achieve the trust and intimacy that God desired for us as marriage partners. Likewise, if there are half-truths in your marriage, it will limit your ability to connect and will create an unsafe environment to trust.

It wasn't until meeting Lori that I understood what real trust was. As I got to know her, I came to the realization that I could trust Lori to be exactly who she said she was. I learned to have complete faith in her, whether we were together or apart, because I knew she was a woman of her word. Peace and confidence were my prevailing feelings on the day I married Lori, and they have remained throughout our 32 years of marriage.

Every marriage requires total honesty. We are meant to have the freedom of trusting our spouse's words without doubt or suspicion. This will bring about the joy and trust God has always intended for marriage.

Being in the Light
Hiding opens the door for shame, guilt, confusion and separation in a marriage.

After 28 years of practice as a marriage and family therapist, I (Barry) have concluded that the single most effective way to overcome shame is to bring shameful thoughts and feelings out in the open in a loving, truthful environment. It is natural to hide things that feel shameful to us, but hiding them will only make us miserable. When we share the things we are ashamed of and experience someone respond with God's truth, love and acceptance, we begin to see ourselves through His eyes of love. This breaks the power of fear that shame brings. Because shame is so destructive in our lives, it is just as important that we do not open ourselves up to someone who is condemning or accusing. This will open the door to more shame.

Often in my counseling, a person will say, "I have never told anyone this before . . ." It is unfortunate how many people live with shameful secrets. The guarantee of confidentiality in professional counseling allows many people to share things they never would have risked before.

Here is an example of how the enemy used hidden shameful life events to destroy a marriage; but when the shame was dealt with, the husband was released into an entirely new realm of freedom. Cliff came to me with his wife, Nancy, to get help for their marriage. Nancy wanted a divorce, but Cliff did not. I sat in my office with this couple and listened while Nancy calmly described how Cliff was emotionally unavailable, how he could not communicate well or understand her feelings. She insisted he was unable to emotionally relate with her. When I asked Cliff to respond to his wife's accusations, he sheepishly and repetitively said, "Yes, it's true." After a few sessions it was apparent things weren't adding up, so I decided to see the husband separately.

For the first time, Cliff spoke of his devastating childhood. His father left when he was very young, and his mother was an alcoholic. Cliff related how, when he was in first grade, his mom would go on drinking binges and leave Cliff with his 12-year-old sister to take care of him. In fear and shame, Cliff went to school each day with tattered clothes, a dirty face and holes in his shoes. He soon became a target for bullies. He was relentlessly teased and got into fights on a daily basis. At seven years of age, his life was a perpetual war zone. He had no safe place and no support. Cliff figured out how to live within this brutal system on his own. He realized that the ones who picked on the less fortunate held the highest place in the social hierarchy.

Out of sheer desperation, Cliff devised a plan he thought would change his world for the better. He knew of one other child who was worse off than he. Cliff brought a knife to school, thinking that if he could hurt this other, less fortunate boy, he would gain some respect. Cliff, who was caught before he could do any harm to the other boy, was labeled a "bad kid." At seven, his world was a swirl of confusion. Nothing worked and nothing made sense. People were all around him, yet he felt completely alone. School became a dreadful place to go five days a week; his academic performance deteriorated.

In third grade, Cliff's mother decided to send him to his father and stepmother in hopes they could help him improve. Cliff now lived in a new state, so he was able to attend a new school; but nothing changed. Living in constant fear, and feeling dead inside, Cliff just sat in the classroom, hating every minute, and put forth no effort. His teacher contacted his father and stepmother and scheduled a parent-teacher conference. The teacher explained how Cliff would not respond to any of her efforts to engage him. He was doing no work and putting forth no effort. His dad and stepmom gave him a pep talk, and he decided to give it a shot. Cliff was a very bright boy, and so his performance went from 0 to 100 overnight. He found that if he tried, the schoolwork was easy for him.

The teacher soon called another parent-teacher conference. Unable to believe that Cliff's improvement was genuine, she told Cliff's parents about the instant and dramatic change in his performance and proceeded to make a life-altering conclusion that was believed by all three adults:

Cliff must be cheating. Cliff's fragile balloon of hope popped. Once again he was seen for who he must be. Once again he could not count on the adults in his life to understand and support him. That familiar feeling of deadness overtook his spirit. He gave up.

The next nine years, from third grade until high school graduation, were torture. Cliff lived in utter confusion, feeling as if there was something terribly wrong with him, but he didn't know what.

Although the man who now sat before me was well liked, he lived in continual fear of rejection. We began to do some inner healing work through counseling. We invited Jesus to speak to him about his childhood, his emotional wounds and the conclusions Cliff had drawn about himself. For the first time, Jesus' love and truth were entering into these areas Cliff had hidden and been ashamed of for so long. He was seeing himself from God's perspective, allowing grace and acceptance into his heart. The Holy Spirit was replacing the lies of darkness with God's heart of compassion and acceptance toward him. These feelings of compassion and acceptance overtook the acutely familiar feelings of shame and inadequacy.

One day, Cliff came to counseling and said to me, "I have always believed that my life was meant for destruction and aggression; but the other day, I was driving when this thought came to me: *I was made to love and be loved.*" Hope and life flooded into the dead, hopeless areas of his heart and mind. Life sprang forth!

Soon afterward, Cliff began to see his marriage differently. He no longer blamed himself for everything, and he stopped taking ownership of his wife's problems. Shortly after these changes, he related some new information to me. For the past year, his wife had been leaving on most weekends to party with friends from high school. He had spent thousands of dollars on cosmetic surgery for her, hoping to make her feel happy. Instead, he only received accusation and criticism in return. As Cliff began to confront his wife and set some healthy boundaries, she was finally truthful with him and confessed that she had been having an affair.

As long as Cliff was filled with shame, he believed that he was bad and deserved rejection. He simply agreed with all of his wife's accusations. Her words only confirmed everything he already believed about himself. The Enemy used those traumatic, destructive experiences from his childhood to construct lies within Cliff's mind about his character and identity. As long as his painful experiences remained hidden, the lies of shame and rejection continued to do their life-stealing work. After being exposed to love and truth, the shame, guilt and confusion were gone. Now, with nothing hidden, Cliff could begin to love himself as God loved him.

Although Cliff's wife proceeded with the divorce, his personal fight against shame completely changed his life for the better. As he learned to love himself with God's love, he could love others better too. He felt much greater security and confidence at work. He became able to assert himself in healthy ways. He could stand against unfair criticism and blame. Cliff eventually entered into a new relationship. This new relationship was much different from his marriage, because it was based on mutual support, love and respect. For the first time in Cliff's life, he could finally rest and fully be himself in a relationship.

Security in Relationship

To have real security in marriage, it is important to give your spouse a complete and full picture of who you are. If you do not risk showing who you really are, you will never have the peace of mind that comes from knowing you are unconditionally accepted. You must be willing to share your inner thoughts and feelings and communicate your current feelings, not just information about the past.

A couple I recently worked with struggled in this precise area. Initially, it was a highly frustrating case because I could not figure out why Bill and Sue remained stuck and unable to make progress. We pressed through several tedious months in confusion before we discovered the key to their breakthrough. Bill's fear of losing his marriage finally pushed him to the point of entrusting his true thoughts and feelings to Sue. He had no deep dark secrets or hidden sins. The problem was not about shameful events from Bill's past. He was simply afraid to talk about things that he believed would cause him to look bad in his wife's eyes. This fear of rejection was so strong that he stubbornly continued to hide even when it was costing him his marriage. He would say the right words to convince his wife that he would change, but then he would deny even obvious failures because he was terrified of being rejected for admitting his mistakes. This pattern resulted in years of frustration for Bill's wife.

Bill loved Sue, and he was not doing horrible things; he just never found the courage to risk being himself, which was negatively affecting their relationship to a great degree. The answer to living with nothing hidden by being completely open with his wife was simple once Bill found the courage to do so. He broke through his fear of rejection. After opening up, it was not only Bill who felt the relief and security that having nothing hidden brings to marriage; Sue also felt hope that she and Bill would be able to connect on an entirely new level.

If you hide shameful events or feelings from your spouse, you will always be questioning what he or she would think if he/she knew how fearful, inadequate or insecure you really feel. Or you might be asking yourself, *What if he or she knew about some of the shameful things I have done in my past?* Until you are able to live with nothing hidden, you will not allow your spouse to know you fully. Hiding prevents you from being all that God wants you to be in your marriage. Your life and your marriage will be far less than it could be.

Living with nothing hidden should begin before a marriage. Openness should be flourishing in the midst of a healthy, growing relationship. You can't make a good, informed decision and feel secure about marrying someone if he or she is hiding important information. If you share all of the significant issues in your life, and you are received with love and acceptance, then you can rest and be at peace inside. You will feel secure because you are truly known and accepted. You will also have the confidence that your relationship is a place where you can openly share who you are without condemnation or criticism.

Please note that when I talk about feeling secure by living with nothing hidden in the context of marriage, I am assuming that the spouse who is opening up and sharing intimately is also trying to change any negative behaviors. When a spouse freely confesses to wrongdoing, but then does nothing to change, it actually creates greater pain, anger, distrust and betrayal.

A couple who has been married for many years and is raising a family takes a much greater risk in sharing hidden, critical issues. With any investment there is risk, but the greater the risk the larger the return. As well as the risk of devastation, living in true vulnerability creates the possibility of deep, meaningful connection. True emotional connectedness—security, acceptance and love—expressed within the context of marriage is one of the most prized possessions in this world.

Living in Faith

To live our lives truthfully and with love for one another is an act of faith, because we are trusting God and His ways, rather than our own schemes. When we trust God and His ways, we are demonstrating our faith in Him. When we trust Him, we can rely on the power of truth to bring God's freedom into our lives. Jesus said, "If you continue in My word, then you are truly disciples of Mine; and you will know the truth" (John 8:31-32). We only know the truth by abiding in Jesus' words. That is the only way to know the truth and the only truth that will set us free.

Jesus calls Himself "the truth" (John 14:6), and the Holy Spirit, "the Spirit of truth" (John 14:17; 16:13). Any time we are not living from Jesus' perspective, the foundation of truth, we are in some way connected to the father of lies, the devil. When we experience negative or painful consequences as a result of choosing to walk in truth, we may be tempted to quit. This is exactly the point where our faith in God's truth gets tested. To choose to speak the truth in love, even when there is great cost to us, confirms our trust in God's ways, rather than our own ways.

Are you willing to risk being truthful in love above anything that you fear or anything that you desire? God is truth. Are you willing to put God, His truth and His ways above anything that you fear or want in your marriage? Are you willing to go beyond your fears and desires and expose whatever needs to be exposed for you to be truly known?

Remember: Truth without love is harsh and destructive; love without truth lacks substance. It must be truth *with* love.

ACTIVITY

1. Share the best thing that happened to you today.
2. Share the hardest thing that happened to you today.
3. Share something the Lord showed you today.

HOMEWORK

Repeat the above activity on three different days this week.

Notes

_____

_____

_____

OUR COMMITMENT TO EACH OTHER AS WE WORK THROUGH THIS MARRIAGE BOOK

*Put on some soaking music and take a few minutes to read
the following commitment out loud with your spouse.*

I commit myself to fully participate in this marriage experience to learn all that I can for the further growth and maturing of our marriage. I am willing to be stretched, to risk and to step out into areas that are not normally comfortable for me.

I promise to make every effort to willingly and freely open up to you. I will not require you to "pull things out of me." I purpose to move toward living with you in a truthful and vulnerable way, withholding nothing of significance and concealing nothing of importance to the health of our marriage.

I will honor you by pursuing relationship with you and by taking the initiative to share things with you that would be important to you, to God and to the wellbeing of our family.

I invite the Lord to "expand my tent pegs" in the area of transparency and vulnerability, to increase my expectation for His highest in our marriage, and to teach me new ways of loving you. I ask Jesus to ignite a new passion in me for you and to give me a new desire to see you and love you as He does.

*Now join hands and look into each other's eyes, holding each other's gaze.
Remember the reasons why you said "I do" to each other.*

3

A DREAM OF HOPE FOR YOU

Soon after Barry and I decided to write this book, I found myself praying, off and on throughout the night, for those who would read it. (The Lord put you, dear reader, and your marriage relationship on my mind.) Whenever I got up to go to the bathroom or turned over in bed, I was conscious of the fact that I was asking the Lord to touch you and bring you the breakthrough you need in your marriage. Obviously, I do not know the specifics of your hopes or the changes and breakthroughs that are needed to bring your marriage into alignment with God's purposes; but He knows. And He wanted me to pray for you!

That same morning, I had this dream: I saw the golden figure of a person hanging on one of the walls in the center of our house. It was adorning the main wall of our dining room. I could not tell if the figure was male or female, even though the figure didn't seem to be clothed. The arms were opened wide as the figure held on to a large fishing net. This person looked like he/she was flinging the net out over the water, as someone might do when working on a fishing boat. There was no boat or water, only the golden figure and the net being flung outward. As I awoke from the dream, I heard the phrase "throwing out the net on the other side" in my mind. This is a very significant dream that was given to me to encourage you and give you some input for this season in your life.

Before I give you the interpretation the Lord gave us, we would like you to take a few minutes and ask the Holy Spirit to help you discern the meaning of this dream. When you have some idea in mind, share your thoughts with your spouse before you start reading again.

SIDE NOTE: The Lord loves to speak to us in so many different ways; dreams are one of them. Many times in our workshops we will share a significant dream one of us has had, then ask the Holy

Spirit to come and give people the interpretation. It is so fun when others share things about the dream that we hadn't thought of. It is also confirmation of the things we discerned. Often, the Lord will give us a dream that reveals the spiritual strongholds couples are struggling with in a particular LAM workshop. This is a tremendous help to us because the dreams give us insight we could not know on our own. We will talk more about dreams in a later chapter; but for now, we just wanted you to get your feet wet.

The Interpretation

Since "throwing out the net on the other side" is a biblical phrase, we went to the two Gospel passages of Scripture and read the accounts. Both times the disciples had been working all through the night, trying to catch fish, but they had caught nothing. They were completely exhausted and discouraged as they dragged their weary bodies up on the beach. They had tried every trick, every technique, everything they knew about this trade of theirs. Jesus said in Luke 5:4, "Put out into the deep water and let down your nets for a catch." In John 21:6, He tells them to "cast the net on the right-hand side of the boat, and you will find a catch." The disciples were probably thinking, *Jesus, we've tried everything already. We've gone deep, we've gone shallow; we've thrown right, we've thrown left; and still no fish. We don't think Your plan is going to work, but since You are the one telling us to try again, we will.*

I awoke from the dream with a strong sense that the Lord was speaking to us about marriages. Just as the disciples fished all night, trying everything they could with no success, we have repeatedly encountered couples who have been working on their marriages for years without achieving the breakthroughs they were seeking. Perhaps you are one of those couples who have "tried everything." You have gone to marriage seminars, tried counseling, read books and prayed; but you are still unhappy in your marriage. You may feel worn-out and want to give up. Possibly, like the disciples, it's been a long, hard, unproductive "night" for you both.

You may be feeling like everything in your marriage is a mess and you cannot sort it out. You may have only a few areas in your marriage that still need a breakthrough. Or you may have slipped into survival mode. Survival mode may keep you together, but over time, passion and intimacy disappear. Perhaps you simply feel that something is missing in your marriage but you don't know what it is. You are not alone. We have had numerous couples come to LAM as a last resort before separation or divorce. When we present our LAM workshops in the United States, as well as in other countries, we hear the same comment over and over again: "Our marriage really needs this!"

Whatever your circumstances, you have not lost all hope, because you have agreed to read this book. Reading this book is like throwing your net out again in spite of the fact that you have already tried everything you know to do for your marriage. Like the disciples, as you listen to Jesus and are willing to try one more time by working through this book with your spouse, the Lord will meet you. If you will both continue to hope, and put forth effort, we believe you will be amazed at what God will do for your marriage relationship. We are astonished at the number of times we have witnessed hopeless couples find intimate connection as they commit to the LAM process.

In the dream, I could not determine if the figure on the wall was male or female. The fact that the body was nondescript represents both husband and wife. The unclothed body speaks of the need for you and your spouse to be transparent and open as you read this book and do the activities. The golden figure and the golden net signify the refining process God wants to do in you. Some of this refining will be completed when you share about your personal issues that have contributed to your marital discord. As you go through this book, welcome this refining process by asking the Holy Spirit to help you take a truthful look at yourself. He does not convict you without bringing hope and power for change.

Though it may not be easy, the refining process will accelerate your and your spouse's journey toward oneness. If you have been in the fire for a long while, it is time for the refining process to be completed. It is time for your marriage, and all Christian marriages, to shine forth like gold to a lonely, desperate world.

A Miraculous Intervention

Bruce and Pam had been laboring hard to press through a long, dark season in their marriage without breakthrough. With only a mustard seed of faith and virtually no hope left, they obeyed the Lord's prodding and threw out the net one more time on behalf of their marriage. As you read their testimony and how spectacularly the Lord met them, allow hope and expectation to flood your marriage.

Dear Barry and Lori,

During the last several years, my wife and I had become so distant that we were like enemies. Our communication had diminished to a few short words about practical things pertaining to our schedule and our three young kids. I wouldn't dare to share anything from my heart for fear it would be criticized or made to sound like I was selfish or wrong. I am sure Pam felt the same.

For the entire 19 years of our marriage, we had been in counseling without seeing lasting breakthrough or change. We tried EVERYTHING! We fasted, prayed, studied the Word and served in the church. We sought counsel, prayed more, begged God, cried and yelled. We even tried leaving the house, giving each other the silent treatment and manipulation. We read books, called the elders, fasted more, prayed more, went on retreats and joined home groups and cell groups.

We thought perhaps more self-sacrifice, listening, waiting or hoping would be the answer. Eventually, the cycle always led to giving up, falling, getting up again, leaving again, yelling again, praying again . . . again, again, again, again . . . for 19 years. It just didn't work, and we knew it.

Despite everything we had done and kept doing, I felt that our marriage was destined to die, and I could do nothing about it. That was the most painful thing I could have ever dreamed up or imagined. Our marriage that once held so much promise was falling apart. The situation was devastating our hearts and the hearts of our three lovely children. We could only watch it decay and feel hopeless as the foundation crumbled beneath our feet.

To compound my frustration, I was trained as a psychiatrist. I had helped many other people sort out their lives, yet I was unable to sort out my own. Addictions, lusts and temptations overwhelmed me in my pain. I began to justify thoughts of having an affair, my struggle with pornography and the many other coping mechanisms I used. Every aspect of my life seemed unmanageable to me as guilt, shame and fear ruled my every move. My mood would swing violently from one side to the other, and I would cry for hours at a time. Over the past year, all I could do was weep before God in desperation as my hope continued to dwindle.

What I hated the most were the constant dreams of sex with other women that I had four to six times per week. I would wake up feeling sick with shame. I wanted so much to be a vibrant Christian and have a deep spiritual connection with God. Instead, every day I felt fresh wounds from the accuser as I woke from my sleep. I believed that I was perhaps the worst sinner I knew. My sleep became hell on earth. I tossed and turned all night long with dreams, anxieties, fears, worries and sweats. Even my health failed me as I began coughing for months at a time. It was only by God's grace that I did not lose my job.

With my spiritual, emotional and physical health failing, I made the decision to be completely honest with everyone and just be myself, as repulsive as I thought I was. I felt like God was happy with this, and that He said, "Now I have you where I want you." That is where LAM came in. Your unpretentious honesty drew my utmost attention. It started when a couple we met last year, who seemed to have suffered to a similar degree, told us about a workshop called Love After Marriage (LAM) that was really able to help them. As desperate as I was, I put aside my lack of faith in marriage conferences and decided to give it one more shot.

At LAM, I was blown away by the two of you! You were very real. I like REAL! I was amazed by the fact that you are older than us, that you have grown kids, that you are very different from each other and yet you have stayed together for 32 years. Intriguing! I was still wondering if you would start telling us what we had already heard many times before. Not so! You told me something VERY different!

You listened to my feelings without fear. You let me know that I was not alone and that my feelings were keys to understanding my spiritual struggles. You validated me. You didn't preach to me. You were honest and poured out your own struggles in a violently vulnerable way. You said things I knew were true in my heart but never heard a Christian say before! You had the guts to talk about truth without shame. You also recognized the indescribable impor-tance of opening your lives to us, which so often reflect our own.

In four short days, you performed open-heart surgery on both of us by acting on what God had given you to do. You obeyed God and went out into the world to set the captives free. You took a risk (a big one) by being leaders who would talk about sex and love in a spiritual way, as well as a human way. You did something that my wife and I had never seen done before in books or in real life; you married SEX and the SPIRIT of GOD. It was a key to unlocking our struggles, both personally and in our marriage. We loved God and wanted Him in every area of our lives, but we both had shame (especially me) that kept us utterly bound.

Even now, eight months later, I cannot believe the transformation that has come over my ENTIRE life! We have begun to truly experience what it means to have a marriage bed free from shame. I feel like we are children experimenting with the pleasures God intended for us to have. For so long we had hyper-religiously gone through the act of sex. No more. It's fun, alive, creative, free and (this is big for me) frequent. My sex dreams have disappeared for good and have not come back. I wake up feeling love for my wife and want to hug her instead of run away every morning. I have learned to connect with Pam in a way that is meaningful to her, and I am no longer put off by her need for my attention and approval; and she is not put off by my need for regular and frequent sex.

Here's another amazing thing. It is shocking and fascinating how this freedom has catapulted my sensitivity to the Spirit of God. I have a new willingness to be open to the leading of the Spirit. I have more confidence in my walk with God, which excites Pam immensely. I am now more willing and able to be the spiritual leader she always wanted me to be. Now that my shame is gone, I have room in my heart for God and His precious Holy Spirit. It is a wonder to me to look in hindsight and see how much of my life was filled with shame and how it prevented the work of the Spirit within me. WOW!

We are now praying together regularly, and I really love to pray with her. That's a BIG change! We have given up the religious regimen that was critical and demanding. We have replaced it with a love that is kind, trusting and accepting. We no longer need to compete as rivals; we are finding spiritual unity in our daily lives and seeing that God can, and will, use us together as a team. We now end our struggles by sharing our feelings about a situation, which results in each of us feeling heard and understood. This is no small miracle, because feeling heard was one of our biggest, deeply rooted issues!

We could go on and on, but to sum it up, God has used LAM in our lives to do a miracle. We are blown away when we think of the degree of transformation that took place in four days. I have to be honest and tell you that I would never have believed it was possible. Our marriage was saved by your willingness to go where few couples would dare to go.

Thanks be to Jesus!
Bruce and Pam

Prayer

In the name of Jesus, we bless you to receive the hope released to "throw the net out on the other side" one more time. Even if you have done all you know to do, Jesus still has something supernatural waiting for you. We bless you to have courage to embrace the purification process as you listen to and obey the Holy Spirit's leading. Thank You, Jesus, that when we willingly follow and obey You, You give an abundant, miraculous catch over and above what we would expect!

"Behold, I go forward but He is not there, and backward, but I cannot perceive Him . . . He turns on the right, I cannot see Him. But He knows the way I take; when He has tried me, I shall come forth as gold" (Job 23:8-10).

ACTIVITY

1. Write your answer to the following question: What would you like the Lord to do for your marriage as you read this book?

2. Share what you wrote with one another.

3. Go for a walk, hold hands and pray for the Lord to do what you are asking of Him.

4. Ask the Lord to bring you hope.

5. Spend the remainder of the walk praying prayers of thankfulness.

HOMEWORK

As you walk and pray three times this week, continue to ask God to give you His hope for your marriage to bring about the answer to your prayers.

Notes

_____

_____

_____

_____

_____

_____

_____

_____

_____

_____

_____

_____

_____

_____

_____

_____

_____

_____

_____

_____

_____

_____

_____

_____

_____

_____

4

GOING DEEPER IN YOUR COMMUNICATION

One of the most common reasons couples come to a Love After Marriage workshop is because they lack emotional connection with each other. They have lost the enjoyment of talking with and learning about each other. Their spouse is not the trusted friend they share everything with. This usually results in a feeling of loneliness and boredom in a marriage where husband and wife have become more like roommates than lovers.

When two people are romantically interested in getting to know each other, they usually love spending time talking, listening and learning about each other. All too often, after marriage and children, communication gets consumed with the *business* of life and a couple stops sharing personally, and therefore stops learning about each other. They talk about work, the children, and their schedules. Who's going to pick up the kids from school? Who's going to take them to basketball practice? Who can take them to their dentist appointment? They talk about finances—can we afford to buy a house or new furniture for the house, or buy a bigger house? They talk about things they want to purchase. They talk about the neighbors, church, vacation plans, but seldom do they take time to talk personally about each other.

I remember a Christian couple that came to me for counseling early in my counseling practice. They were not angry or mean to each other. They were not hopeless about their marriage. They just needed to connect better. Their problems seemed minor compared to other couples that came to counseling filled with anger toward each other. We would talk through their problems during counseling, and they seemed to understand one another.

Because I was a new counselor, and idealistic, I falsely assumed they were working on communicating like this at home. But after a few months of counseling, nothing seemed to be changing. I asked them a question:

"How much do you talk together about these issues outside of your counseling session?"

"We don't," they replied. "We only talk about day-to-day issues."

They were good at talking about what I call the *business* of life. But they were missing the best part! They were living together, but they were virtually alone. They had stopped connecting on a personal level. They were no longer continuing to learn about each other.

For many of us, and especially for men, it is not natural to listen well. A few years ago, I was talking with my sons, when one of them commented, "Dad, I'm surprised that you can listen to people all day long in your counseling because you don't like small talk."

I had already thought about this. It's true, I am task oriented, but I really care about people and I like to help people. People come to counseling specifically for help with their problems. Because I have a clear purpose when counseling, I can listen to people all day long, but I struggle to listen well when people are simply talking. This is not a trait I am proud of. My wife and I do talk a lot about what is going on inside of ourselves, but she is much better at it than I am.

ACTIVITY

Take a couple of minutes and ask yourself the following question: "How well do I do at listening and sharing on an intimate, personal level?" Rate yourself on a scale from 1 to 10, with 1 being the worst and 10 being the best. Share your answer with your spouse and why you chose that number. Answer only for yourself; you will not be rating each other. You can give feedback to your spouse *only* if he or she asks you to!

Ideas for Going Deeper

Here are some ideas to help you get to more personal, intimate communication as you move forward in strengthening your marriage.

1. Talk About Your Dreams and Hopes

Talk about the things that excite you—especially the things that persist in your thought life. Did you know that it may very likely be the Holy Spirit putting those exciting ideas in your head? You need to pay attention when you feel enthusiastic about something. The first definition for the word "enthusiasm" in the *Merriam Webster Collegiate Dictionary* is "belief in special revelations of the Holy Spirit." The origin of the word "enthusiasm" comes from two Greek words meaning "in-God." Pay attention to your thoughts that come with excitement, especially thoughts that persist; it may be the Holy Spirit giving you important information about you or your spouse.

I'll never forget a comment my father-in-law made many years ago. He said, "Whenever I hear one of my children get exceptionally excited about something, I really pay attention, because it may be revealing a key part of who they are." You need to pay attention to enthusiasm in yourself and talk about it. Talking through the feelings with your spouse and getting input is a good way to distinguish whether it is God speaking or just your flesh wanting something. Either way, it is important to know the difference, and to share with each other. Lori and I continually do this, and our times of sharing dreams that the Holy Spirit puts in our hearts are some of our most cherished connections. Sharing our hopes and dreams with each other keeps us united as we work out our future together.

2. Talk About Your Purpose and Destiny as a Couple in These Last Days

It is so easy to be led by the tyranny of the urgent that we lose the big picture and our actual spiritual purpose in life. We all need to do daily life well, but God has much more than this for us as couples. Remind each other of the prophetic words that have been spoken and confirmed in your life. Talk about the higher goals that God has for you as a couple. Seek God's direction together. It is tremendously unifying to hold to common spiritual goals.

3. Talk About Revelations the Lord Is Speaking to You

Open up and talk about the things the Lord is speaking to your heart. It may be things He speaks during your Bible study time, during Sunday morning worship or as you go about your day. Don't talk in an intellectual way, spouting truths that you know but are not living. Talk about the things the Lord is showing you personally about Him and about you. As you think of important revelations while you are away from each other, make a note on your calendar or put an alert on your phone to remind you to talk to your spouse when you return home. Sharing revelations the Lord is speaking keeps you focused on His direction for your life and your marriage.

4. Talk About Things You're Learning

It is okay to talk about things you're learning at work or at school, but intimate relationship is built by sharing from your personal experiences. Don't wait until you've learned what you need to learn and then announce to your spouse what you have learned. Talk about what you are learning while still in the process. Let them support you in the process. It is much more vulnerable to share while you are still learning than it is to share afterwards. The Lord often tells us to share our learning experiences in the LAM workshops as we are still going through them. It is very vulnerable and humbling at times, but it is also a powerful tool to bring change to others when we are in the midst of dealing with an issue in our own relationship.

5. Share Dreams from the Night Before and Talk About Interpretations

We regularly write down our dreams that we feel are from the Lord, even if we don't understand them at the time. God wants to speak to us and instruct us in our sleep, but as was spoken to Job, no one notices it: "Indeed God speaks once, or twice, yet no one notices it. In a dream, a vision of the night, when sound sleep falls on men, while they slumber in their beds, then He opens the ears of men, and seals their instruction, that He may turn man aside from his conduct, and keep man from pride" (Job 33:14-17). You must learn the language of the Spirit in order to understand dreams; it is a tragic loss to ignore any way that God wants to speak to you. In a later chapter, we will share how God has led us to make major life decisions for our family through dreams.

6. Review and Discuss Prophetic Words You Both Have Had

A prophetic word is an invitation to walk into the calling of God that is much bigger than you are. Prophetic words carry with them the enabling power of God to accomplish things you could never accomplish on your own. Abraham, the father of our faith, received the promises of God because he wanted them, and because he believed for them when everything in his life was going the opposite direction of God's words to him (see Rom. 4:18-21). In 1 Timothy 1:18-19, Paul tells Timothy to fight the good fight of faith by using the prophecies that had been spoken over him. We need to do the same thing as the men and women of faith who have gone before us. What better way to strengthen your spouse's faith than by encouraging each other to believe in the prophecies God has spoken to you?

7. Talk About Your Children, Family and Friends in a Meaningful Way

It is easy to get in the habit of talking about the problems of the people closest to us instead of talking about what is good and about what God is doing in their lives. As parents, you provide a spiritual covering for your children. It is extremely rewarding to identify and bless what God is doing in your children. It is also important to be aware of ways that the Enemy is coming against your children and stand together with them against his schemes. It is too easy for your conversation about family and friends to be driven by the things that frustrate you. Choose to make your conversations edifying and life giving.

8. Talk About How You Are Feeling—Good or Bad

Talking about feelings adds another vital dimension to communication in your marriage. It is not healthy to allow feelings alone to dictate your choices and behaviors; however, communicating your feelings to each other brings a deeper level of mutual understanding. Women generally have a deeper need to have their feelings understood than men do, and they generally possess greater skill in communicating those feelings. Women who are patient can help their husbands who want to develop this skill. When Lori and I did our first LAM workshop and spoke about communicating feelings, a man came up to me afterward and said, "It would help to have a list of feeling words, because I can't think of them even when I try." So we have put together a simple list of feeling words at the end of this chapter to help you get started practicing.

9. Talk About How You Are Doing Spiritually

As we will talk about in detail later, the Enemy loves to divide and accuse people. When you begin to recognize what he is doing, you can stand together against him instead of being used by him to accuse each other. Talk about what you are struggling with spiritually and where you are growing spiritually. Learn to create a safe and comfortable environment for each other to share where you are at spiritually.

10. Talk About What You Appreciate About Each Other

Many times, I have heard men say that they think about how much they appreciate their wives when they are away from them, but somehow they never say it out loud when they are together. Speaking kind, tender words to each other feels just as vulnerable as opening up about shameful areas in your life. If there has been considerable emotional wounding in a marriage, without reconciliation and restoration, it may be very difficult to open up and speak tender words to each other. You must not let unresolved hurts keep the tender and kind words out of your marriage when these words are meant to promote deep trust and closeness.

11. Pray Together
Although this is last on the list, it is by no means the least important. Lori and I have been consistently walking and praying together (about five times per week on average) for the past 22 years. We walk, pray and talk together. We pray for our marriage. Sometimes we end up working through an argument. Many times we pray through spiritual battles we are experiencing. Every morning we talk about and pray through challenges or victories concerning our boys and discuss what God is doing in their lives. We love to pray for our church leaders, our spiritual kids, our families and our neighborhood. We just talk to God about what's most present in our hearts at the time. As we talk freely with Him, there is something that powerfully joins our spirits as well.

We happen to love to pray while walking, which also gives us some of our physical exercise for the day. Find whatever works best for you, but be sure it is something you can easily incorporate into your everyday routine. Maybe you are coffee drinkers, so your prayer time can be out on the front porch or in front of the fireplace having coffee together. Be creative. Just make sure your prayer time is meaningful and consistent. Soon you will be looking forward to it and missing it when you cannot pray together!

Listening Exercise
Take some time now for each of you to practice the *Listening Exercise* in this section. There is a list of feeling words at the end of the exercise to help.

> *The purpose of this exercise is simply to connect with your spouse by understanding each other's words and feelings. When responding to your spouse, try to use individual feeling words as much as possible, rather than long, wordy explanations. Fixing problems or giving advice is not allowed. There is a time for problem solving, but this is not it! The husband will go first, and then repeat the exercise with his wife sharing an issue.*

1. Husband: briefly describe one part of an issue—up to 20 seconds maximum and only three or four sentences. Talk about anything going on inside of you. It could be about your marriage relationship or any other situation or issue of significance to you. (If needed, use the list of *Feeling Words* provided at the end of the chapter to describe how you are feeling.)

2. Wife: listen for what your husband is *saying and feeling*.

   a. After your husband talks, your job is to respond with words that let him know you understand him, what he is feeling and why this is important to him.

   b. Once you have responded, ask for feedback to find out how closely you understood him.

   c. If you did well, your husband should let you know that he felt understood by you.

   d. If you did not understand him well, ask for more explanation (a maximum of 10 to 20 seconds) and try responding again.

   e. Continue this process until your husband can say, "Yes, you understand me and know how I'm feeling."

3. Ask your husband to let you know how it felt to be listened to and understood.

When each of you has done this correctly—both of you have been the one who is sharing and the one who is listening—this exercise will lay a solid foundation for selflessly understanding one another with the capacity to deeply touch the person who is sharing.

Feeling Words

If you have trouble expressing what you are feeling, use some of the words from this list. You can go online and get a more extensive list if needed.

Affection
close   loving   passionate   sexy
tender

Anger

annoyed	bitter	enraged	frustrated
furious	hateful	indignant	
infuriated	irate	irritated	
livid	offended	ticked off	

Doubt

defeated	distrustful	dubious	helpless
hesitant	hopeless	powerless	skeptical
unsettled			

Eagerness

anxious	enthusiastic	excited

Fear

apprehensive	fearful	frightened	horrified
nervous	petrified	scared	terrified
threatened			

Fearless

bold	brave	courageous	daring
determined			

Hurt

aching	afflicted	betrayed	crushed
distressed			

Happy

amused	carefree	cheerful	delighted
ecstatic	elated	excited	exhilarated
joyful	playful		

Interested

curious	excited	fascinated	intrigued

Sad

choked up	disappointed	discouraged	heavy-hearted
low	sorrowful	unhappy	

HOMEWORK

Repeat the *Listening Exercise* three times this week, with both you and your spouse sharing something important that is going on inside of you.

Notes

5

OVERCOMING SIN AS A SPIRIT

Hector struggled to thrive in an environment of violence and poverty while growing up in a barrio of Orange County, California. Our son Jeremy had attended kindergarten with Hector. Even as a young boy, Hector's innocent young eyes witnessed much violence, both inside and outside of his home. He disclosed stories of his father's alcoholism and rage, and shootings and deaths he had witnessed on the street where he lived. This was simply "normal life" to Hector. After the sixth grade, Jeremy and Hector attended different junior high schools. As a result, Hector had no regular contact with our family except for an occasional visit to our home.

Years later, while Hector was in college, we ran into him working at a local restaurant. We talked a bit, catching up with each other, and then Hector asked, "Do you know anyone I could talk to about God . . . like a pastor or something?"

We couldn't pass up this opportunity, and said, "We would love to talk to you about God. Would you like to come over for dinner?"

Later that week Hector sat with our family at our dining room table and talked about his life. Hector was living a "party" life at the time. He drank a lot and was sleeping with a lot of girls, but what bothered him was a growing anger inside. It scared him. He said, "I'm really a nice guy, but I'm afraid that my anger is going to take over and make me do something I don't want to do. I'm afraid I'm going to really hurt someone."

We began to talk to him about how Jesus loves to help people with emotions like anger. After considerable discussion back and forth, we asked Hector, "Would you like to ask Jesus to be in charge of your life so that He can help you with your anger and any other things that you need?"

"Absolutely!" was his immediate reply.

We moved from the dining room table to the living room sofa, where we could pray. Lori sat on one side of Hector, and I sat on the other so we could lay hands on him as we prayed. I led him through a prayer to confess sin and receive Jesus into his heart. Then I asked, "What are you feeling inside?"

Hector hesitated for a moment and then said, "Well, I don't want to scare you, but I feel like choking you right now."

That was not what I was expecting. Fear flashed through me for an instant and then the Spirit spoke: *Of course he wants to choke you. The Enemy wants to shut you up. You just gave him the keys to be free from the realm of darkness and a spirit of rage!*

I composed myself and calmly repeated what I had just heard from the Lord. Then I asked, "Can Lori and I pray for you about this rage?" Again he eagerly agreed. Together, we simply bound the spirits of anger and rage and then commanded them away from Hector, in the name of Jesus Christ.

A second time, I asked Hector what was going on inside of him. With a calm excitement, he said, "I always wondered if God was real. Now I know He is; the anger and rage are gone!"

What Hector experienced was a spiritual exchange. A spirit of rage (which he did not want) was exchanged and replaced with the fruit of the Holy Spirit (peace and faith). What a great exchange! Hector still had many things to learn and to walk out, but the spiritual realm of darkness manifesting as anger and rage had been torn down and replaced with the Spirit of God.

When Hector came to us that night, he was feeling much more than "feelings" of rage; there was a *spirit* of rage trying to control him. There was a power behind the feelings that came and bothered him. All of his effort and desire for the rage to leave did not make it go away, but the power of Jesus' name made it go. Hector had a responsibility to guard what God had done in him when He delivered him from the spirit of rage. He could choose to refuse the anger, or he could choose to listen to rage the next time it spoke and tempted him. Hector was not "demon possessed," but rage did have a stronghold in his life that needed to be dealt with. It was working on the inside of him, and he could feel that rage wanted expression through physical violence.

Spirits and Feelings

It seems that when we get our outside behavior cleaned up, the Enemy works even stronger on the inside, attacking our minds. Every day we must deal with various spiritual temptations that come against us: frustration, anger, discouragement, disappointment, fear of the future, fear of what others think, anxiety, worry about things out of our control, pride, selfishness, depression, hopelessness, and so on. These and many other spiritual forces assault people daily, and sometimes numerous times a day.

These experiences are common even to believers who are sincerely trying to walk by the Spirit of God. No worries. Do not allow the work of the Enemy to cause you fear. There is always a way to overcome whatever the Enemy throws at you. In the next chapter we will teach you simple but divinely spiritual weapons that, if practiced diligently, will make you an overcomer too.

You may be thinking, *Now wait a minute, I thought that fear, anger, worry, anxiety, depression, hopelessness and the like were* feelings, *not* spirits.

Well, they are experienced as feelings, but most of the time the source of these feelings is not within us, but outside of us. One of the reasons I believe these feelings originate outside of us is that so many people experience these feelings in spite of years of painful and arduous effort to get rid of them. The feelings come to us without us choosing them. They come when we don't want them at all, and even when we are fighting hard against them. They do not leave just because we want them to leave. They have a power of their own.

Many times our negative, tormenting feelings reveal the fact that we are dealing with a spiritual force of darkness, such as anger, fear, worry, depression, discouragement or hopelessness. We must learn to recognize the origin and fight the right battle. If we are fighting against ourselves when the source of our battle is spiritual, we will only end up going around in circles and feeling defeated.

Personal Experience

I (Barry) have had to battle with anger in my life. I am not physically violent, and I do not yell or scream at my wife or children. I do not cuss, or call them names. But I would, all too often, become irritable and grumpy to such a point that the rest of the family would want to stay away from me, especially when I was working. I was impatient and no fun to be with.

When I started practicing some of the spiritual principles we will explain in the next chapter, my temper began to change. It was a gradual process over a couple of years, but I became much more patient. One of the greatest compliments I have ever received was from my son Justin. One evening, about 10 years ago, our family was standing in the kitchen talking together when Justin unexpectedly remarked, "Dad, I'm glad that you learned about dealing with sin as a spirit. I have watched you master your anger." Wow! That felt so good to hear from my son! He could see the difference in me. I love it when people can see a change without our needing to speak a word.

Understanding Sin as a Spirit

Is sin first a spirit, or is it first a behavior? The first time the word "sin" is mentioned in the Bible occurs in Genesis 4, when God is speaking to Cain about his anger toward his brother, Abel. God accepted Abel and his offering, "but for Cain and for his offering He had no regard. So Cain became very angry and his countenance fell. Then the LORD said to Cain, 'Why are you angry? And why has your countenance fallen? If you do well, will not your countenance be lifted up? And if you do not do well, sin is crouching at the door; and its desire is for you, but you must master it' " (Gen. 4:5-7).

The Lord explained to Cain that he had a battle against *sin*. God did not say to Cain, "You have sinned and need to repent." The Lord further described *sin* as an intentional, purposeful, crafty creature that had plans for Cain—"its desire is for you." God made it clear that sin was coming to Cain in the form of anger. Someone was going to win this battle—either Cain or sin. The Lord told Cain he "must master" the sin that was crouching at his door.

As we read the story, we find that Cain did not master sin when it tempted him; sin had its "desire" with Cain. Sin's desire was to turn Cain's anger into a murderous rage. Sin led Cain to kill his brother, which describes the nature and work of the Enemy, who steals, kills, and destroys the abundant life the Lord offers us (see John 10:10).

Sin began working in the world when Adam and Eve invited it in by obeying the voice of Satan. Sin, as a spiritual force of anger, led Cain to do Satan's handiwork. The Lord was warning Cain that his battle against sin began when he was tempted with feelings of anger. Up to that point, Cain was not yet guilty of sin. It was only after Cain failed to master sin's temptation and acted according to the temptation that he became guilty of sin.

It is important to recognize sin first as a spirit coming against you, and secondly as a behavior. Overcomers learn to resist and master sin when it comes in the form of temptation so that they don't act according to the temptation and then need to repent. The more we learn to recognize and master the work of sin when it comes to us as temptation, the less we will need to repent.

Spiritual overcomers do more and more *resisting* of temptation, which results in less and less *repenting*. I am talking about the internal temptations of our minds, as well as the temptations to act out sinful behaviors. We can be tempted in our minds with fear, anger, hatred, anxiety, hopelessness, depression, despair or worry that never get acted out in sinful behaviors. But these internal attitudes will stop us from living in the freedom and the fruit of the Spirit that God desires for us.

There is no guilt in being tempted, but we must recognize our spiritual battle, which begins when we are tempted. Jesus was tempted in all things as we are, yet He never sinned (see Heb. 4:15). If we set the standard that we have overcome when we are no longer tempted, then we place a higher standard on ourselves than God placed on Jesus. If we accept the idea that a "mature Christian" is not tempted, we will either live in constant condemnation because we know we are tempted, or else we will reduce our Christian life to a few rules we can keep in order to feel good about ourselves. We will also probably pride ourselves in recognizing others' faults while remaining blind to our own.

Since we are all tempted, it is what we do when we are tempted that truly matters. We must focus on finding a godly response to temptation, rather than trying to eliminate temptation from our lives.

Overcomers

When we are tempted, we overcome by speaking and acting according to the Spirit of God. The Old Testament prophet Nehemiah understood this principle. We read in Nehemiah 6:13 that a prophet was hired to lie to him and tell him that people were trying to kill him "that I might become frightened and act accordingly and sin." Nehemiah did not act according to the temptation and follow the spirit of fear. He probably felt fear, but he boldly acted according to faith and did not sin. If he had acted according to the temptation of fear, he would have sinned and then needed to repent.

If you learn to recognize the work of sin when it comes to you as temptation, and then you deal with it spiritually, you can prevent it from spreading to your spouse and doing damage to your marriage. Remember, when the Lord had no regard for Cain or his offering, Cain became angry at his brother, Abel, for whom the Lord had regard (see Gen. 4:4). It is interesting that Cain took out his anger on his brother instead of being mad at God. In your marriage, you need to recognize and deal with the darkness that comes against you or else it will come into your marriage and get between you and your spouse. Then the darkness will do all it can to infiltrate, divide and destroy the rest of your family relationships.

It is not okay to just passively wait and hope that sin, in the form of temptation, will leave. The Bible makes it clear that we are to resist the devil, and stay firm in our faith until he leaves (see 1 Pet. 5:8-9; Jas. 4:7-8). We must deal directly with the work of the devil through temptation; the battle and the weapons are spiritual, not natural. Like Cain, we either learn to recognize and resist sin when it comes in the form of temptation, or else we will end up acting out the temptation and will need to repent. The choice is ours.

By actively resisting sin when it comes against you as temptation, you develop your "spiritual discernment muscles" and become trained to discern the more subtle differences between good and evil (see Heb. 5:12-14). Overcomers do a whole lot more resisting than repenting, because they learn discernment by doing the right thing when tempted. Discerning Christians recognize that their spiritual battle begins at the point when they are first tempted.

The Recycler

About 10 years ago, after I had significantly overcome the issue of anger in my life, I had an experience that clearly demonstrated this spiritual task of resisting sin as a spirit coming against me. One Friday night on my way home from work, I picked up a copy of *The Recycler* (a paper that advertises used items for sale) to look for a used mountain bike for my oldest son, Caleb. I placed *The Recycler* on the dining room table because I didn't have time to look at it that evening. Interestingly, I was preparing to teach this very message about sin at a Christian university the next day.

The next morning, when I had finished my preparation, I went to look for *The Recycler*. It wasn't on the dining room table or anywhere else in sight.

"Have you seen *The Recycler*?" I asked Lori.

"Oh, I put it out in the trash," she nonchalantly replied.

After digging through the trash for a while, I found *The Recycler*—soggy and wet, covered with last night's dinner scraps. I began to get angry, thinking, *At least she could have asked before she threw it away. Couldn't she see that it wasn't even opened?* Then my thoughts took me even further. *It sounded like she didn't even care about what she had done when she told me she had thrown it in the trash!*

Then the Holy Spirit gently spoke and reminded me, "This is anger speaking to you again, remember?"

Yes, I remembered this old enemy. After years of familiarity and conscious spiritual battle against it, I immediately spoke to the spirit of anger. "Anger, I know what you want to do with me. I am *not* going to let you interpret my wife to me. I will not let this spirit of anger convince me that I have a right to be angry, and instruct me how to deal with my wife! Lord, by Your grace, I will be patient instead of angry."

As soon as I spoke these words in my mind, the anger lifted and the Lord revealed another insidious level of spiritual attack. When the Enemy put this thought in my mind, *She didn't even seem to care when she told me she had thrown it in the trash,* he was trying to get me to believe the idea that Lori had done this intentionally. However, after dealing with the anger, I could see clearly, and I spoke again to the Enemy: "That is a lie! Lori has never done anything like that to intentionally hurt me in our 20-plus years of marriage."

If the Enemy can get us to buy into one of his lies, he will see how far he can take it. After getting me to accept his temptation to anger, he also tried to persuade me to accuse Lori of intentionally trying to anger me. Once we accept the lies of the Enemy, our minds get clouded, and it becomes easier to accept another deception. This is why we must actively use the weapons of our warfare, which are simple but divinely powerful, to break down strongholds. We must take every thought captive to the obedience of Christ. Our weapons are not of the flesh, but of the spirit (see 2 Cor. 10:3-5).

We are no longer under the law—limited to the strength of our flesh to make us good. We now have a New Covenant of grace, and a Helper, the Holy Spirit, to open our eyes to the spiritual realm and then fortify us to overcome anything that comes against us spiritually. We must learn to hear and use the voice of the Holy Spirit, not just rely on our natural sight and understanding. We have authority to command spiritual forces of darkness (see Mark 16:17). If we do nothing, they may fade into the background for a while, but we will not gain any ground in the spirit realm.

In the above incident over *The Recycler,* the battle was strictly in my mind. Lori did nothing wrong or malicious toward me. When I reentered the house, my heart and my mind were settled. Believe me, if I had returned to the house angry, Lori would have felt it immediately. She felt no anger, frustration or accusation from me, and so the spirit of anger had no opportunity to spread through me to Lori.

For the sake of example, let's change that scenario and say that Lori was angry at me and had intentionally thrown out *The Recycler* in order to hurt me. I would have had the same battle against the spirit of anger that I described above, but I would also have had an issue to work out with Lori. If I did not first deal with the anger, it would have come out against Lori.

Generally, it is far better to work out our heart issues with God before we try to work out our personal issues. This is essential because whatever is in our heart will eventually come out of our mouths. Jesus said, "The mouth speaks out of that which fills the heart" (Matt. 12:34). If I am still harboring anger when I go to Lori to work out our differences, chances are that the anger will find a way to express itself through my words and attitudes toward her. Even if I am trying hard to be patient, the anger will rise up to find expression.

Continual Overcoming

A few weeks ago, I tried to begin a conversation with Lori about something she had said that felt judgmental and condescending to me. I did my best to use the communication skills that I teach. I tried to speak calmly without judging her in return. She was doing the best she could to listen and understand me; however, all she heard was criticism from me, while I was feeling misunderstood and criticized too. We remained calm in our speech, but we both felt very frustrated and hurt.

Eventually, Lori burst into tears at the frustration she felt and in desperation she suggested, "Let's pray." I said okay. She prayed out loud, and I silently agreed as she prayed against a spirit of confusion and accusation that was misinterpreting and confusing our words to each other. When she finished, it was as though the atmosphere between us had completely changed. The veil of confusion was gone, and we could see and understand each other clearly again. It was definitely a spiritual reality working between the two of us.

Lori and I strongly believe in the value of good communication skills. We practice them and teach them. However, sometimes our natural skills will not break through if the battle is spiritual in nature. By practicing good communication skills and praying against spiritual forces, we can learn to discern when we need a spiritual intervention and when we need to use more natural interventions. Most times it is a combination of both.

In the next chapter, we will teach you simple but powerful spiritual tools to use when the battle in your marriage is a spiritual one.

Proceed to the next chapter for the practical application that will teach you to overcome sin as a spirit.

Notes

6

PRACTICAL WAYS OF DEALING WITH SIN AS A SPIRIT

In this chapter you will learn to use a tool called *1-2-3 Skidoo,* which can be easily incorporated into your daily life. This tool will enable you to take your thoughts captive to overcome sin that comes against you. Remember, sin is something outside of you that comes at you to steal, kill and ultimately destroy you. It is a spiritual force sent by the Enemy to cause you to miss out on all that God has for you.

Here are some descriptions of sin as a spirit coming against you: frustration, impatience, a critical attitude, accusation, fear, worry, inadequacy, entitlement, disappointment, hopelessness, depression, feeling overwhelmed, confusion, unbelief, doubt, withdrawal, isolation, resentment, bitterness, offence . . . and more. I'm sure you have experienced more than one of these forces in your life, some to a stronger degree than others. The good news is, you don't have to let any of these spirits of sin control you.

Introducing 1-2-3 Skidoo

(Although we are presenting the tool to you now, you will have an activity later in this chapter to practice it.) First, bless your spirit to be prominent over your soul and body as you answer these questions and follow the instructions.

1. What is coming against you spiritually?

2. How is it affecting you, and what is it trying to steal from you? Remember our example of "anger" trying to get Barry mad at Lori for throwing away *The Recycler*?

3. Take yourself through the *1-2-3 Skidoo* tool with each thought you've mentioned that has come against you.

1-2-3 Skidoo Tool

a. In the name of Jesus, I nail _____ to the cross. The thoughts could come as a feeling (anger, depression, hopelessness, rejection, self-protection, and so on). They could also come as words or thoughts you're hearing, such as, "Nothing is going to change" or "This is impossible" or "Nothing really happened." Insert the feeling or thought that is coming against you. There may be more than one.

b. I break all agreements I have made with _____, known or unknown, and I repent of joining with _____.

c. I ask You, Father, to send _____ away from me.

d. Father, what do You want to give me in place of _____ _____?

(It will be critical to remember the Father's words and use them to win your spiritual battle.)

Discerning What Is Coming Against You Spiritually

If you are going to stand against the sin that comes against you, you must first discern what it is. Sin starts as a thought sailing through the mind. If you don't catch it, check it out and deal with it, sin as a spirit will begin interpreting your life and affecting your relationships. It is not enough to say it is the devil or an attack. That is like saying you are sick without knowing what disease you have. Just as it is necessary to know what disease you have in order to choose the correct treatment, you need to learn to specifically discern the Enemy's strategies so that you can accurately stand against them.

It is helpful to practice identifying the particular way the Enemy most often comes to you. For example, is it through fear of failure, fear of being criticized or fear of being abandoned? Instead of just saying, "I'm afraid," and leaving it there, you will need to go through a process. Here is an example of the discerning process that evolved from a situation in my (Lori's) life.

A year ago, I started feeling insecure about Barry's relationship to another lady. At first, I simply felt uneasy, like something was wrong, but I couldn't really identify what I was feeling. My first thought was to look at what I thought Barry might be doing wrong. I began to tell him that he needed to set some boundaries with the lady. This was not the real issue. Eventually, I realized that I was feeling jealous. In all our years of marriage, Barry has never given me a reason to feel jealous; but I was, in fact, feeling jealous. It was a new and unfamiliar feeling to me, but the emotion was incredibly real and the jealous thoughts were convincing.

The jealousy was more about my spiritual battle than about what was going on between Barry and the lady. As Barry and I continued to talk and pray about it, we realized this was not just a feeling; it was a spirit of jealousy. Jealousy was speaking to me, trying to persuade me that its intrusive thoughts were actually my own thoughts. Thoughts like "he is more interested in her than he is in me" came to my mind, tempting me to join with jealousy. While I was under the influence of fear and jealousy, I could not discern accurately. It was vital for me to process my inner feelings out loud with Barry. By honestly talking through my feelings, we were able to discern what the Enemy had insidiously deposited.

Whenever sin comes to your mind like this, deception will be present as well. Satan is called "the deceiver" and "the father of lies." If you cannot overcome your spiritual battle on your own, process it with your spouse or someone you trust so that he or she can help hold you to the truth.

What Is this Spirit Attempting to Steal?

The jealousy coming between Barry and me made both of us feel frustrated, disconnected and miserable. The spirits of jealousy and fear incited me to accuse Barry of mistrust and view him as my enemy. Their goal was to undermine our relationship and bring separation to our typically harmonious marriage.

We have found these types of assaults to be on the increase in marriages as our ministry through LAM increases. The purpose of these forces coming against us now goes beyond hindering our private marriage relationship. The Enemy wants us to feel guilty about ministering to marriages around the world while our own marriage suffers assault. As we overcome these temptations, they equip and qualify us for more empowered service with authority. Our authority does not come from knowing about the Enemy but from faithfully following the Lord in the midst of temptation.

The 1-2-3 Skidoo

I finally knew what I needed to do, even though everything inside me was screaming, "No!" I was feeling angry and like I wanted to cry, scream and run out of the room. The battle was so strong! I could not believe how much opposition I was feeling to do this simple tool and pray the prayers.

When you are going through this kind of spiritual assault, just identifying the spirit of jealousy, fear or whatever is coming against you is not enough to get free. You must continue to the next step and use spiritual weapons against the spiritual forces.

Despite my extreme feelings of wanting to scream and run, I made the choice to stay and, with great effort, pressed on. I made myself repeat out loud as Barry led me through the *1-2-3 Skidoo* tool found at the beginning of this chapter:

1. *I nail the spirit of jealousy and fear to the cross, in the name of Jesus.* (Jesus died so that we could overcome *every* spirit of sin that will come against us. This first step helps us appropriate what is already ours by reminding us of the authority His blood has gained for us. Jealousy and fear must bow to the King of kings!)

2. *I break all agreements I have made, known or unknown, with the spirits of jealousy and fear.* (The only thing worse than listening to the lies of the Enemy is agreeing with them. When we agree, we end up believing his lies, instead of God's truth, and living under his power. When the serpent came to Eve in the Garden of Eden, he had no power until he persuaded her to agree with him. Once she gave in and agreed with Satan's words rather than God's truth, Satan gained authority. Jesus took care of everything at the cross, but if we agree with the lies of the Enemy, those lies will become our reality.)

3. *I ask You, Father, to send the spirits of jealousy and fear away from me.* (First John 1:9 tells us, "If we confess our sins, He is faithful and righteous to forgive us our sins and to cleanse us from all unrighteousness." Declaring what is coming against us and what it is doing to us *is* confessing our sins while sin is still just a temptation. When we confess our sins according to this verse, the Father *will* forgive them. The word "forgive" comes

from a Greek word meaning "to send away." Whenever we discern and expose a spirit coming against us, the Father will send it away. It is a spiritual certainty we can count on.)

Asking the Father to Replace It

I asked the Father to show me what He wanted to give me to replace the jealousy and fear He had just sent away. As I listened, I heard the Lord say, "This was not you. It was a spirit sent to separate you and Barry." When the Lord spoke those words to me, He was giving me His perspective and truth. As a result, His peace returned, and almost instantly, I felt relief.

When you ask the Lord to speak to you, He might put a thought in your mind, as He did with me; He might show you a picture in your mind; He might give you an impression or a feeling. He will choose the best way to speak to you as He replaces the lie with His truth. Receiving the Lord's *spoken* word, and believing it, is vital to this process of gaining victory in your battle against sin. Hold on to what He shows you; write it down and declare it as often as needed.

Hearing and believing God's specific words to us are the most important aspects of the spiritual gift of discernment. We are not fully discerning if we only see what the Enemy is doing. We are not fully discerning if we are only skillful at identifying what others are doing wrong. A mature Christian will have his or her senses trained to discern good and evil (see Heb. 5:14). If we are not able to discern the good word of the Lord, we will miss out on the power of His words to overcome evil.

As the day progressed, I gained a clearer perception in my spirit and more understanding about what jealousy had been trying to do. When I was out from under the delusion of the spirits of jealousy and fear, I saw the scenario in an entirely different way. As if I had come out of a fog, I realized there was nothing going on between Barry and this woman that was inappropriate.

Barry has never stepped over appropriate boundaries with another woman in all the 32 years of our marriage. I really trust him. The Lord has faithfully covered and protected us in this area. But when I joined with jealousy, I saw everything through jealousy's grid. Jealousy and fear were challenging what I knew to be true. The Enemy was trying to steal my peace and bring separation and mistrust to Barry and me. He was even trying to harm our connection to this other woman. Having won the battle, I saw that jealousy was a huge liar, and fear was nothing but an illusion.

The Cost of Spiritual Ignorance

Imagine, for a moment, what would happen to our marriage if we had never discerned and overcome this spiritual attack. What would it do to our relationship if I had continued to allow the spirit of jealousy to interpret Barry and his behaviors to me? What if I had continued to tell him that he needed stricter boundaries when, in reality, there was nothing wrong with his boundaries with women?

In a similar vein, imagine what would happen to our relationship if Barry continued to believe that I intentionally did things to hurt him, like throw *The Recycler* out in the trash when I knew he wanted to read it. What if these lies about each other were never overcome and they replaced God's truth about each other? Probably, like many other couples, we would give up trying to do the "right thing," because we would still feel accused and mistrusted. As many other couples do, we would begin acting in a way consistent with the lies being spoken about us. This would absolutely destroy our intimacy and connection.

Even though my thoughts were scattered, and I could not immediately identify them, I knew something was wrong. (Feeling that "something is wrong" is a first warning that should cause you to stop and investigate what is at work.) My feelings were beginning to affect my thoughts. My bad feelings increased as the thoughts in my mind were allowed to run free. My peace was gone! I could not rely on my feelings to lead me; I could only trust the Holy Spirit. When I got to this point, I had to use *1-2-3 Skidoo*, even though I didn't feel like it. It was not until I actually did the third step of the *1-2-3 Skidoo* that I started to feel the shift away from jealousy and fear.

Remember: Discerning what is coming against you starts with deliberately paying attention to your thoughts and feelings. When your peace leaves, it is a big red flag telling you to grab those thoughts and evaluate them. When you reach this place, you must realize that your feelings are not your friends. Spiritual discernment begins with hearing and obeying God's voice.

The Spirit Realm Is Real

We have a friend who sees and hears God in ways that Barry and I do not. She has open-eyed visions like the type the apostle John described when he was on the Isle of Patmos (see the book of Revelation); and like Daniel described while standing beside the Tigris River (see Dan. 10). One day, she and her husband were in a pizza parlor when she saw a churning green mass moving around the room near the ceiling. She watched this phenomenon for some time and then asked the Lord what it was. He told her she was seeing a spirit of confusion. No sooner had the Lord said these words to our friend than a man in the kitchen suddenly yelled out in a loud voice, "I'm so confused!"

The Lord revealed this spirit to her by allowing her to see it in the spirit realm, and then He confirmed it in the natural. When the Lord exposed the spirit of confusion to our friend, she prayed, sent it away and watched it leave!

Whether the Lord shows you a churning green mass, or you simply sense when something does not feel right, it is God wanting to expose the spiritual forces coming against you. He wants to give you spiritual discernment. Once you identify the opposition and what it is trying to do, use the *1-2-3 Skidoo* tool to appropriate the power over darkness that Christ has given you.

He has given us the authority to get rid of any spirit of sin that comes against us. When we resist the Enemy, he has to flee. After the Father has sent it away, ask Him what He wants to give you in place of what He has just sent away. Hold on to His spoken word for you; it is powerful!

ACTIVITY

As a couple, follow the instructions below to activate these truths in your life.

1. Start with blessing your spirits to be prominent and to lead your souls and bodies. Take a minute to ask the Holy Spirit to bring to mind one thing that has come against you (anger, self-criticism, offence, worry, fear, and the like) that you have not dealt with today, in the last week or maybe for a while. There may be many things that come to mind. Jot them all down, but for now choose only one for this exercise. We ask the Holy Spirit to help you choose. He knows exactly what He wants to help you work through and get freed from in this moment.

2. When you both have it, write it down.

3. Go to the *1-2-3 Skidoo* tool at the beginning of this chapter.

   • Husbands, go first and lead your wives through this tool,
     step by step.

   • On steps #1 and #2, you'll be reading the instructions
     out loud and have your wife answer the questions. On #3,
     have her repeat the italicized print after you.

   • Be sure to give yourselves plenty of time to let the Lord
     speak to you.

4. Asking the Lord to replace the spirit that has fled is a very important step. When the Lord gets rid of something that's been
   coming against you, He always wants to give you something
   in place of it. He will replace the lies of the Enemy with His
   truth. He may speak something to you, show you a picture,
   give you a feeling, remind you of a dream or remind you of
   something you've seen or done. He talks to us in many different ways. Don't discount what you sense from the Lord. Remember, you're asking for the Holy Spirit to reveal the mind
   of Jesus and the Father (see John 16:13-15). We can trust the
   Holy Spirit to reveal God's heart to us when we ask sincerely
   with the right motives.

When a husband has finished leading his wife through the tool, then she
will lead her husband through the tool.

A Maintenance Plan

When you overcome the Enemy, he will usually try to weasel his way back
in, so you must continue to stand (see Eph. 6:13). The Enemy does not
like to give up his strongholds easily, especially if he has held you captive
for a long time. You may need to do the *1-2-3 Skidoo* 20 times a day for a
while in order to seal your victory. To illustrate the importance of holding
on to your breakthroughs, I want to tell you an astounding story about
a friend of mine. I will never forget her story of faithfully holding on to
God's work in her life.

Lauren had a cancerous tumor in her throat. She had already gone through two operations and was devastated when the doctors told her the cancer was back and they wanted her to have surgery a third time. The doctors gave her a 50 percent chance of survival after the surgery; and if she lived, she would definitely have no voice. When Lauren heard this news, she cried out to the Lord, desperately asking Him what to do. He answered by placing it on the heart of a friend of hers to gather some believers together to pray for her healing. I was one of those called to participate in the prayer time.

As we prayed, Lauren started choking and coughing. This caused her to throw up a bunch of what looked like phlegm. Some of the women, who were well acquainted with this type of healing ministry, started digging through the phlegm she had just thrown up on the floor. I was shocked, having never experienced anything like this before. I was completely grossed out when they started digging through all that yuck.

Finally, one of them said, "Yep! There it is."

At first I was appalled, and then I was totally and utterly shocked. They had found the tumor they were looking for. Lauren, who was scheduled for her third cancer surgery, had supernaturally thrown up her tumor right before my eyes! I thought to myself, *That is impossible . . . people do not get rid of cancerous tumors by simply throwing them up.* She started to feel the difference in her body right away and was confident the Lord had truly healed her of the cancer she had battled for years.

When Lauren went to her doctor for a checkup, he could not believe what he found. His tests showed her to be completely *cancer free!* Isn't that incredible? Every time I tell this story, I am filled again with amazement at what a powerful, loving God we serve. Listen carefully to the next part of the story; it contains encouragement and power to hold on to your breakthroughs as well.

A week or so after Lauren had been declared cancer free, she started feeling all of the symptoms returning. The Enemy was right at her door, feeding her thoughts like, *You're not really healed. It is all coming back.* Lauren did not accept one word from the Enemy. She knew exactly what was going on. She put on a pink T-shirt with the words "I Am a Promise" printed on it. Next, she began standing in the truth of what God had said and done. God had healed her, and she had been declared cancer free. One day, two days, three days passed, with no change. Imagine waking up each day to all the familiar symptoms of fatigue and pain she had felt as she battled years of cancer. It tested her faith in God's healing to the very core of her being.

Even with the threat of cancer screaming through her mind—four days, five days, six days went by—still Lauren did not budge in her belief that God had healed her. She relentlessly stood against these thoughts from the Enemy and, on the seventh day, that spirit of the fear of cancer turned tail and ran. She held on to the truth. She persevered. She chose faith and did not give in to what she felt or saw. The spirits of doubt, unbelief and the fear of cancer were breathing down her neck for seven days, but she held on to what God had said and she believed what He'd done. On the eighth day, all symptoms were completely gone. Lauren remained cancer free. Lauren's faith worked because she remained faithful to what God had done and what the doctors had confirmed. Thank You, Jesus!

I have had people leave my office after receiving a tremendous breakthrough from the Lord only to hear words in their mind like, *Nothing really happened* or *You won't be able to hold on to this.* This doubt and unbelief is a spirit trying to climb back in a window after the Lord has just thrown it out the door. It is imperative for us to recognize the responsibility and the right that Jesus gave us to hold on to our breakthroughs, just as Lauren held on to her healing in spite of Satan's lies and illusions.

Our Prayer Over You

We ask the Lord to release the gift of spiritual discernment into your spirits so that you would begin to see as He sees. [Insert your names here], we bless you to have the mind of Christ, that the eyes of your spirits would be open to all truth, understanding and wisdom. We pray that the Lord will expose the spiritual work of darkness that comes against you so that you can clearly distinguish it from your own thoughts and emotions. We ask that any spirits and lies that are familiar, and that seem normal, would no longer feel normal to you. We pray for spiritual acuity to quickly detect these intruders. We ask Jesus to teach you to unmistakably recognize His voice.

Thank You, Lord, for the power and anointing You have given this couple to take every thought captive. Break down every stronghold You reveal to them and replace it with Your freedom. We ask this in the name of Jesus. Amen!

ᘔᕼᕼᕼᕼᕼᕼ᙮ HOMEWORK ᕼᕼᕼᕼᕼᕼᕼ

Here's some homework for this week to help you begin to make this process of "taking your thoughts captive" not just a one-time exercise, but a way of life (see Heb. 5:12-14). Do this homework individually, but discuss it when you're finished.

1. Once a day, evaluate your life and ask this question: Is there something that spiritually came against me today that I didn't deal with? For example: anger, frustration, impatience, lying, a critical attitude, accusation (toward God, self, others), fear, worry, anxiety, self-pity, inadequacy, fear of failure, entitlement, disappointment, despair, hopelessness, depression, feeling overwhelmed, confusion, unbelief, doubt, withdrawal, isolation, shut-down, resentment, bitterness, offense . . .

2. Use the *1-2-3 Skidoo* tool!

3. If you don't experience immediate results, you may be dealing with a spiritual force that has been speaking to you for a while, and it may require persistence to overcome it. Remember, you will be strengthened spiritually through your perseverance.

Your goal is to become an overcomer. If you persevere and don't see any significant change, ask your spouse to join with you in praying and standing against it. If you still can't get breakthrough after having prayed together, ask the Lord to identify another couple you trust to join with you and the Holy Spirit to pray through what is coming against you. The Lord loves to bring breakthrough through community. We've watched Him do this again and again in our workshops. Give Him the opportunity to do this with you as well. It does require more vulnerability, but if you're willing to step out, He will meet you.

Notes

_____

_____

_____

_____

7

SEEING YOUR SPOUSE THROUGH GOD'S EYES

Can you imagine what life would be like if we could see each other just as God sees us? What would our marriages be like if we could feel for each other just as God feels for us? Think about what we would experience in our relationships if we knew and understood each other just as God knows and understands us. Jesus truly wants us to see each other exactly as He does. It is a gift He longs to give, and it is ours if we choose it.

The Lord continues to use the following testimony and activity to bring many couples into the amazing place of seeing their spouses through God's eyes. And it is His desire to bring you into that place as well!

Awakening Love

We had a tall, beautifully regal couple in their sixties come to one of our workshops. They were steadfast, supportive and a real strength within their small group. As we drew near to the end of the workshop, this couple volunteered to come up in front of the entire group to be led through a "couples' coaching" session. In their home country, it was culturally uncomfortable to share emotions openly with one another, much less with a roomful of people. The fact that they were volunteering to be coached in front of the entire class should have been terrifying, yet both of them were utterly determined to receive their breakthrough and were resolute that fear would not direct them.

The Lord directed us to talk and pray through many different issues as they shared their story. At one point, the husband shared with us a significant part of his relational history. As a young man, he had been encouraged by his spiritual mentor to turn away from a passion-filled relationship he was involved in. He was dating a beautiful young Christian woman who was the equivalent of a movie star. His mentor told him the passion he felt for this woman was ungodly and needed to be stopped and directed toward a more holy end.

As a man of integrity, and desiring to be a devoted follower of Jesus, he felt that he needed to heed this "righteous" counsel from the man of God who was directing him. Heartbroken, he ended the relationship, even though they were engaged to be married. Sadly, he also came into agreement with the belief he had been fed that a passion-filled relationship was both base and carnal. As a result, he later made a choice with his head, not with his heart, to find a godly woman and marry her, which he did after five years. Trusting that his heart was unreliable, he allowed duty and obedience to take the place of emotion and desire. Furthermore, he began to agree with the lie that passion, pleasure and enjoyment did not have a realistic place within a godly marriage. Maybe you can see where this is going.

His beautiful young bride came into their marriage full of expectation; she dreamt of love, life and a beautiful family with the wonderful man of God the Lord had brought her. As her husband's lack of pursuit and his lack of expressed desire began to materialize, a subtle but harsh reality began to settle into her soul. As a result, lies began to form that shouted, "You are not lovely" and "You are undesirable as a woman, a wife and a lover." Being a strong, godly woman, she threw herself into making the most of this passionless marriage, as so many couples do. She went into survival mode, praying that hope deferred and the tremendous shock of what marriage had become would not be her undoing.

As a married couple, they basically did life "well." They worked hard to do what was right; they functioned effectively as partners raising their kids, ministering to others and doing all things properly in order to be a godly couple; but there was little to no connection emotionally when they had sex. They didn't really see or know one another. They didn't let each other into the inner courts of their lives and, consequently, there was very little real or significant exchange that occurred outside of the everyday duties and demands of life.

But here they were, attending this workshop and stepping out to risk uncommon vulnerability as they began the twilight years of their lives. Despite bad counsel and years of loneliness, somehow the Spirit of God within this precious couple had kept hope alive; and now, in the fullness of time, God was bringing forth a desire for more.

First, we dealt with lies about the wife's self-image and worth, which had been stealing from her long before she married. These lies cut into the core of who she was as a woman—her value, beauty, femininity and desirability. We asked Jesus to show her where these lies started. As the Lord brought memories into her mind, we invited Him into the memories. The Enemy had used those painful memories to interpret her world since the time when she was a young girl; but Jesus spoke the truth to her. He broke through the shame, failure and regret that had ruled in their relationship. The lies ended on that day, and God's goodness, joy and passion filled her.

At one point, Barry felt led to give this gentleman—who was 10 years his senior and about six inches taller—a father's blessing. This precious man had been looking for a father's input and a father's blessing his entire life. Having lacked an example of fatherhood in his life was, in part, what caused him to mistake religiousness, duty and performance for true fathering. The husband later shared with us how Barry's "father's blessing" was very significant in bringing him the breakthrough he desperately needed at that time. He had never received or felt the blessing of a father, so the Lord brought it right then and there, using Barry as a stand-in.

Now that they were free from so many lies and false mindsets, Barry asked if they would recommit themselves to one another as he led them through some vows. This is where we all lost it! As this man took his wife's hands, gazed into her eyes and affectionately spoke her name, with tears in his eyes, we saw on his face the evidence of something awakening. It was as though he were seeing her for the first time. The realization of her beauty; lost passion stirring within him; an emotional, sexual and spiritual connection all poured forth in one glance as he finally saw his lover. They both continued on and finished their new marriage vows before God and man.

Their declarations of newly awakened love were so intimate and passionate that both of them were crying. As for the rest of us, there wasn't a dry eye in the room. Finally they were seeing each other as the Lord had always intended them to. They were seeing each other through God's eyes for the first time, after 30-plus years!

We all whooped, hollered and screamed as though they had just been married. And no one had to tell him, "You may now kiss your bride." If you measured passion on a scale from 1 to 10, that kiss was at least a 15. It was as if we had all disappeared from the room. They could not have cared less that they were in a room full of people. They were passionately making out. It was the "making up for a lifetime" kiss of the century. It was such a beautiful transformation and example of the awakening of love and passion. No one who was there will ever forget it.

An Invitation

There is something very powerful in seeing your spouse as the Lord sees him or her, through heaven's perspective. The enemy will do everything in his power to keep us from stepping beyond our own pain, offence and hurt. He is desperate to prevent us from truly seeing each other's heart. Even if the enemy has been successful throughout your life and prevented you from desiring to understand or see your spouse's heart, give the Lord an opportunity right now. He wants to break through with the revelation and truth of who your husband/wife is. This is an invitation: Do you want to see your spouse as He does?

Prayer

Lord, we ask that You would release grace and anointing for the precious couple reading this book. We ask that even now, they would receive impartation to see each other through Your eyes, and we pray for the power of this testimony to be showered all over their marriage!

Epilogue

About half a year later, I had the privilege of meeting two of our couple's beautiful daughters. They shared with us about how much the Lord had changed their parents' relationship and how thankful they were. It had literally affected all of their lives, as you could imagine. We sat there and cried together as I shared with the daughters the details of what had happened on that day when the Lord changed everything and let their parents see one another through His eyes.

And now, more than two years later, this dear couple tells us that after that staggering coaching session they decided to become each other's best friend and lover. They are enjoying much more loving, caring and openness—spiritually, emotionally and sexually; and even their praying together became easier! Oh, the goodness of God and His faithfulness that never lets go until we are walking in all He has for us! This is such an amazing story of how God worked to heal a marriage and helped a broken couple reclaim the passion in their love for each other that He'd always intended for them.

ACTIVITY

There's nothing more beautiful than being able to see each other as God sees you. Would you like to see your spouse through God's eyes? If you are willing to go with Him and let Him lead you, He will take you there.

A Word of Encouragement: In doing the following activity, we have seen God bring breakthrough to countless marriages. Regardless of their hurt or their history, as couples have truly joined with the Holy Spirit in this activity, He has supernaturally met them and broken through strongholds to help them see each other's heart.

Put on some soaking music.

1. List your spouse's God-given strengths, abilities, gifts and talents. Share your list with each other—(spend a minimum of 10 minutes to write and share). Take time with this; it is not just a "fill in the blanks" exercise. Ask the Holy Spirit to help you see everything good that God has put within your spouse. When you are finished sharing with each other, proceed to number two.

2. A Letter from God to Your Spouse: Read the guidelines below. (You can transfer the letters you write to the "notes" page at the end of the chapter after you've written them out. They will be keepers!)

   • Ask the Lord to write the letter to your spouse and you record what He's saying.

   • Just start writing, and allow it to come out in the first person. God will be speaking directly to your spouse. Don't second-guess what you are hearing; just keep writing. When we ask for the Holy Spirit, He doesn't trick us and give us something other than Himself.

   • Give yourselves plenty of time to write. Don't be afraid to sit and wait in order to hear all that God wants to say to your spouse.

- When you are both done writing, take turns reading your letters out loud to each other.

- Pray over your spouse and over the things the Lord has said to him/her. Bless and affirm what the Lord has said.

Barry and I have done this activity several times, and it has been so encouraging! The first time I was writing my letter to Barry, I began evaluating what I was writing, and I thought, *This isn't right; this isn't Barry. He isn't even thinking about this type of thing.* Even though it wasn't what I knew to be true of Barry, I continued writing anyway and then read it to him. When I finished, he told me that what I had written was amazing! I wrote about the same details the Lord had been personally speaking to Barry, but he hadn't had a chance to share them with me. He told me that when I read my letter out loud to him, it confirmed what he had been hearing from God, and he was quite encouraged. It was so fun to be used as God's messenger to my precious Barry B!

Most of the time when we do this activity in the workshops, husbands and wives all over the room are touched or they weep at the wonderful, life-giving message the Lord is saying to them.

Prayer

We bless your spirits to be prominent; souls and bodies, step aside.
We bless your spirits to join with the Holy Spirit and receive all that the
Lord has for you and your spouse as you write and receive from one
another and from the Lover of your soul.

ഇരുന്ന HOMEWORK ഇരുന്ന

1. Each day this week tell your spouse three ways you saw God in him/her. For example: beauty, creativity, order, ability, generosity, the fruit of the Spirit, sacrifice, gifting, compassion . . .

2. Keep a daily log of the things you say to your spouse; at the end of the week, give it to your spouse.

3. Thank God every day for the good things you see in your spouse. You can do this out loud during your prayer time.

4. Continue praying together daily.

5. Practice the *Listening Exercise* (from chapter 4) two times this week.

Notes

_____

_____

_____

_____

_____

_____

_____

_____

_____

_____

_____

_____

_____

_____

_____

_____

_____

_____

_____

_____

_____

_____

_____

_____

_____

_____

_____

_____

_____

8

EMOTIONAL INTIMACY

Few delights can equal the mere presence of the one whom we trust utterly.
GEORGE MACDONALD

To achieve intimacy in marriage, we must be willing to risk being vulnerable. If we choose not to share the deep parts of our heart, we may achieve safety but still feel isolated and empty. You see, the desire to deeply know and be known is fundamental to all human beings. Just like a plant needs sunshine, fresh air and rain, we also need to live in a place of openness to grow. Truthfulness and vulnerability in love will bring healing and wholeness to a marriage.

For those who have been deeply wounded through life experiences, the thought of risking vulnerability may sound stupid or scary—why would you open yourself to more pain? But every human heart has an innate desire to be deeply known and loved by at least one other person. Letting down the protective walls you have developed to ward off pain is the only way to fulfill that desire. However, in our broken world, many people have asked, "What is *healthy* intimacy and how can we cultivate it in our relationships?" I recall the story of one couple in particular who came to a LAM workshop looking for that answer.

William and Julie were trapped in an all-too-common cycle: living in a marriage without true emotional intimacy. William was miserable; he believed he was incapable of making his wife happy, even though he deeply longed for a real and loving connection with his wife. Sadly, William became infected with the fear that his marriage was failing, and every tense conversation he shared with Julie merely reaffirmed this thought. Hope had become both dangerous and out of reach for him. He was convinced that he could never be the man Julie needed, despite his deep love for her.

Overtaken by his inadequacies, William would bring every problem and issue to Julie. Because of the baggage that she had brought into the marriage, she took on the crushing burden of responsibility for everything in their relationship.

As their personal tensions increased, so did the distance between them. Desperate to connect, they would try over and over again to talk through things, but it always ended in more misunderstanding and pain. William would walk away feeling like a failure as a man and in his marriage. Once again he had not been heard and he had failed to connect with the one person in his life he longed for. Julie, feeling overwhelmed and overburdened, would dissolve into tears of hopelessness because her efforts to resolve things always fell short.

This pattern of relating had gone on for years. William and Julie knew they needed outside help to overcome it, so they decided to try the new workshop at their church, "Love After Marriage."

The very first topic we cover in our LAM workshop is the power of transparency and vulnerability—having "Nothing Hidden." The most basic component of an intimate relationship—to know and be known—requires that a couple has no secrets. Each spouse must both understand and be understood. In our workshops, we ask the participants to listen to the Holy Spirit and be willing to share whatever He is prompting, no more and no less.

Something started churning in the pit of William's stomach at the mention of "nothing hidden." It was the first session, and the class was being challenged to pray and share whatever hidden things God brought to their minds. Like a siren blaring in his conscience, the pornography he'd been engaging in for the last two years screamed at him. He had heard the speaker say that in order to have the connection he so deeply desired with his wife, he could have no secrets. With his heart burning inside him, he resolved to confess to Julie his consuming addiction to pornography. Although he was terrified, this was exactly what God needed him to act upon if he and Julie were to move forward.

During their weekly homework assignment, William ventured out and asked the question, "Babe, are there any deep, dark secrets that you've hidden from me and need to tell me about?" in hopes that he wasn't the only one. Julie carefully thought about the question and replied that there was nothing. With his stomach in knots, William knew it was his turn now. Determined to face his convictions, he told her everything, holding nothing back. The pornography had been shameful and so debilitating. Although it was hard to expose his sin, the moment he did, a weight immediately lifted from his spirit. Riding high on this wave of transparency, William was reminded of another shameful sexual experience from before he was married and risked sharing that as well. Everything was finally out, and it felt so good! All of the hiding—all of his believing that he was inadequate, shameful and despicable—was over now. The relief was exhilarating! He felt like a brand-new man.

Celebrate Risk

Life with God is meant to be full of freedom! God celebrates when we take a risk in order to follow Him and be true in love. William took a huge risk when he shared openly with his wife. He overcame his feelings of embarrassment and shame and his fear of Julie's anger and rejection. Until he was willing to do this, his shame and guilt kept them separated by an invisible wall that prevented them from progressing any further in intimacy. William's confession demonstrates the kind of faith, risk and trust that attract God's presence and power into a marriage. However, confession is just the first risk.

After William exposed his hidden sin, Julie did not experience the same exhilaration that he did. She knew William needed to say all that he had said, but that knowledge did not avert the crushing pain and devastation she felt. She had always worked hard to offset any lack in their marriage; so in addition to the painful betrayal, she felt as though she had failed. Even though she could see the hope and life in William's countenance that she had patiently waited for, the burden she was now carrying felt oppressive and all consuming. To make matters worse, it was difficult for William to feel the depth of Julie's pain while experiencing the rush of his newfound freedom.

Julie needed some time away to process all that had transpired. Fortunately, she made a conscious choice to go to a friend that she knew would give her godly counsel. Her friend was able to gently guide Julie to a place of faith and trust for God's work in her marriage. After crying, praying and processing for an entire afternoon with her friend, Julie realized there was something greater at work than the pain she felt. She was able to see God's plan in spite of her hurting heart, and she returned home with hope and resolve to press through to the intimacy she foresaw coming on the horizon.

Armed with this new perspective, Julie was able to push past her feelings of offense and join William in pursuing God's purpose for their marriage. Questions still raced through her mind: *Could this truthful, vulnerable communication actually lead to what we have always been looking for? Can I trust William to remain truthful? Will this pain ever go away? Could we really be on the road to a meaningful, fulfilling relationship?* Despite the questions and the unknown, she chose to celebrate William's risk and take a risk of her own.

In marriage, we will regularly be confronted with choices—one of the most crucial is whether or not we will choose to look at our spouse through God's eyes and place our focus on what is good. The apostle Paul teaches about love in 1 Corinthians 13. In verse 7 he says that love "rejoices in the truth." He continues by saying that love "bears all things, believes all things, hopes all things, endures all things" (v. 7) before he says his famous closing line: "Love never fails" (v. 8). When we rejoice in the truth and choose to believe God's truth about our spouse, hope will strengthen our hearts to continue moving us deeper unto His unfailing love. As we do so, we are actively demonstrating our faith and trust in God.

A vital question for Julie at this point was, "Lord, can You help me see the truth of what is in William's heart?" Julie wisely chose to hear God's heart and thoughts about her husband and the situation, rather than following her overwhelming feelings of hurt, offense and betrayal. This was critical to a positive outcome for their traumatized marriage.

Remember: When you are in a time of crisis and trauma, your feelings are not your friend. What would have happened if Julie had listened to her feelings and gone to a friend who would have joined in her pain and offense? She would have gained ammunition to blame and accuse her husband, which would have resulted in more separation. Choosing to believe and hope involves risk, but it's God's path to the trust, love and freedom we so desperately desire.

Healthy Intimacy

Here is the definition of healthy intimacy in marriage that we use:

> Healthy intimacy exists in a relationship between two people who both know and are known by each other in a deep, personal way; and that deep, personal knowledge is talked about openly and is then handled with trust and respect.

So there are three main components to healthy intimacy:

1. There must be a deep, personal knowing that goes both directions.
2. There must be intentional talking about that deep, personal knowledge.
3. That deep, personal knowledge that is shared must be handled with trust and respect.

Deep, Personal Knowing

Being vulnerable and allowing someone full access to your heart is probably the greatest risk you will ever take. Many people will easily and gladly take physical or financial risk before they ever risk opening up their hearts. Others will even risk being sexually intimate without being emotionally intimate. The truth is, healthy intimacy should never begin with sexual contact; it must begin with knowing.

Recently, a woman came to me and told me that for a long time she had suspected her husband was having an affair. Because of her desperate need to be loved, and her fear of rejection, she could not risk directly asking him about this. Whenever she had tried to question him, he would be very critical and demeaning; so she settled for just hearing what she wanted to hear. Most of all, she was scared to death of hearing that maybe her husband was not being faithful to her.

While attending LAM, she decided to be bold and risk complete honesty. She finally confronted her husband and heard the truth that she already knew: He *was* having an affair. After this confrontation, she realized how deeply she had been controlled and paralyzed by fear. For years, she had never actually known who she was or who her husband was until she began to speak out what she really thought. She had to speak up in spite of his frequent angry responses and false accusations. Although it was terrifying for her to face her fears, she had finally arrived at the place where she could no longer live with all the lies and half-truths. After choosing complete truthfulness, her eyes were opened to see clearly that they had never developed authentic intimacy in their marriage.

Sadly, this marriage did end in divorce when the husband chose to continue his affairs and self-deception. She could not control her husband's choices, but she chose to risk living in the truth rather than in fear. In spite of the divorce, this woman is grateful to have learned how to be truthful in love. Armed with new awareness, she has blossomed in her self-confidence and grown by leaps and bounds in her relationships with her friends and family.

Intentional Talking

Years ago, a Christian family came to my office for counseling concerning their teenage daughters. When asked about communication in the family, the oldest daughter in her late teens piped up, saying, "We don't really talk in our family; we just work on vibes." They were missing out on one of the greatest gifts for building healthy, intimate relationship—intentional, purposeful talking. Instead, they worked on "vibes" and just guessed their way through the family relationships.

Sometimes, you may think you understand your spouse simply because you have observed him or her for years. While it is true that you can learn a lot by observing, real intimacy requires that you talk openly. Is it hard for you to communicate? Are you able to communicate about your own personal thoughts and feelings—the ones only you are aware of? It is only by talking openly and honestly that you can really work together on issues that affect your marriage. It is only through open and honest talking that you can confirm what you think you know about your spouse.

- If speaking the truth in love is difficult for you, read the following prayer out loud together: *Lord, we pray that You will help us to have a desire and willingness to go beyond what is familiar and what is comfortable in the area of deep, personal communication. We pray that if one of us is stronger and more skilled in communicating, we will be patient and supportive, using our gifting to help our spouse. We pray for courage where we feel inadequate, so that we can willingly take gradual risks and increasingly open up, learning to speak the truth in love. Amen.*

- Next, pray the following out loud: *In the name of Jesus Christ, I nail to the cross of Jesus Christ the fear of opening up myself and risking vulnerability. I break any agreements with this fear that I have made in my thoughts, and any agreements I have made through my choices. In the name of Jesus, I break every agreement that I have made with this fear, known or unknown to me. Father, send this fear away from me. I give You permission, Lord, to teach me to risk being vulnerable. Father, what do You want to give to me to replace this fear of vulnerability?*

- Now listen for what the Lord wants to give you instead.

Handling Intimate Information with Trust and Respect

Throughout our marriage, Lori and I have never allowed ourselves to yell at each other, call each other names or swear at each other. Interestingly, since we have been teaching the LAM workshops, we have had greater testing in our relationship than we have ever experienced in the 30 years prior.

A few months ago, as I was dealing with some hurt and misunderstanding between us, a door was opened for the Enemy to assail my mind with angry, vile thoughts about her for an entire day. It felt horrible! I had never before experienced this kind of anger in my mind toward her. Until we were able to work through this, all I could do was refrain from speaking out the destructive words attacking my mind. I knew I could not unleash the feelings inside of me; they would have devastated her. At times, we may not understand the barrage of feelings churning inside us. During those times, it is important to keep from acting upon what we feel, and look prayerfully into our hearts. We simply cannot allow ourselves to use the information and the position of influence we have to hurt our spouse and damage our marriage connection.

At the time of that particular testing, we were teaching a LAM workshop at Bethel Church in Redding, California. On Sunday morning, we shared our experience with the class. Afterward, we asked how many of them were experiencing the same kind of onslaught of anger or had experienced this throughout their marriage. More than half of the couples in the workshop stood up. We prayed for the Lord to break this destructive power in their marriages as He had done for us that week.

Lori and I have discovered that many times these unusual experiences are a type of "word of knowledge." They are no fun to go through, but the Lord reveals critical information to us through these life experiences. He showed us what many of the couples had experienced or were experiencing on a regular basis. As we have overcome these tests that come into our marriage, the Lord has given us authority to help others. As leaders or teachers, we must remain teachable and be able to live out in our own marriage the precepts we teach.

Opening your heart to your spouse is a precious gift to give and to receive. One of the quickest ways to destroy blossoming intimacy is to use the personal information entrusted to you to hurt the person you love. However, if you value the connection you have made through intimacy, you will protect the vulnerable areas your spouse has shared in love. Only then will intimacy, trust and respect have fertile ground to grow and bear good fruit.

Cultivating Healthy Intimacy

A prerequisite to your intimacy with another person is self-knowledge and taking ownership of the truth about yourself. It is vital that you acknowledge your strengths and your weaknesses. If you don't recognize and use your strengths and good qualities, you won't have the ability to bring these qualities into your marriage. As a result, your marriage will not be able to live within the strength of its true potential.

When you do not fully face your weaknesses and faults, you typically end up "placing" these negative attributes on your spouse. In psychology, this is known as "projection." When you use the defense mechanism of projection in your marriage, you attribute to your spouse the negative qualities you have not personally taken responsibility for.

James and Christy came to my office wanting to work through some difficulties in their marriage, at least that's what they said. After meeting together for months, we had seen very little progress. As I sat in my chair listening to James criticize his wife, Christy, once again, I couldn't help but feel somewhat frustrated. During the sessions, James simply pointed out all of his wife's faults; while Christy, although hurt and confused, seemed to be trying hard to make the marriage work. Something wasn't adding up.

After some time, the truth finally came to light. James was in the midst of an affair with a woman from their church. Because of his internal struggle with guilt, his defense mechanisms of self-justification and projection had made him blind to the truth about himself. In his heart, he blamed his wife for all of their problems and could not see his wrongdoing. Until James was willing to be honest about his own life, all he could see were Christy's faults. As absurd as this may sound, it happens all the time. I could share dozens of similar stories where one person does not see his or her own problems and literally "puts it on" the spouse, blaming the spouse for his or her own stuff.

Happily, this man set his heart in earnest to make things right once the affair was exposed. He fully confessed to the adultery and allowed the leaders in his church to develop a plan for personal and marital restoration. Interestingly, soon after confessing and repenting of his adultery, he saw himself and his wife in a completely different light. He was finally able to see that his wife was trying her best to love him and serve him despite her struggles with being codependent. He saw the true beauty of her heart for him. After repenting, he could also see how deeply he had hurt his wife, his church family and God. Most of these truths were hidden from him while he continued in the deception of the adultery. James and Christy's marriage was restored, and to this day they continue to live in greater oneness and enjoyment than ever before.

Confession and Repentance

In spiritual terms, there is a simple solution to the blindness that projection creates—it is called confession and repentance. In the Bible, the Pharisees give us a clear example of projection. Blinded by their own self-justification and pride, they chose to reject the ministry of John the Baptist. Three of the Gospels record this critical fact (see Matt. 21:25; Mark 11:30-31; Luke 20:1-4). John preached a baptism of repentance and confession for the forgiveness of sins. This baptism was the exact preparation necessary for people to recognize the kingdom of God in Jesus. The multitude of sinners who had accepted the baptism of John and confessed their sins were able to see that Jesus was from God. The Pharisees could not.

Ironically, the Pharisees, who were the spiritual leaders of Israel, failed to see the anointing and call of God in John the Baptist and in Jesus. When they observed Jesus casting out demons, they accused Him of having power from Beelzebub, the ruler of demons (see Mark 3:22). The Pharisees called Jesus a sinner (see John 9:24). It was also recorded that they believed John the Baptist had a demon while Jesus was a "gluttonous man and a drunkard, a friend of tax collectors and sinners" (Luke 7:33-34).

Jesus explained that the Pharisees were not spiritual leaders but rather hypocrites, fools, blind guides, sons of hell, serpents and a brood of vipers who would not escape the sentence of hell (see Matt. 23:13). Of course, we know it was Jesus who spoke the truth; but let's imagine it from a counseling perspective. Who was right? Jesus and the Pharisees both believed they were right! Sadly, the Pharisees were projecting onto Jesus and John the sins they themselves had never confessed or repented of. In the end, while the Pharisees schemed, slandered and finally murdered Jesus, they were convinced that He was the evil one, while they were upholding what was right. Their unconfessed sin brought such strong deception that they fully believed they were serving God and the nation of Israel by murdering Jesus!

I've already stated that a prerequisite to intimacy is taking ownership of your weaknesses and faults. You must admit *and* deal with (*confess* and *repent*) the sinful, destructive attitudes and behaviors in your life or you will end up blaming and accusing your spouse of those same things. You will have no real intimacy. There will be no deep knowing of one another. Your marriage will be characterized by codependency and confusion over which issues are yours and which belong to your spouse. Healthy intimacy requires that you know yourself and deal with any spiritual darkness that has a hold on you. It is for this reason that Lori and I devote so much time to emphasizing the importance of overcoming sin as a spirit in the LAM conferences. If couples do not learn to recognize and overcome the spiritual darkness that comes against their marriages, it will cause them to see their spouses as the enemy.

The enemy is passionate about dividing the greatest human union God created—marriage. We forfeit the intimacy and oneness that God intends for us if we allow the enemy to accuse us to each other. We must learn to stand together and fight our real adversary so that he does not make our spouse the enemy. We must learn to overcome the schemes of the devil together so that our intimacy is not hindered.

It's Not Only Who We Are, but Also What We Do

The final step in cultivating intimacy is learning to live life in such a way that we will feel good about ourselves before God. If we feel guilty about something we are doing, we won't want to let someone else into our private internal life. Shame wants to keep things hidden!

Do you remember James and Christy? James was hiding his adultery from his wife. The true reality of sin is that even though he was caught up in the exhilaration of illicit sex during the moment, most of the time he was utterly miserable. He lived in daily torment because of his perpetual guilt and fear of being found out. Every time he looked at his children he felt deeply ashamed because, instead of living honorably and working diligently to improve the covenant relationship with his wife, he chose a destructive course that fed the sinful pleasures of his flesh. As a Christian, he could not live with this dichotomy between his belief and his behavior and still feel good about himself. Compromising your core values and morals will severely limit your capacity for intimacy, especially within marriage.

Please understand that I am not saying we will always be perfect, never making a mistake. Rather, we are to recognize that our values and words must carry such weight that they are seen and reflected in our life choices, big and small. It's common to hear statements like, "What matters is who you are; not what you do" or "God doesn't care about your performance; He cares about your heart." Well, I don't think those statements are true! It isn't only your heart, nor is it only about what you do—it is BOTH! While God looks at our hearts to judge us justly, it is our actions that reveal what is in our hearts.

Let's take another look at John the Baptist. He was chosen to bring a message that would prepare people to see and receive the Kingdom of God in the person of Jesus Christ. By admonishing the Pharisees and Sadducees who came to him for baptism, and by saying, "Bear fruit in keeping with repentance" (Matt. 3:7-8), John is telling us that words of confession are simply not enough; there must be more. There must be true repentance—a change of mind and behavior that joins hands with the confession. True repentance will always bring about real change and bear good, desirable fruit.

One final note: We deceive ourselves and betray the trust of others by continually saying the right things without examining ourselves to see if we are actually doing the right things. Hear me again: I am not saying, "be perfect and never make a mistake." I am clarifying the importance of putting forth real effort to live with your spouse in a way that validates the sincerity of your words. Most spouses are satisfied when they see genuine effort. They don't need perfection, just honest and consistent effort. God desperately wants you to have the intimacy you desire. Can you see that God desires for us all to confess and repent of sin so that we will be free to invite our spouse into the innermost places of our heart? It is a necessary path to experiencing intimacy with Him and with each other (see 1 John 1:7).

Prayer

Father, I pray for the grace needed for every reader to trust You and Your ways. I pray for the humility to confess to You, and to their spouse, any area where darkness is ruling over them. I pray for the grace to go beyond just a remorseful confession and into a heartfelt commitment to continually turn to You, to let You bring lasting changes. I pray this in the name of Jesus. Amen.

ACTIVITY

1. Name any areas in your life where you have significant feelings, thoughts, discomfort, distress, fear or anxiety that you've never taken time to understand.

2. What patterns, habits or behaviors in your life make you unhappy with yourself?

HOMEWORK

1. Just for fun, try to think of three interesting facts about yourself that your spouse doesn't know; share them with each other.

2. Continue to walk and pray (or whatever works best for you) three or more times this week.

3. As you pray with each other this week, ask God to reveal more about the things that make each of you unhappy with yourself. Pray together about those things. If appropriate, use the *1-2-3 Skidoo* tool (from chapter 6).

4. Practice the *Listening Exercise* (from chapter 4) two times this week.

Notes

9

STEPS TO RECONCILIATION

Even though I (Barry) am 33 years older than my youngest son, Brendon, he and I can relate to each other in many ways. We have very similar tastes in music. He is a thinker, as I am, and both of us are strongly led by our convictions. He is a psychology major, as I was. We have had issues and misunderstandings to work out through the years, but over all, there has been a lot of mutual respect and comfort in our relationship. That's why I was surprised by a verbal exchange we had last fall.

One evening, I was sitting at the dining room table when Brendon was passing through on the way to his bedroom. It was the middle of August, and the unprompted thought went through my mind, *I haven't heard Brendon say anything about registering for college classes in the fall.* I remembered that in the spring of that year Brendon had made a decision to remain at home and work so that he could save money and be able to pay for his college education. So I asked him if he was registered for the fall semester. Rather abruptly and without further explanation, he replied, "No." Already feeling some resistance, I cautiously pressed on and asked if he was planning to take classes. He informed me that he was planning to apply for some grants to help pay for tuition and wait to take classes in the spring. Again I pressed on, confused at the resistance I was feeling, and asked, "Do you know the deadline for applying for grants?" Once more he tersely said, "Yes," and then walked away.

Confused and a bit shocked, I asked Lori, who had overheard the interchange, "Did Brendon seem upset to you?"

"Yes, he did," she answered.

Soon Brendon reappeared, passing through the dining room, so I grabbed the opportunity and said, "Brendon, were you upset when I asked you about registering for classes?"

He thought for a moment and then replied, "I wasn't really upset. I just feel like I have to give you the right answer so you wouldn't be upset." After a little more dialogue, he stated, "I just feel like I can't fail or make a mistake with you."

Once again I was surprised and knew that I had to pursue some understanding, knowing that I would probably have to listen to some way that I had unknowingly caused Brendon to feel this way toward me. With some apprehension, I asked, "Why do you feel that it's not okay to fail or make a mistake with me?"

He said, "Well, it probably goes back to when I was young."

We launched into a discussion that proved to be extremely frustrating for both of us. We just could not connect, and neither of us felt understood. He gave me an example: "Like when you would teach me to use the weed eater. I would start to use it and then you would take it from me and do a whole bunch of the weed eating and then hand it back to me. I felt like I had to do it exactly like you or it wasn't good enough."

I defended myself, stating that I had seen a TV show years earlier that talked about modeling as a way of teaching. I thought it was a good way to teach. In my mind I thought I was helping him by showing him what I had learned about weed eating. My explanation did not help at all. I did not see it at the time, but my defending myself left Brendon feeling like I was frustrated with him! I was trying my best to listen while I wanted to be understood at the same time. It was actually agonizing work to put aside my need to be understood and try to listen. Although there was much tension in the room, we continued to talk calmly for quite a while but still could not connect with each other.

Lori listened silently to the discussion.

At one point, in spite of my frustration at feeling misunderstood, I mustered up all the skill and energy available to me at the time and tried to empathize with Brendon's feelings. I heard his next comment as frustration toward me.

"Dad, you haven't heard anything that I have been trying to tell you!"

This pushed me over the edge. For the first time that I can ever remember, in the middle of a conversation, I said, "I can't take this anymore!" (Inside, I was thinking, *I can do this all day with my clients; this can't be all my fault!*) Then I stood up and began to walk away toward the kitchen.

Brendon cried out in desperation, "Don't leave! I'm doing the best I can! Sometimes I f— up, but at least I'm trying!" This was not normal language for Brendon. It shocked me and got my attention. I finally heard his heart. In spite of the tremendous frustration on both our parts, I knew he was trying just as hard as I was and doing his best to communicate.

Finally, a voice of sanity broke through, and Lori suggested, "Why don't you go through the *Steps to Reconciliation?*"

Wow! A novel idea! Actually use one of the tools that I teach in my counseling and in LAM!

I sat down again on one side of the table while Brendon sat at the end. I looked directly at him and started by stating that I had hurt him by acting in ways that communicated to him that he could not do things well enough for me, and I left him feeling that he could not make a mistake in front of me. I made this statement without any explanation or justification for my behavior.

Earlier in our conversation, I had been completely oblivious to the fact that I was creating frustration and feelings of disconnection inside of Brendon by defending myself. This time I made no excuse even though the hurt was truly unintentional.

Next, I tried to empathize once again. "I can see that you never felt safe to fail in front of me. I can see how my behavior left you afraid of failing. I'm sorry that you had to deal with this for so many years."

Third, I told Brendon how badly I felt that I had caused him this pain and confusion for such a long time. At this point, he dropped his head into his folded arms on the table and began to sob. I waited a few seconds and then moved to the end of the table and put my arms around him. He continued to cry for a while and then he turned and embraced me and sobbed on my shoulder. "I love you," he said to me.

"I love you too," I replied. I asked if he could forgive me for the pain I had put him through.

"Yes," he said.

The atmosphere was completely different now. I needed to connect with the pain in his heart—and I finally was able to give him what he had needed for years. Neither of us really knew what was needed; we stumbled into it by trying our best to talk. He simply needed me to understand the pain I had caused. He needed me to understand it and to care about it— without justifying myself at all.

It was amazing to experience the new level of trust and closeness between Brendon and me. Beyond feeling closer and more comfortable, there was a spiritual change as well. This process brought growth in our mutual love and respect for each other; we could honor and receive honor from each other in new ways. At the time of that conversation, God was bringing freedom to Brendon in the area of shame. As he shared what he was learning with me, I received freedom from shame in my life as well.

Authentic Reconciliation

True reconciliation is motivated by love for the other person and a genuine concern for his or her pain. We must let ourselves feel the pain of the other person and then put those feelings into words. With Brendon, I had to get past my pain of wanting to be understood and let myself feel the pain that he had gone through for years. I had to feel the pain of acknowledging that my best efforts as a father to love him and raise him well still fell short of really understanding him at times. I needed to simply understand him and care about what he felt without turning the conversation to me. After all, I was the one who invited him to open up and tell me about what was bothering him.

To help a person feel understood, we must find words that touch the part inside of them that is hurt. It is best to use feeling words that clearly describe the other person's pain, such as: You probably felt unloved . . . betrayed . . . insecure . . . embarrassed . . . humiliated . . . lonely . . . unwanted . . . afraid . . . terrified . . . worthless . . . trapped . . . controlled . . . undesirable . . .

It can take considerable thought and effort to find the right words to connect with our spouse's pain. When we can describe the other person's pain well and with sincerity, it is an exceptionally powerful tool to restore two hearts that have been separated by hurtful words or actions. Precise words that communicate understanding create intimacy. Proverbs 24:26 tells us, "He kisses the lips who gives a right answer." Giving just the right words of understanding to our spouse's feelings can be as intimate as a kiss.

By the way, simply saying "I understand" does not mean that you really do understand. You need to use words that describe what the other person feels inside in order for them to be confident that we truly understand what they are going through.

Going Beyond "I'm Sorry"

I have often observed that saying "I'm sorry" or "Will you forgive me?" is not enough to reconcile a wrong. When there is a very deep wound or repetitive wounding, reconciliation requires a more extensive process. Brendon needed me to go beyond saying "I'm sorry."

Perhaps you have experienced times when "I'm sorry" did not bring the necessary healing, and the feelings of hurt and pain remained or even increased. One reason the pain remains even after saying "I'm sorry" is because the person who has been hurt still does not know if the one who is reconciling really cares or is just trying to do the right thing. Saying "I'm sorry; please forgive me" *can* be mostly about getting out of trouble. It can sound right, but actually it can be selfishly motivated.

In true reconciliation, we need to care more about the pain we have caused than about our own comfort. When we go beyond simply saying "I'm sorry" and allow ourselves to feel and care about the pain we put our spouse through, then we move from only caring about what we did wrong to caring about how we affected our spouse—we move from just doing the right thing to loving. When I connected with Brendon's feelings, he felt deeply understood and loved. His first words to me were, "I love you."

Jesus said, "If you love Me, you will keep My commandments" (John 14:15). Jesus was saying that love is the greatest motivator for obedience. The greatest motivator for change is love, not an obligatory adherence to what is right. If we reconcile out of genuine love and concern for our spouse, our spouse will have the most confidence that the change will last because it is motivated out of love. If our heart is motivated by the desire to get out of trouble, then our words and behaviors will be about us rather than the person we have hurt. This will never bring the healing touch needed to heal another person's heart.

Reconciliation and Conflict Resolution

There is a difference between reconciliation and conflict resolution. In the reconciliation process with a spouse, we are simply and fully acknowledging the way that we have hurt or wronged our spouse. Reconciliation repairs wounded hearts; it does not solve problems. Conflict resolution is the process of coming to agreement and making decisions together. If a couple cannot agree on where to go and how much to spend on summer vacation, that is a conflict resolution issue. It requires a solution. It is best to reconcile any hurts and restore a heart connection before trying to work through conflict.

Jesus said, "The mouth speaks out of that which fills the heart" (Matt. 12:34). He is saying that whatever we feel in our hearts is going to find a way out through our words. If we do not reconcile our hearts before we try to work through conflict, it will be natural to speak out of the hurtful things that remain in our hearts. Trying to work through conflict while our heart is still filled with hurt and offense is one of the reasons why people get stuck going around the same issues over and over.

I recently met with a couple that had significant trust issues. Every time they tried to talk about finances, they got stuck repeating the same issues without any progress. They needed to reconcile their resentment and distrust of each other before they could resolve their conflict. Once they were able to reconcile the conflict, resolution became much easier. They were much more able to be patient and think the best of each other. A heart that is filled with love and concern for a spouse will generate healing. Thorough reconciliation reconnects a husband and wife at the heart level.

Here is a reconciliation tool you can use to restore your heart to your spouse when you have hurt him or her.

Steps to Reconciliation

If your goal is true reconciliation, you need to care more about the pain you have caused than about your own comfort. So, your responses must be clear, concise statements without any explanation or justification for your own behavior. The numbered list that follows provides the five steps to reconciliation and the general context for what you are to say:

1. This is what I did wrong, or this is what I did that hurt you.

2. This is the pain that I believe I put you through because of what I did—this is what you felt because of what I did. (Ask for feedback to verify that you have accurately identified the person's pain.)

3. This is how I feel about putting you through that pain.

4. Express your sincere desire and your intention to change this behavior and not bring this pain into the relationship in the future.

5. Look at the other person and ask, "Can you forgive me for this pain I have brought to you, or this wrong I have done to you?"

Note: If you go through this exercise with empty words and do not follow through with sincere and diligent effort to change, you will only succeed in disappointing your spouse again and betraying his/her trust in you.

Now let's look at the steps in a little more detail.

Instructions

The first instruction, "to respond with clear concise statements and without any explanation or justification," is extremely important. It requires a lot of self-discipline to go through this exercise without explaining or justifying your behavior. Some of us feel that we must use a lot of words and explain everything in great detail in order to be understood. To the contrary, it is important to be clear yet as concise as possible, because the more words you use while in a state of pain, the more likely you are to trigger more pain. Use just enough words to be clear.

The reason that you don't give any explanation or justification for your behavior is to keep the reconciliation focused on the other person's pain, and not on you. As soon as you begin explaining or justifying yourself, the conversation becomes about you rather than about how you hurt the other person. When you explain or justify yourself, the other person must work to understand you rather than you fully understanding them. This is a one-directional exercise. (You can do reconciliation the other direction after one person finishes.)

Reconciliation is a pure focus on owning up to how you hurt the other person. In the example of my talk with my son Brendon, it would have been very easy and accurate for me to say, "It wasn't my intention to hurt you. I even thought that I was doing a good job of training you." This would have been a true statement but would have shifted the conversation to me rather than remain focused on Brendon's pain. It would have required Brendon to start understanding me rather than me fully understanding him. Whenever we justify ourselves, we shift the focus to ourselves, and that requires that the other person place his or her pain on hold and deal with our need to be understood. This greatly diminishes the reconciliation process.

What I Did Wrong

Step one asks the person who is reconciling to state simply and clearly what he or she did wrong or did to hurt the other person. It is easy to see what we need to reconcile when we do something seriously wrong, like infidelity or an ongoing destructive addiction. However, the wrong done could be something common like a "small" lie or being irritable or controlling. It is important to note that you can benefit from reconciliation even if you did not do anything wrong but simply did something unintentionally hurtful. I didn't do anything wrong or malicious to Brendon, but I failed to see how my behavior was hurting him. Still, he lived with the pain of feeling like he couldn't make a mistake with me. I could either defend myself, expecting him to understand me, or I could care about how I affected him. If I care about how I affect him, then I will take the time to reconcile the pain.

What You Felt

This is probably the hardest step because it is painful to choose to feel the pain you cause another person. If the other person is your spouse or anyone that you love, it will hurt you to realize that you brought pain to a person you love. In my example with Brendon, I made a few statements to try to communicate the pain I had caused him—"I can see that you never felt safe to fail in front of me. I can see how my behavior left you afraid of failing. I'm sorry this has affected you for so many years."

Step two is best accomplished by using words that express feelings and simple clarification when needed. The goal is to find words that accurately convey what the other person felt inside as a result of what you did. Using the phrase, "What I did may have left you feeling . . ." and using a word to describe what the person felt, for example, "humiliated, betrayed, worthless, unloved, lonely, hopeless, powerless, rejected, deflated, unimportant, invisible, discouraged, crushed, frightened," is a good way to communicate understanding of the other person's pain. It is best to avoid lengthy explanations of the other person's feelings. Try to stay focused more on what the other person felt about himself rather than what he felt toward you. (Reference the list of *Feeling Words* in chapter 4, "Going Deeper in Your Communication.")

I Feel Bad About Hurting You

The third step is a simple statement about how you feel after realizing the pain you put the other person through. I told Brendon that I felt very bad that my behavior had caused him to live with insecurity and fear of failing. In this step, you are trying to communicate that it hurts you to know that you hurt your loved one. Do not use self-deprecating phrases like, "I feel like such an idiot" or "I feel like a jerk." Statements like these tend to make the other person want to take care of you. It is a digression from staying with the other person's feelings.

I Intend to Change

Step four is a sincere statement of intent and purpose to not bring the pain into the relationship again. It is a statement of genuine repentance. When there have been severe issues, like adultery, child abuse or violence, a complete and immediate change is required. When you are dealing with less serious but repetitive behavior patterns, I recommend that you stay clear of expressions like "I promise I will never get angry at you again." It is better to express your sincere desire and intention to change and then follow through. Usually, any reasonable spouse is encouraged by honest and persistent effort and does not need an immediate and complete change. Here is an example, "I promise that I will do all I can to remember how I hurt you and get whatever help I need to keep from hurting you with my anger in the future."

Notice in my example with Brendon that I did not include step four because I had already changed my behavior. He only needed me to understand and care about his pain. He no longer needed me to change my behavior.

Can You Forgive Me?

This is a clear request to be forgiven for the pain you've caused your spouse. Giving forgiveness releases the offender from the wrong he or she did and the pain the one offended experienced. Forgiveness lets go of any longing to hurt back. If I forgive Lori for saying something disrespectful to me, and she has understood how she hurt me, and then repented, I will need to let go of any impulse to pull away in self-protection. I will not remind her again of what she did to me as a way to control her. Forgiveness means that I am choosing to respond out of what is best for Lori, not out of my hurt feelings.

Forgiveness is not the same as trust. If there has been a longstanding pattern of wrongs and hurts done, it is wise to gradually give trust as a person waits to see if there is fruit from the repentance—is there real and lasting change? We must still forgive, but we may realize that we cannot trust the words of a spouse who promises to change but does not.

Some spouses fall into the trap of repeatedly trusting words without waiting to see if there is follow-through. They repeatedly believe their spouse's words even though there has been no actual lasting change. This leads to great frustration from repetitive broken promises. Others have trouble risking vulnerability even when genuine repentance and consistent change have occurred. If the offending party is truly changing, and stopping the wrong or hurtful behavior, then we need to risk trusting again at some point.

> **Note:** Reconciliation must be done in sincerity and there must be follow-through, or else you will only succeed in hurting and betraying with the tool that is intended to mend broken hearts. It will be a betrayal to draw your spouse in to trust you with kind and understanding words but then not follow through with sincere effort.

The Holy Spirit Helps Us Reconcile

A couple from Europe came to one of our workshops last year. During the workshop they volunteered to allow us to "coach" them in front of the group of 52 couples. The husband wanted God's help for a long-standing issue with anger. After asking the Lord to show him where this anger came from, he saw a picture in his mind's eye of himself as a young boy. He said, "I see myself reaching for my father and there is none." He then let out a gut-wrenching scream at the top of his lungs. Immediately, he started sobbing; and then for about 15 minutes he alternated between wailing and laughing. This whole experience was so intense that he fell to the ground in the midst of it all. When it was over, he lay stretched out on his back with his eyes closed and a smile on his face, calmly declaring, "It is gone!" The Lord did an astounding, supernatural work in this man, and he was truly free! The anger pattern was broken.

A day or two later, this husband and his wife again volunteered to come up in front of the class to model the *Steps to Reconciliation*. The husband felt the need to reconcile the wrong and hurt he had done to his wife by his years of anger. When we led him through the second step, where he tried to find words to express the pain that he had put his wife through, he got stuck. As hard as he tried, he could not feel what she might be feeling, nor could he find the right words to express this. So we asked the Holy Spirit to show him how his anger had affected his wife. After a few seconds of listening, he began to speak and weep simultaneously. "I see myself like a huge wave pouring over you and pushing you down and crushing you and suffocating you!" Tears were now streaming down his face and his wife's face.

For the first time ever, his wife felt him truly connect with the pain he had inflicted on her for years. Seeing her husband so deeply understand her pain gave her the freedom to address ways that she also had hurt her husband by manipulating and controlling him. Words of ownership and understanding began to pour out of her. They went through the rest of the *Steps to Reconciliation* with tears and smiles.

At the end of the reconciliation, as they stood smiling at each other in front of their captivated audience, the husband looked tenderly at his wife and spontaneously blurted out, "I feel my body being drawn to you!" The entire room erupted with joy and laughter. I quickly commented, "This is the way reconciliation is supposed to work. When our hearts are reconciled and joined as one, we will *want* to be physically close to each other." Our hearts must be reconciled in order to feel completely comfortable in our physical connection.

In the case of this couple, the Holy Spirit helped them the first time they tried to reconcile. We can trust that He will always be there to help us even if we do not obtain the desired results the first time we ask. The Holy Spirit knows things about us that we do not. He will show us things that we have pushed out of our conscious memory. He will help us feel emotions that we cannot get in touch with on our own. Be sure to ask for the Holy Spirit's help if you get stuck somewhere in this process.

You Cannot Reconcile a Victim Spirit

Often when Lori and I teach this tool of reconciliation, someone will ask, "What do you do if one person always wants you to reconcile and blames you for everything but won't do the reconciliation himself?" This pattern probably represents what is often called a "victim spirit." A person under the influence of a victim spirit will be highly skilled at finding fault with others and equally skilled at avoiding ownership of his or her own faults and weaknesses.

Here are a few of the common characteristics that describe a victim spirit:

1. The victim spirit or attitude enters through real pain, hurt, trauma or mistreatment. In other words, there is a real victimization in

the person's life and the enemy takes advantage of the pain to bring the victim attitude.

2. The victim spirit keeps the person keenly aware of others' faults while remaining blind to his or her own. The victim spirit teaches an ungodly way to avoid dealing with pain by focusing on others' faults.

3. The victim spirit brings a strong sense of entitlement. The person who has been victimized and then joins with a victim spirit feels a sense of entitlement to be pitied and excused from taking risks again.

4. The victim spirit leads a person to demand that his or her feelings of pain be taken care of by those around them. They do not take the responsibility to deal with their own pain.

5. The victim spirit leads a person to demand his or her rights rather than continuing to love, give and serve.

6. The victim spirit teaches a person to become suspicious and protect themselves instead of trusting God as their protector.

7. Often the victim spirit will lead a person to vacillate between being a victim and being a perpetrator and hurting others; but he or she will remain blind to being a perpetrator.

8. The victim spirit harms a person's gift of spiritual discernment by being overly alert to find fault rather than to accurately discern who is safe and who is not. People with a victim spirit will often use phrases like, "I don't feel safe" as a way of avoiding the risk of walking by faith and trusting God to show them who is safe.

9. A victim spirit steals away faith, hope and courage and replaces it with hopelessness, accusation and manipulation.

The victim spirit is insidious and a destroyer of intimacy in marriage. Earlier this year, Lori and I recognized the beginnings of a victim spirit

creeping into our marriage. This is not characteristic of us. I was beginning to feel hopeless, thinking that I could never change a pattern of
being distracted when I was listening to Lori. I began to expect to fail
when I tried to listen to her. I felt like a victim to this growing pattern in
our marriage. Understandably, Lori was hurt by my constant distraction
and she began to feel entitled in being irritated with me when I was not
listening well. One morning, while we were still lying in bed and talking,
the Lord opened our eyes to see how this victim spirit was taking root.
We prayed against it by acknowledging its work in us, and using the
1-2-3 Skidoo tool. Then we reconciled with each other. I began to weep,
which I do not easily do, as I thought of how I had hurt Lori by not
listening. She wept as she saw me genuinely care about her pain. Lori
reconciled her impatience with me. After praying and breaking agreements with the victim spirit, most of my pattern of being distracted was
broken. Immediately, Lori noticed a difference; I could pay attention
much better and with far less effort.

Because the victim spirit teaches a person to deflect blame so well, it is
usually very difficult to minister to a person with a victim spirit. However,
the week after we worked through this issue we did a five-day intensive
LAM workshop and were able to minister corporately to the entire group
regarding a victim spirit. We shared what we had gone through and how
the Lord had helped us. We then taught on the characteristics of a victim
spirit and offered to minister corporately to those who felt that a victim
spirit was affecting them. Every couple but one stood to receive ministry!
This is very unusual. One woman stated that she had been struggling for
many years to be rid of the victim spirit, and now she felt it was truly gone.
Apparently our personal sharing helped us break through the typical resistance and enabled the people to receive ministry from us.

If you find yourself doing sincere reconciliation over and over with
no results, while your spouse blames you continually, you are probably
dealing with a victim spirit in your marriage. You can do one-sided reconciliation forever and never remove the victim spirit from your marriage. If you are dealing with a victim spirit, it is imperative that you
speak the truth in love even in the face of your spouse's anger or threats
of rejection.

A person who is under the influence of a victim spirit must choose to
own his or her stuff and take risks to trust or he/she will never be free. If
we try to take responsibility for all of the wrong and hurt in our marriage

when our spouse unjustly blames us, we will only succeed in reinforcing our spouse's control through the victim spirit. They will remain blind to their own issues. It is very important that you only reconcile those things that are legitimately wrong or hurtful.

If you are trying to deal with a victim spirit in your marriage, you will need more than the reconciliation tool. Many of the attitudes and skills you will need can be found in chapter 12, "Honoring God Through Godly Assertion." We recommend that you study that chapter well and apply its principles. Remember, this victim spirit is something coming against your spouse. *It* is the enemy, not your spouse.

ACTIVITY

1. Take some time right now and individually ask the Holy Spirit to bring to mind any ways you may have brought pain and hurt to your spouse that has not been reconciled. (Remember, just saying "I'm sorry" or "Would you forgive me?" is not true reconciliation.) This is not you telling your spouse how he/she has hurt you; it is letting the Holy Spirit help you see the ways you have brought hurt to your spouse. You will take turns going through the five *Steps to Reconciliation*.

2. Now take turns going through the five *Steps to Reconciliation* in one area that you have brought pain to your spouse as the Holy Spirit showed you. (Step 1. This is what I did wrong, or this is what I did to hurt you . . . state it simply and clearly . . . finish all five steps and then switch roles). If you insert what you did to hurt your spouse and follow each step carefully without adding to the tool, you'll have success. This tool has changed many relationships in amazing ways when it has been used correctly and regularly.

Prayer

*We bless your spirits to be prominent as the Holy Spirit leads you,
and we tell your souls and bodies to sit down. Lord, release
Your anointing and grace on the use of this tool, on this couple
and on this time. Amen.*

HOMEWORK

1. Use the *Steps to Reconciliation* to get your hearts reconnected in any remaining areas the Holy Spirit has shown you or any new areas that arise. Remember to follow the tool step by step.

2. Continue to pray together at least three times this week.

3. Use the *1-2-3 Skidoo* tool to deal with any spiritual forces that come against you this week.

Notes

_____

_____

_____

_____

_____

_____

_____

_____

_____

_____

_____

_____

_____

_____

_____

_____

_____

_____

_____

_____

_____

_____

_____

_____

_____

_____

_____

10

RULES FOR WORKING THROUGH CONFLICT

After completing the entire 30 weeks of LAM at Bethel Church, Jim and Natalie were enjoying a greater emotional connection than they had ever experienced; yet a critical issue of unresolved conflict remained. Jim loved Natalie deeply, but he lived with built-up frustration and fear as the result of feeling unappreciated, devalued and helpless, with no voice in their marriage. These feelings rose up on a regular basis like a tall brick wall between them, keeping them separated emotionally. Jim was afraid of confrontation and tension, so his habitual response was to withdraw and walk on eggshells around Natalie.

One of these potentially explosive incidents occurred one day and brought to the surface all of Jim's familiar pain and frustration. Natalie wanted to talk about what Jim was feeling and thinking. But Jim was not ready to talk, because they would not be able to work through the issue in the short amount of time available to them. He did not want to repeat what was their common pattern of talking and then feeling rushed to process all that had been said. This situation always resulted in his feeling misunderstood, unappreciated, powerless and devalued.

Jim took about 10 days to think through and identify what exactly was bothering him, and he was able to identify a recurring pattern. Natalie would come to him with an important issue that needed to be taken care of but was not a crisis. After talking it through, she would continue to over schedule her life, having forgotten about the task she had brought up to Jim. Jim, however, would continue to think about the task and develop questions and strategies to take care of the problem; but when he approached Natalie to discuss it, she would put him off by saying she was too busy. This would continue until the problem reached crisis proportions and had to be taken care of immediately.

At this point, Natalie would bring the problem to Jim once again and expect him to drop everything on his agenda to take care of her crisis. Over and over, he felt that he was at the mercy of living out the consequences of her procrastination. This was the frustrating ongoing pattern Jim needed to tackle.

In spite of the tension they were feeling, Jim and Natalie were determined to work through their conflict. They planned a picnic for two and took along their LAM workbook. They began by reading through the *Rules for Sharing* so they would have some ground rules for talking. Then they launched into the tool *Rules for Working Through Conflict*. As best they could, they walked through the tool step by step. Opening up discussion about this conflict forced Jim to acknowledge his deepest fear—that he did not have value in Natalie's eyes.

Facing his fear head-on, Jim carefully explained his side of the conflict while fully aware of the risk he was taking. He and Natalie conversed back and forth, clarifying and stating what they could agree with, and presenting various aspects of the issue. At one point, Natalie interrupted Jim to remind him that the *Rules for Working Through Conflict* stated that he needed to be concise and not cover every detail. Jim accepted Natalie's correction. They both avoided the temptation to take offense at each other and chose to get back on track. It was a great victory!

When in the midst of intense conflict, a couple must follow the instructions and use the tool exactly as written. Without a supporting framework, they typically will return to old patterns and repeat the same arguments without any progress. We often encourage couples to methodically work through the tool step by step in order to break out of their usual patterns of communicating. That is exactly what Jim and Natalie had to do.

They spent more than an hour working through the *Rules for Working Through Conflict*. They spent another three hours, over the course of the day, clarifying and discussing until they gained new understanding of each other and their conflict. Jim realized he had incorrectly concluded that Natalie saw herself as the "queen." He now knew that she did not see him as her slave who was expected to drop everything to take care of her problems.

Natalie could see how she was setting Jim up for frustration and failure. After hearing and understanding his heart, she could feel what she had done, and she began to care about how she had affected him. When Jim felt validated by Natalie, his feelings toward her immediately changed. Relief flooded through him when Natalie realized how hard he was trying to serve her, despite his intense frustration. For the first time, she saw how unfair her expectations of her husband had been; and for the first time, Jim felt understood. They continued to work through this conflict until they came to a mutual understanding and began gaining a new respect for each other.

By intentionally venturing into conflict resolution, Jim was finally able to face his fears. Instead of walking on eggshells around Natalie, he found his voice and asserted himself in a constructive, caring way. This act of courage produced dramatic, life-changing results for both Jim and Natalie. After successfully resolving his conflict, Jim felt tremendous relief and hope that the long-standing pattern of their communication would change. As a result of removing this conflict from their relationship, their spiritual and emotional connection has grown by leaps and bounds.

Several months later, Jim said that he no longer felt like a slave to a queen; now he felt like a co-laborer with Natalie. Because he had felt spiritually inferior in the past, he had relinquished spiritual leadership to Natalie. She had never wanted to carry this responsibility on her own; she was just trying to make up for the lack.

Now, Jim is actively watching for the spiritual forces working in their home and he is standing against those forces, rather than fighting against Natalie. He now realizes how he had not been a protector for his wife. As he has stepped into the role of leading spiritually and is consciously protecting Natalie, she says that he has become much more attractive and even more sexually appealing to her. In fact, one day, as Jim was telling Natalie about his desire to be her protector, to his delight, she exclaimed, "Wow! I am so turned on by you right now!" Working through their conflict took them from feeling like enemies to desiring one another as lovers! This is exactly how God wants it.

Jim now sees Natalie in a completely different way. His fear and hurt feelings had not allowed him to know her accurately. Things about her that used to annoy him, he now sees as her cute little idiosyncrasies. By taking his stand and facing his fear of conflict, Jim went from feeling help-less to having a voice; he went from the place of walking on eggshells to being a spiritual warrior in his marriage; from feeling hopeless to enjoying a wonderful connection with Natalie.

They are now leading a LAM home group in their home where they meet with other couples biweekly to train them in working through conflict and practice the LAM tools. Resolving conflict needs to become a skill that is used regularly until it develops into a lifestyle.

Conflict Resolution and Marital Success

While it is usually easy for couples to enjoy each other during good times, it is the constant tension created by unresolved conflict that creates separation in a marriage. After more than 20 years of research with thousands of happy and unhappy couples, Clifford Notarius, Ph.D., and Howard Markman, Ph.D., concluded, "Relationship success depends on the ability of two people to *manage* the conflicts that inevitably occur in all relationships."[1] If you cannot resolve conflicts, you are left with the futile task of trying to build a loving relationship in an environment characterized by unending pain and frustration.

As a result of working through their conflict, Jim and Natalie are now living on a new level of intimate connection and marital happiness.

Looking at conflict resolution from a spiritual viewpoint, we see that relational conflicts entered the world with the entrance of sin. Sin brought relationship conflict, sickness, death and all sorts of misery into the world. Overcoming conflict in marriage actually deals with the work of sin and defeats the Enemy's attempts to damage a couple's relationship oneness.

Conflict Resolution or Reconciliation?

Conflict resolution is different from reconciliation. The purpose of reconciliation is to restore two people's wounded hearts; whereas, the purpose of conflict resolution is to solve problems and come to a mutually agreeable solution to those problems.

In conflict resolution, you are attempting to find answers to problems that both spouses can agree upon. We have already emphasized how very important it is for a couple to be sensitive to each other and listen to each other; but sometimes problems must be solved and decisions made. Much of the time it requires more than listening, empathizing and understanding to solve a problem. When a couple talks through the issues with the goal of coming to a mutual agreement about the answer to the problem, they honor their words and abide by their agreements. Just like Jim and Natalie, anyone can build trust and confidence in his or her marriage by working through conflicts to the point of resolution.

When you are in the midst of a conflict, and your emotions are running high, it is difficult to be rational, calm and slow to take offense. Yet this is exactly what is needed to resolve conflict. If you approach conflict resolution with the attitude that you have to win or you have to be right, you will create an atmosphere of competition rather than cooperation. A competitive attitude will thwart your efforts at resolution and mutual agreement; but an attitude of cooperation is indispensable to conflict resolution.

The first thing you need to do when entering into conflict resolution is to check your attitude. You must get yourself to a place where you want the best solution for everyone concerned in the conflict. You must take the time to get your heart right before the Lord so that you care more about doing what is best than getting your own way. This is the attitude Jim and Natalie adopted as they determined to resolve the conflict in their marriage. Even if you need to leave the discussion and spend time before the Lord to correct your heart attitude, you must prepare your mindset before entering into conflict resolution.

What follows are the *Rules for Working Through Conflict* tool that Jim and Natalie used to break through the conflict in their marriage.

Rules for Working Through Conflict

A couple is prepared to use this tool when both parties are actively and willingly working toward understanding each other in a mutually respectful and honest relationship.

Begin with Prayer

Pray together, asking the Holy Spirit to empower you to keep the following attitudes as you discuss your conflict.

We bless our spirits to lead us and remain prominent as we do these things:

- Approach the discussion with the attitude, "I don't have to win this argument, and I don't have to be the one who is right."
- Make of paramount importance whatever is best for everyone concerned.
- Present an honest, accurate picture of the conflict.
- Fully own up to my part in the conflict.
- Follow these principles above anything I fear or desire.
- Humbly listen to and learn from my spouse.
- Validate any good ideas coming from my spouse.

1. The First Person Talks:
   - When one person speaks, the other person listens (the listener will have an opportunity to speak later).
   - Stay focused and concise.
     - ➤ Don't try to cover every aspect of the issue in one communication.
     - ➤ Don't try to do a "sales job" on the other person.
     - ➤ Do give reasons why you believe your ideas or opinions would be the best choice for everyone affected by them.
   - The longer one person talks, the more complicated the discussion becomes. When many issues are raised in one communication session, it can be confusing and overwhelming for the other person to choose which issues to respond to.
   - The longer a person talks without hearing from the other person involved in the conflict, the more likely he or she is to hit sensitive issues and stir up hurt, resentment and the like.

2. The Second Person Listens:
   - Try to pay more attention to what the other person is saying than to what you are going to say in rebuttal.
   - Try to hear not only the words but also the heart attitude of the person talking.

3. The Second Person Responds:
   - First, ask questions to *clarify*, or state what you heard to be sure you've understood correctly before you respond.
   - Next, *state the things you can agree with* that the first person has said, and why you agree.
   - *Only after these two steps are completed is it okay to give your contrasting or opposing view and the reasons for it.* When giving your opposing view, follow all of the guidelines listed in the #1 guideline.

Resolution

1. Repeat the three steps until you reach a mutual agreement.

2. Be patient. Give the process time even though it may feel tense and seem tedious.

3. *Do not* agree to decisions or conclusions that you don't really believe in just to end the conflict, make the other person feel better, or prevent anger.

4. Continue talking and listening respectfully until you come to the place where each can honestly say, "I can live with that," or "I think that would be the best choice for both of us."

5. Honor your agreements by keeping them until you make a new agreement.

6. If you do this process well and still cannot come to a consensus, you may need the help of a third-party mediator. There may be individual issues that need attention before you can resolve conflict well.

ACTIVITY

1. Go through the numbered list that follows and mark the ways that you respond to conflict.

    ___ 1. I deny it, gloss over it or cover it up.
    ___ 2. I hold it and hold it . . . then blow up.
    ___ 3. I blame and accuse.
    ___ 4. I hold a grudge and put up walls; then I live with hurt and unforgiveness.
    ___ 5. I am easily triggered and respond destructively.
    ___ 6. I shut up, stuff it and appease the one who's angry to make everyone happy.
    ___ 7. I get defensive and justify everything—I can't listen to or hear the other person.
    ___ 8. I withdraw and retreat emotionally and/or physically.
    ___ 9. I look for something wrong in myself, or I blame myself.
    ___10. I talk it out and work it through.
    ___11. I joke and laugh it off.
    ___12. Other . . .

2. Talk about your patterns of dealing with conflict.

3. Each spouse will choose an area of conflict in the relationship that has not been worked through to a point of resolution. Decide which conflict you

will address first. Set aside enough time to go step by step through the *Rules for Working Through Conflict* tool with each spouse's area of conflict.

Note: If you are having trouble resolving your conflicts, you may need to go through the *Steps to Reconciliation* in chapter 9 to work through any hurtful ways you have responded to your spouse in the past.

When Conflict Becomes Explosive

Efforts at resolving conflict that quickly become explosive will require help to de-escalate. If we act on our strongly antagonistic feelings while trying to resolve conflict, we can do great damage to our marriage. Lori and I have developed the following tool—*When the Poop Hits the Fan*—to help couples in those situations. This tool is specifically designed to stop highly volatile situations from becoming destructive and enable couples to arrive at a place where they can remain calm and listen to each other.

A while back, one of our pastors was at Whiskeytown Lake, several miles north of Redding, California, when he recognized a couple from church standing back to back, apparently talking into the air. He asked what they were doing. They explained that they were using the tool *When the Poop Hits the Fan*, right there in the parking lot. As with all of the other LAM tools, be ready to use this tool whenever you need it. This "de-escalating conflict" tool is fairly simple to use; just follow the numbered steps.

When the Poop Hits the Fan
(A godly option to deal with your disagreements in the heat of the moment)

1. *Choose not to leave.* If you need to cool down or get control of your tongue, tell your spouse that you are going to leave for a short time and that you will be back. If it is longer than five minutes, give your spouse a time when you will come back to talk. Stay in the battle, even when you are tempted to physically leave or emotionally withdraw/shut down . . . don't do it!

2. *Stand back to back.* Ask Jesus to come as the Wonderful Counselor, and pray in English or in tongues for a few minutes until you feel a slight shift in your spirit or emotions.

3. *Continue to stand.* Take turns nailing to the cross whatever you're feeling that is not from God. Break agreements with whatever is coming against you, and ask the Father to send it away. *Say it out loud.* Example:

   • In the name of Jesus, I nail _____ (anger, frustration, separation, accusation, fear, rejection) to the cross of Jesus.

   • I break all agreements I have made with _____, known or unknown.

   • I ask You, Father, to send _____ away from me.

   • Father, what do You want to give me in place of _____ _____?

4. *Now turn and face one another and join hands.* Discuss the issues respectfully, not allying with accusation, anger or the like.

5. *If discussion is going well, finish.* But if not, stop and declare the truth about what you are dealing with. Start with overall truths about yourself and your marriage. Then get specific. Don't rush this.

6. *If either spouse needs to ask forgiveness, do so.*

⌇⌇⌇⌇⌇⌇ HOMEWORK ⌇⌇⌇⌇⌇⌇

1. As areas of conflict arise this week, use the tool *Rules for Working Through Conflict* to come to resolution and agreement. Do not let your conflicts go unresolved.

2. If you and your spouse find yourselves in a heated argument, use the *When the Poop Hits the Fan* tool.

3. Continue to walk and pray at least three times this week.

4. Use the *1-2-3 Skidoo* tool as needed.

5. Use the *Steps to Reconciliation* for any hurts that arise.

Notes

Note

1. C. Notarius and H. Markman, *We Can Work It Out* (New York: Perigee, 1994).

11

SPIRIT BLESSING

We couldn't write this book without including a chapter to introduce you to the concept of "blessing your spirit," as taught by Arthur Burk. Because Love After Marriage is all about passing on the things the Lord has used in our lives, it is with great joy that we pass on this invaluable perspective and strategic tool.

In his teachings, and in his book *Blessing Your Spirit,* Arthur Burk says that problems arise when we have placed our souls in the most prominent place instead of our spirits. The Lord gave him revelation through a picture that depicted our spirits as emaciated stick figures, while our souls looked like big sumo wrestlers. We have all learned many ways to nurture the body, mind, will and emotions; but our spirit is left relatively unnourished. He teaches the practice of speaking to and blessing each other's spirits as a way of nurturing our spirits. This must be done intentionally, just as we must intentionally nurture our bodies and our souls for growth. The Lord wants us to live out of our spirits, because this is the part of us that connects with God and hears Him. A person who is led by the Spirit of God is one whose spirit is ruling over his or her soul and body.

Here are some specific situations in which Lori and I have seen spirit blessing bring breakthrough when other methods have failed:

1. A spouse who was *unwilling* to work on the marriage and/or had given up
2. A spouse who was *emotionally cut off* and unable to feel
3. A couple that was at an impasse relationally and *unable to connect*
4. A couple that was gaining significant ground and wanting to *maintain their breakthrough*

Unwilling or Given Up

Years of unresolved feelings of disconnection, hurt and misunderstanding can take a spouse to the place that he or she no longer wants to stay in the marriage. When this happens, there is always the potential that the spouse will move on and start looking elsewhere for love and relationship. But Barry and I have seen the "spirit blessing" tool bring breakthrough. The unwilling spouse doesn't even need to be in the room to use this tool. Praying that the despondent spouse's spirit will rise up and lead opens the door for the Holy Spirit to come and bring another perspective. As heaven's perspective materializes in the spirit of the resistant spouse, it will often result in disarming the pain that made him or her unwilling to change.

A woman in one of our workshops had come to the point of wanting to leave her marriage. The hurt and disappointment of her relationship led her to the point of complete emotional withdrawal. She stated that she no longer found her husband attractive, and she had decided to look for someone else. Remaining in the LAM workshop to work on her marriage was no longer an option. Through tears of anger and hopelessness, she informed her small-group leaders that she was done with the marriage.

Her husband, who certainly had his part in contributing to this disconnection, was desperately looking for any possible help. Because his wife was unwilling to even pray with him, we encouraged him to get the Arthur Burk book *Blessing Your Spirit*. This prayer book of scriptural topics and insights was written as a guide to pray over someone's spirit-man with the goal of nurturing and growing a person's spirit. We instructed this husband to find blessings in the book that would address the angry, resistant spirit affecting his wife and then pray those blessings every morning and evening. He agreed to do it. He was determined to pursue his wife in this way even though she had no desire to be with him.

Unbeknownst to her, he fervently prayed Scripture and truth over her spirit every morning and evening. After only two weeks, they returned to LAM together. The Lord had heard the husband's prayers, and his wife's spirit had begun to respond. Her spirit grew as he nourished it daily through prayer. She completely turned around in her attitude and her desire for her marriage. Hope and emotional desire for her husband returned! She decided she wanted to stay with her husband, make the marriage work and continue in LAM to work on it.

We could hardly believe what the Lord had done through the earnest and consistent prayers of this husband. I think he was the most surprised of all, and he was definitely the most relieved. With resolve and expectation, they continued on with the healing process for their marriage. They finished the LAM course filled with hope, having seen many significant changes in their relationship.

We ran into them the other day—it has now been a couple of years since this turnabout—and they're still together, emotionally connected and doing very well. Yay, God!

A great miracle took place when this wife's heart—so dead to her husband—completely turned back to him. Because her husband prayed and blessed her spirit, her spirit was able to navigate the necessary heart change with the Holy Spirit's help. In just two weeks, her spirit became strong enough to lead and direct, even though her soul had been leading for so long.

Your soul consists of your mind, will and emotions. When you are in pain, trauma or crisis, your feelings are not your friend. During those times, you cannot count on your feelings to lead you into God's ways. It is best to let your spirit lead; blessing your spirit achieves this in incredible ways!

Emotionally Cut Off

Barry and I have had numerous opportunities to deal with individuals who absolutely cannot identify or express their feelings. Their emotions remain bottled up inside, even though they strongly desire to connect emotionally with their spouse. This is obviously painful for a spouse married to someone who is emotionally shut down; however, it is equally excruciating for the spouse who tries but cannot communicate his or her feelings. People in this state have no idea how to wake up from the emotional coma that continues to wound and separate them from the ones they love.

We encountered this phenomenon in a young couple married about one year. During a LAM workshop, we invited this couple to do a couple's coaching and found out that he couldn't feel much of anything. His bride had never seen him cry. He couldn't really feel love and he had a very hard time expressing it.

As the Lord led us through the coaching time, we discovered that his father had been very angry and, at times, abusive. As a small boy, he had been terrified when he saw his dad unleash this rage in inappropriate ways—usually at inanimate objects. At that time in his young life, he made an unconscious vow never to be angry like his father was. He had a very tender, compassionate heart and could not bear to imagine ever becoming uncontrollably angry like his father. Because of this vow, he not only cut off any negative emotions, but all of the God-given positive emotions as well. Love, passion, joy, excitement—all had been locked up in his emotional prison along with his fear of anger.

We prayed through this with him and guided him to forgive his father for allowing the spirit of anger and rage into the family. He broke agreements with the unconscious vow he had made in an attempt to protect others from ever experiencing the terror he had felt from his father's rage. Even though it was right and good for him not to be angry like his father, the vow he made as a young boy had bound him to the fear of having *any* strong feelings. He was left to suppress his passions in his own human strength. He did stop the anger, but he was still controlled by the fear of anger. Anger is a spirit and must be dealt with spiritually. Natural remedies to spiritual issues carry little authority or power to produce change.

After we ministered to this young man for a while, he began to feel some peace, but emotionally and relationally he did not recognize any change. So we had him and his wife do the "blessing your spirit" tool we call *Face-to-Face*. (We will teach you this exercise at the end of the chapter.) We blessed this couple's spirits to be in a prominent place, and we asked their souls and bodies to be led by their spirits. We had them look into each other's eyes, spirit to spirit, as we invited the Holy Spirit to come and connect with their spirits and help them see the beautiful, wonderful things God had put in each of them.

As they took turns declaring this out loud to one another, something very wonderful began to happen. The wife spoke out first about what the Lord was showing her about her husband. It hit the mark for the first time in their marriage; it bypassed his mind and went straight into his spirit. His countenance noticeably changed as he felt her words of affirmation and blessing. When it was his turn to speak, he struggled for a moment as he attempted to formulate words to express his heart. He pressed through and stammered the words, "I . . . I love you!" As he spoke, tears began to flow along with a flood of feelings. He was now weeping freely. They cried, embraced and enjoyed experiencing the deep, passionate love he had locked away for most of his life.

The next day was the last day of the workshop. During the last session, we invited every couple to stand and share what the Lord had done for them during the last five days. When it was their turn to share, this previously silent, unemotional man in lockdown mode stood up and calmly said, "I just have one thing to say." Then, erupting like a volcano, he thrust both arms up into the air and jumped with all his might, screaming, "Breakthrough!" The whole room exploded in screams, cheers and praise for what God had done, as this man continued to jump around unable to contain his joy and laughter.

This young husband's exuberant expression was evidence of what God had unlocked, first in his spirit, then in his emotions and, finally, in his body. He had felt some relief during the inner healing prayer, but the real breakthrough came when his wife blessed his spirit. The spirit blessing and the *Face-to-Face* exercise have been key tools for many couples that have been stuck. When your spirit is leading, it allows you to connect with the Holy Spirit, who has the power to awaken the soul!

Cannot Connect

When a couple continually misses each other's heart and misinterprets each other's actions and intentions, it provides opportunity for bitterness, resentment, frustration and anger to become part of daily life together. Over a period of time, if left unchecked, these ingredients make for a giant batch of debilitating separation.

In one workshop last year, we were engaged in a couple's coaching for about an hour and fifteen minutes with no sign of any breakthrough. The couple repeatedly accused, blamed and condemned each other, in spite of our efforts to connect them to the Lord's heart of compassion for them. We just could not help them find any common ground. It was painfully clear they had been hurting and missing each other for a long time.

Finally, we remembered the *Face-to-Face* exercise and, as a last effort, we led them through it. We blessed their spirits to be in a prominent position and told their souls and bodies to be quiet, since their souls had been carrying the offence so persistently. We instructed them to look into each other's eyes and into each other's spirits. We then invited the Holy Spirit to help them see what He saw. As they started to speak, something finally started to shift in them. There was a softening and understanding, almost as if they were seeing each other clearly for the first time in a long time. We heard love and tenderness given and received as they continued to speak the truth of what they were seeing in each other. We all breathed a sigh of relief as they embraced and held each other with affection.

The next morning, when they came to the workshop, there was quite a noticeable change in them. The heaviness and depression that had been on the husband all week was gone. His demeanor was lighter and joyful, and he was cracking jokes at his table. Many commented that he didn't even look like the same man. His wife was equally changed—carefree, relaxed and happy.

As a result of ongoing bitterness and resentment, their souls had grown strong in claiming their right to be offended. We tried everything we could think of to turn them around, but it took calling their spirits to lead over their souls to get the breakthrough.

Maintaining the Breakthrough

When a couple receives a breakthrough, no matter how significant or life changing it seems to be, it must be maintained until it becomes a lifestyle. We have found that blessing the spirit is an effective component in turning marriage breakthroughs into lifestyle changes.

Not long ago, a couple came to one of our five-day workshops. They had never had the depth of connection they longed for. There were important hidden events they had never told each other about. Additionally, in their 20 years in ministry, there were some significantly damaging things that had come against them, which they had never taken the time to work through. During the first day, the wife got so upset that she wanted to leave and go home. Fortunately, they had travelled a long distance, so this was not an option. As they gingerly maneuvered their way through the workshop, dealing with the unexpected issues that arose, the Holy Spirit brought tremendous breakthrough and hope. To their surprise, they began experiencing the depth of emotional intimacy that had always eluded them. It was incredible to see the change the Lord was bringing to this precious couple.

About a year later, we had the privilege of spending some time with this couple. It was so exciting to hear and see how well they were doing. They definitely had continued to use the tools from the LAM workshop and were being very intentional about using them. One of the tools they used almost daily was the *Spirit Blessing for Couples*. This had become so much a part of their lives that they felt the loss keenly on the days they were unable to do it. It was so confirming to hear how much this simple little tool was not only maintaining their spiritual and emotional connection but was actually nurturing and growing it as well.

Testimonials and Evidence for Spirit Blessing

Because the concept of blessing our spirits is new to many people, we thought it would be helpful to give you more background and some examples of how God has powerfully used these spiritual principles.

Blessing Babies in the Womb

Many years ago, Arthur Burk began working with the spirits of babies in the womb. He believed that if he could teach parents to nurture their baby's spirit from the moment of conception, it would have a priceless head start over the soul by the time his or her mind, will and emotions were fully developed.

Arthur began praying Scripture over these little lives almost immediately after conception and taught the parents to do the same. Though the babies' minds were not developed, their spirits were fully operational. Through these prayers, something wonderful was happening, and these little spirits were growing by leaps and bounds. Within these budding lives, their spirits were already leading their souls and their bodies.

What we are about to share with you is powerful, because the minds, much less the bodies, of these babies could not have accomplished what happened without their spirits leading. Their minds were unable to comprehend, but their spirits led their minds and bodies to do something amazing. There are recorded accounts of babies who were about to be born but were coming feet first in the breech position. Throughout the pregnancy, parents had been nurturing their babies' spirits by regularly praying over them. As a set of parents spoke to their baby's spirit, telling it to turn around and prepare for birth, the baby immediately turned and was born head first! This happened again and again in families.

When I shared this story at a workshop one time, a man raised his hand and said he and his wife had done the same thing with their child when it was coming down the birth canal in the breech position. They said it was incredible. Their baby heard them, obeyed and immediately turned around to be correctly positioned for a normal birth.

We read in Luke 1:15, "He will be filled with the Holy Spirit while yet in his mother's womb," and in Luke 1:44, "For behold, when the sound of your greeting reached my ears, the baby leaped in my womb for joy." It was the spirit within each of these children who were set to be born in breech position that responded with understanding. Their minds were not fully formed yet. They lacked the ability to comprehend and send a message to their bodies. But with their spirits leading, they understood, and their bodies obeyed.[1]

A Troubled Youth

This teaching and this tool are not for babies and marriages alone. Barry and I started seeing God use it with children and youth as well. Here's one example my assistant shared with me one day. She was talking on the phone to a friend who worked at a boys' correctional facility. He explained to her that he had been assigned to work with a young man who had been incorrigible since he'd been at the facility. He was continually on detention and was very difficult to work with.

In about five minutes, my assistant explained to her friend some of what we had been learning through Arthur Burk's teaching. She shared with him how, before praying, to call forth the spirit of the person, bringing it into a prominent place over his body and soul. She explained how to ask the soul and body to follow the spirit—that is, to give over the place of leadership to the spirit. And finally, to begin praying the truths of Scripture and the words the Holy Spirit gives you for that person.

He thought it was a great tool, but he wasn't allowed to pray with kids in this manner at the boys' correctional facility. My assistant told him it wasn't a problem. He could just look into the boy's eyes and pray silently, spirit to spirit.

Her friend decided to try "the stare" with this troubled boy. At first, the boy hated this exercise and would fight it every time. But as they continued, he began to enjoy it and actually looked forward to the few short minutes each day when they would connect in this manner. In a short time, this young man's behavior changed, and he became considerably calmer. He was even taken off detention.

After a while, it was time for his parents to come and visit him. When they arrived at the ranch and saw their son, they could hardly believe it. The improvement was so dramatic that they told the ranch directors they didn't even know who he was. They had *never* seen their son like that. He was truly transformed!

A Mental Patient

Arthur tells a similar story about a nurse in a mental hospital who had a patient who was really tough to work with. She couldn't pray out loud for him, so for about five minutes a day she tried just sitting down and looking into his eyes. She called his spirit into a prominent place, and his soul and body to submit to his spirit. She then started to pray over him silently, spirit to spirit, her spirit speaking truth, Scripture, hope and life into his spirit. Pretty soon, he began to show improvement. She continued ministering to him on a regular basis. As she did this, he began to show great improvement. He was finally moved to a facility for higher-functioning patients. He had progressed so remarkably that he'd outgrown the hospital where he was. After they moved him, he requested to come back on a regular basis to continue his sessions with the nurse because they were instrumental in his continuing to heal and grow!

Emotional Detachment During Sex

We had a couple in one of our three-day workshops where the wife had experienced some significant spiritual, emotional and sexual abuse as a child. As a result of the abuse, she was unable to stay emotionally present in their times of lovemaking. All their married lives, her eyes would glaze over during sex, and her husband could tell that, once again, she had checked out emotionally. Because they loved one another and were working hard at going deeper in their love, this was painful for both of them. She didn't want to "leave," but she didn't know how to "stay." And her husband didn't just want her body; he longed to express his love with all of her engaged—spirit, soul and body.

This precious couple had experienced some great breakthroughs in the workshop, but we were now moving into the sexual portion of the course, and both of them were quite apprehensive. We introduced the sex challenge as homework for that night, and they, along with Holy Spirit, decided on what that would be.

We always encourage couples to invite the Holy Spirit to be present and call each other's spirits to be prominent, leading their souls through the whole time of lovemaking. This couple did just that; but as they began to engage sexually, the husband felt his wife begin to withdraw emotionally. He again called her spirit to attention and called it to stay in a leadership position. As he spoke, he felt led to hold her gaze while continuing to bless her spirit. As he did this, her spirit responded, held his gaze and remained emotionally present throughout their entire time of lovemaking.

The husband wept as he shared the next morning that this was the first time this had ever happened. We rejoiced with them at what the Lord had done and how He'd led this husband and wife to overcome what the Enemy had been stealing from them for years.

This little tool of blessing each other's spirits is so simple and easy to apply. At one particular three-day workshop, we didn't have much time to fully teach or explain the spirit blessing tools. But what we said was evidently enough for this husband to listen to the Holy Spirit and apply this tool in a way that overcame something he and his wife had wrestled with all their married life. Thank You, Jesus!

The hardest thing about blessing your spirit is that it's so simple it can be easy to forget about it. But don't! It carries the potential, when used with the Holy Spirit, to change your life.

ACTIVITY

We call this tool *Face-to-Face.*

1. Looking face to face into each other's eyes, call your spouse's spirit to attention, and tell his/her soul and body to follow his or her spirit.

2. Begin speaking positive truths about what you see in your spouse.

3. Go back and forth, five to ten times, speaking positive truths over each other.

HOMEWORK

Spirit Blessing for Couples:

• Before you go to sleep each night, take turns saying the following to each other: "_____, I call your spirit to come forth and be prominent over your soul and body so that you may receive all the rest and revelation the Holy Spirit brings to you through the night. 'He gives to His beloved even in his sleep' " (Ps. 127:2).

• Every morning, when you wake up, take turns saying the following to each other: "_____, I call your spirit to attention to operate in a leadership role over your soul and body. And, _____, I call your spirit into alignment with the purposes of Jesus for your life today."

· Do the *Face-to-Face* activity three or more times this week.

Notes

_____

_____

_____

_____

_____

_____

_____

_____

_____

_____

_____

_____

_____

_____

_____

_____

_____

_____

_____

_____

_____

_____

_____

_____

_____

_____

_____

_____

_____

_____

Note

1. Sylvia Gunter and Arthur Burk, *Blessing Your Spirit* (Birminham, AL: The Father's Business, 2005).

1 2

HONORING GOD
THROUGH GODLY
ASSERTION

"This is crazy. This is not you," Lori calmly but firmly said to me. Off and on for two days we had revisited the same issue with no progress toward resolution. Once again, Lori resolutely held her ground.

I had spoken strongly and convincingly (at least I was convinced) that Lori was not connected to me and that she was putting one of her friends ahead of me. Feeling my intense conviction made it very challenging for Lori to stand against my strong assertions, but she could not agree with the accusations I had been making about her. Her ability to hold firm to her own inner convictions while respectfully addressing me was the key to breaking through the work of accusation between us. The spirit of accusation wanted to divide us. Lori did not allow it.

At Lori's encouragement, we finally prayed together against that accusation, which quickly ended an argument that had gone unresolved for two days. We discovered that my feeling of Lori putting her friend ahead of me was not the issue at all. The issue was spiritual, and so we needed to pray against the spirit of accusation. By holding on to her inner convictions and respectfully persevering with me rather than becoming angry, offended or manipulative, Lori superbly demonstrated what I call godly assertion.

We use this definition of godly assertion:

Godly assertion occurs when we take the time to find out what God wants to say and do through us, and then we exercise the faith and courage to resolutely speak and do those things with respect and humility.

There is a very important difference between self-assertion and godly assertion. In self-assertion, we are taught to stand up for ourselves and to firmly assert what we want or what we believe to be fair and right. Sometimes this is a very good thing, especially for people who are very passive, shy or timid. Jesus made a clear distinction between self-assertion and godly assertion. In John 7:18, He said, "He who speaks from himself seeks his own glory, but He who is seeking the glory of the One who sent him, He is true, and there is no unrighteousness in Him." The first half of the verse describes self-assertion, which is speaking from self and seeking one's own glory. The second half of the verse describes godly assertion, which is seeking to glorify God rather than self. This can be a subtle distinction that is recognized only by the condition of our heart.

For example, I may be kind and giving to a person so that I will be accepted by him and, therefore, I am seeking my own glory. I might be telling someone about some great thing the Lord did through our ministry, but in my heart I want my gifting to be recognized and validated. This is self-assertion rather than godly assertion. If I can tell about great things God has done, and in my heart I want the Lord to be honored instead of me, that would be godly assertion. Jesus perfectly asserted only what was important to His Father rather than what was important to Him. This is what we call godly assertion.

The person who "speaks from himself" is asserting himself and wants personal recognition. If we are simply asserting our own desires without regard for what God wants, then we are promoting ourselves and trying to make ourselves important in the eyes of others. This does not mean that we must ignore everything we want or desire. It means that we must check the motives of our heart to be sure our words and actions are exalting God more than ourselves. We check the motives of our heart by asking the Spirit of truth to show us exactly what is motivating us.

Our senior pastor, Bill Johnson, had one question for his son-in-law, Gabe, when he asked permission to marry Bill's daughter. Bill asked Gabe, "Will you love God more than you love my daughter?" He was confident that the best way for Gabe to love his daughter was to love God more than anyone. Gabe's love for God would lead him to assert God's ways rather than his own ways in the marriage. We bring God's truth and righteousness into our marriage best by asserting God's ways above our own ways. This is true whether we are in the role of headship or the role of submission in the marriage.

God is looking for couples that will boldly manifest, demonstrate and communicate His kingdom truths and His heart to the world. God uses people who are led by His Spirit to manifest Him to the world. These are the only people who will be able to represent Him well. Self-centered, selfish Christians will not be able to represent Jesus and His kingdom. Likewise, fearful, passive Christians and angry, domineering Christians will not be able to accurately represent God.

A Fearful Wife

Sheila was controlled by her husband's fear and anger until she learned to assert herself in a godly way. She had grown thoroughly frustrated and exhausted after living for 20 years in the same dysfunctional pattern. Each evening, when Sheila's husband, Phil, came home from work, she instantly went on high alert to discover and prevent whatever might trigger his anger that night. She would mentally and physically prepare herself to preempt or defuse her husband's nightly tirades. Sometimes she would succeed and feel good that she had done her duty as a wife to submit to her husband and appease his anger. Other times she would fail, and then she would stuff the familiar feelings of frustration and failure until she could hold them no longer. Eventually, she would blow up and unleash her pent-up anger and frustration against her husband.

Neither the years of manifesting selfless, passive compliance, nor her occasional angry outbursts changed the pattern. Sheila had to learn how to assert herself in a godly way in order for Phil to begin to recognize and deal with his controlling anger.

First, Sheila needed to learn that it was not her responsibility to appease her husband's anger. In fact, she had been rewarding and strengthening his anger by her fearful, compliant responses. With some help, Sheila was able to keep from getting pulled into her husband's chronic angry tirades. She learned to courageously speak the truth to him without using anger to drive her words. She became able to speak up and say things like, "I'm sorry you're so upset about what happened at work today, but I don't think your anger is going to help you." She was able to be kind while asserting the truth without taking responsibility to control her husband's anger. She learned to assert God's truth and compassion.

At first she felt guilty for not trying to appease her husband, but eventually she could feel the freedom of simply representing God to her husband and taking no ownership of her husband's anger. Like so many of us, Sheila vacillated between the two extremes of aggressive anger and passive fear. When facing her husband's anger, it was easier for her to silently follow feelings of fear than to speak up courageously. It was also easier to use anger to empower her words rather than risk asserting the truth when she was likely to meet with his resistance.

A Fearful Husband

I (Barry) recently counseled a husband who had been afraid of his wife's anger for the entire 15 years of their marriage. To counteract his fear, he had developed a pattern of using anger to feel strong. He was depressed and took several medications to combat it. Through the process of counseling, he came to the place where he learned to meet his fears head-on by speaking up calmly and with honesty in the face of his wife's angry accusations.

It was terrifying for him to choose to face her anger, because she had been extremely hurtful and destructive with her words for many years. In spite of the terror he felt as he asserted God's truth in love, afterwards he always felt considerably better. His depression began to lift and he stopped getting pulled into the old patterns of using destructive, angry words to retaliate. As he learned to seek God's glory instead of his own, he could respond to his wife with God's truth and righteousness instead of responding from his flesh. Godly assertion enabled him to honor God by speaking the truth in love instead of asserting the anger he had so often felt in response to his wife's hurtful words.

Fear and anger will never allow us to represent God in our marriages. Wives cannot use submission as an excuse to be passive and silent. Fear will prevent us from bringing what God wants us to bring to the marriage. Anger cannot be justified as a husband's right because he is the head. Both husband and wife must seek to actively bring God's truth and righteousness into the marriage.

Godly Assertion and Headship

The essence of spiritual headship for a husband is to live so closely connected to Jesus that Jesus is clearly manifested through him to his wife. If you look at Jesus as the perfect model of headship, our description of godly assertion is completely compatible with the biblical roles of headship in a marriage. As our head, Jesus' role was to manifest the Father to us. He lived in a bold, conspicuous way, asserting the Father in all He said and did. In a similar way to how Jesus manifested the Father to us, husbands are called to represent Jesus to their wives and to love them as Christ loved the Church. Just as we, the Bride of Christ, see the Father through Jesus, wives are intended to see Jesus through the spiritual headship of their husbands.

We often associate the role of headship with making decisions for all of those under our authority. We think headship means, "I have the right and responsibility to make the final decision." Paul tells us in 1 Corinthians 11:3 that Christ is the head of every man, and God is the head of Christ. So we can use Jesus' relationship to His disciples as a perfect example of the role of headship. As the head of the disciples, Jesus did not focus on making decisions for them. He made decisions for Himself and He told His disciples about the Father. He did whatever the Father told Him, and He invited His disciples to follow Him. Even though He sent out His disciples, He was never forceful. Jesus let His disciples choose whether or not they wanted to follow Him. His goal as their head was always to manifest the Father to them and connect them to the Father.

In Mark 10, we read that James and John asked Jesus to give them the authority and privilege of sitting on the right and the left of His throne. They wanted the first place of authority to rule with Jesus. Instead of agreeing to give James and John the highest place of authority, at His right and left, Jesus cleverly got them to agree to drink from the cup of His sufferings and His baptism of death to self. The other disciples then became indignant at James and John's request. (They probably wished they had thought of it first.) Jesus chose to use their request for authority and the offense of the other disciples as an opportunity to give some instruction about how Christians are to think and act when in roles of authority.

In Mark 10:42-45, Jesus plainly described the difference between a godly approach and a worldly approach to exercising authority. He explained that the Gentile rulers, people who did not know God, used their power and authority to rule and dominate those in subjection to them.

If we apply this same principle to marriage, a husband who uses his role of headship to get his wife to do whatever he wants is exercising his authority like a person who does not know God. The husband who follows Jesus will have the opposite attitude. He will serve his wife by demonstrating God's love and truth, without dominating.

Any Christian who wishes to be the greatest must become the servant of others, and the one who wishes to be first will become the slave of others (see vv. 43-44). Then Jesus applied His teaching to Himself and said, "For even the Son of Man did not come to be served, but to serve, and to give His life a ransom for many" (v. 45). Jesus is the perfect example of what we call godly assertion while in a role of headship. As our head, He was able to serve, love and die for the people, without ever dominating anyone. Although He loved and served the people to the point of giving up His life for them, He still trusted God above any person. Even though Jesus had all the authority of the Father behind Him, He never forced anyone to act against his or her own will. Jesus' disciples always followed Him willingly, never under compulsion.

If we use Jesus as the example of headship for husbands, we will recognize that a husband's headship is not about making decisions for his wife. The primary element of godly headship in marriage is uncompromisingly manifesting Jesus and His Father to his wife. This is godly assertion—asserting what God wants to do and say through us, with humility and respect.

In response to Jesus' manifesting the Father to the world, some loved Him and some hated Him, but He never turned away from glorifying God to follow men or to represent Himself apart from the Father. In John 17:14, Jesus said that He gave His Father's words to the disciples, and the world hated them for it. The world hated them for lovingly and powerfully representing God as Savior, Healer and Deliverer.

Jesus never intentionally created conflict, but boldly representing God's love and power will often provoke great offense and hatred from those in darkness. He never stopped asserting His Father's words, even in the face of great conflict. Jesus never stopped boldly doing what the Father was doing, in spite of life-threatening opposition.

One result of living out godly assertion is that it will reveal people's hearts. It will stir up either the love or hatred of God. Godly assertion requires that we must be willing to face conflict, offense and even hatred in the process of clearly representing Him through our words and actions.

As husbands in the role of headship, our challenge is to lead by revealing Jesus to our wives and serve them without following them. We must represent Jesus no matter how difficult or frightened we might be. This type of godly assertion will attract and inspire those who love God more than their own lives.

What Does Godly Submission Look Like?

Godly assertion is just as important when in a role of submission as it is when in a role of headship. If we use Jesus' example of submission to the Father as our model for godly submission, we see that Jesus freely and willingly did only what He saw the Father doing and spoke only what the Father was saying. When Jesus humbled Himself to leave heaven and come to earth as a man, to die for us, I am quite confident that the Father did not say to Him, "You must go down to earth, suffer, and die for those people whether you like it or not!" Or, "You *are* going to obey every word that I tell You!" No, it was a completely mutual agreement between the Father and the Son, a plan they had made together before they created the world. As a man, Jesus happily chose to submit to His Father and give Himself for us. Although Jesus was in perfect submission to the Father, they operated in complete harmony.

When the roles of headship or submission in a marriage are operating in harmony and unity of purpose, as they did between Jesus and the Father, it is difficult to distinguish between the two. Both the head and the person in submission will be asserting what God wants, not what he or she wants. That is what will unite them and bring harmony to the relationship. A wife can be submissive by always being respectful of the role that God has chosen for husbands, while her husband must always focus on representing Christ in everything he does and serve his wife as God desires. This is the relationship that God gives us to work out in our marriages.

In Ephesians 5:22–24, Paul talks about the role of submission in marriage: "Wives, be subject to your own husbands, as to the Lord. For the husband is the head of the wife, as Christ also is the head of the church, He Himself being the Savior of the body. But as the church is subject to Christ, so also the wives ought to be to their husbands in everything." Many godly scholars have undertaken to describe and explain this role of submission in marriage, and there are very intelligent men and women with strongly contrasting opinions regarding what this role looks like. I will not try to address all of those differing opinions, but I do have an opinion of my own about the role of submission in marriage.

In order to do this, I first took the word and the role of "submission" out of the limited context of marriage. I wanted to understand the larger biblical concept of submission. When was the last time you heard a message on men in submission? Yet, we are all—both men and women—in roles of submission. Paul tells us, in Romans 13:1-7, that every person is to be in *subjection* to all governing authorities. The same Greek word is used in Romans 13 and Ephesians 5 in reference to submission. All men and women are commanded to be subject to both godly and ungodly authorities. Every man and woman must submit to church authorities, to various levels of governmental authority, to the authority of their employers, and so on.

Paul goes on to tell the Christians in Rome that all authority is established by God. To resist authority is to oppose the ordinance of God. The point I am making is that both men and women are in roles of submission. In the Church, we seem only to talk about the role of submission with regard to women in marriage. Do we hold men to the same standard of submission that we hold women to in marriage? For example, do we tell men in submission that they must be quiet and not question a decision made by church leadership or their employer? Do we even try to define what it means for a man to be in submission?

Rather than trying to precisely describe the general role of submission, I took a different approach and asked myself, "What right does *any* person have to assert himself or herself in a godly way while in a role of submission?"

Biblical Evidence for Godly Assertion in a Role of Submission

To answer this question, let's review four stories from Scripture. Each story illustrates a person in submission who asserted himself or herself in a godly way while challenging the person who had a role of headship and authority over them. I have specifically chosen these four examples because, in every one, God Himself responded directly to the person in submission who challenged the person in headship. I could add many more biblical examples, but in the following four stories we have the benefit of observing and learning from God's direct response.

Let me first remind you of our definition of godly assertion:

Godly assertion occurs when we take the time to find out what God wants to say and do through us, and then we exercise the faith and courage to resolutely speak and do those things with respect and humility.

Godly Assertion When Face to Face with God

The first two stories involve Moses while he was in direct submission to God. In Exodus 32, it is recorded that the children of Israel decided to fashion a new god out of gold. Moses had been up on Mount Sinai with the Lord for 40 days and nights. The mountain was covered with smoke and fire. Even the people down on flat land were terrified. I can easily imagine that after 40 days, the people had concluded that Moses must be dead in the fire and smoke.

The Lord saw that the people and leaders had not remained faithful to Him, so He told Moses to go back down the mountain. Then the Lord gave Moses His solution to the problem of the people's unfaithfulness. He told Moses that He would destroy all of the Israelites and start over to make a great nation out of Moses.

Even though he heard these words directly from the mouth of God, Moses did not passively and silently obey. Instead, he humbly entreated the Lord. Moses asked God why He would destroy the people He had delivered from Egypt with His own mighty hand. He reminded God of how this would harm His image and reputation in the eyes of the Egyptians. Then Moses reminded the Lord of His promises to Abraham, Isaac and Jacob. Astonishingly, God Almighty, the highest authority that exists, listened to His servant Moses and "changed His mind" (Exod. 32:14). He did not destroy the people.

In Exodus 33, the Lord told Moses to continue the journey to the Promised Land. He then said that He would not go with Moses and the people, because the people were so obstinate that He would likely kill them along the way. Moses spoke face to face with God. He heard directly from God's mouth that He would not go up to the Promised Land with Moses and the people.

Would you ever suggest to a friend who had heard the audible voice of God that he should go back and make sure that God had thought of everything? Would you suggest he try to give God a better idea? Moses was not silent, even before God. He humbly entreated the Lord and told the Lord that he needed to know who He would send with him to help with the job. Moses reminded the Lord of His own words, that he had been given favor in God's sight. Lastly, and very importantly, he said that the nation did not belong to him, but to God.

Moses willingly served God, but he never became possessive of the people or the mission to get them to the Promised Land. In response to

Moses, God again "changed His mind" and said that His presence would go with Moses on the journey to the Promised Land.

What Moses said to the Lord, his ultimate authority, could appear presumptuous or even arrogant, but he didn't stop there. He went on to say, God, if Your presence does not go with us, then do not send us to the Promised Land. How would we be any different than any other people if Your presence is not with us, manifesting to everyone how great You are by Your wonders!

The Lord could see that Moses was concerned about God's reputation and not his own. Moses' statement sounds a lot like a statement made by the late John Wimber, the founder of the Vineyard Churches, years ago. He said that if God was not present in his ministry to do signs and wonders, he did not want to minister. To some people, a statement like that sounds like arrogance. It could be arrogance, but God looks at the heart. (I attended John Wimber's church for several years, and I believe that the same heart attitude about wanting God's reputation to be great was true about him as well.)

Moses never became possessive of the people God called him to lead. He was never deceived into believing he could accomplish the mission without God. Moses even rejected God's offer to destroy the children of Israel and make him into a great nation. Instead, he asked God to be merciful to the people.

We read in Numbers 12:3 that Moses was more humble than any man who lived on the face of the earth. Sometimes we get humility and arrogance completely mixed up. We think that a humble person would never challenge God or suggest that God should do something different than what He has spoken. We sometimes judge people according to our own standards, rather than accurately discerning their heart. God, the ultimate authority, chose to listen to His friend Moses, who was in submission to Him. This is a great example of godly assertion while in a role of submission. Moses clearly had the right to humbly assert his own differing thoughts, even while speaking face to face with God.

Moses Asserts His Opinions to God a Second Time

A second incident between Moses and the Lord demonstrates again that a person in submission has a right to respectfully assert what God has placed on his heart. We read in Numbers 13–14 that Moses had a very similar encounter with the Lord, where he humbly entreated the Lord, and the Lord changed His mind.

The children of Israel had reached the land of Canaan, the Promised Land. The Lord told Moses to choose 12 spies, one to represent each of the 12 tribes, who were to spy out the land "which I am going to give to the sons of Israel" (Num. 13:2). God did not say to go and spy out the land and come back and tell Him *if* He could give it to them, but that is what they did. God expects us to believe His words to us, especially when circumstances appear completely impossible.

Ten of the 12 spies decided that the people of the land were too great to overcome in battle, and they convinced the Israelites that it was impossible to conquer the land that God had promised them. These 10 leaders stirred up fear in the people. Then, all the people began to grumble against Aaron and Moses, saying it would have been better to die in the wilderness; and they spoke of appointing a new leader to take them back to Egypt.

At this point, Moses and Aaron, along with Joshua and Caleb, fell on their faces and implored the people not to be afraid and not to rebel against the Lord. But the people wanted to stone them.

For the second time, the Lord suggested the same solution: He would destroy the people and make a completely new nation out of Moses. This was another test of Moses' heart. I am quite sure that if I were leading these people and they wanted to stone me and choose a new leader to take them back to Egypt, I would have said, "Okay, God. The first time I talked You out of Your idea to destroy them, but now I think You must be right." Besides, "The Nation of Barry" has a nice ring to it. I'm sure I would have been offended at their unwillingness to follow me.

Moses was far more humble and merciful than I am. Once again, Moses thought only of the Lord and His reputation. He selflessly entreated God to consider His reputation. Once again, Moses reminded the Lord of His words and he quoted what the Lord had spoken about His goodness in Exodus 34:6-7. He concluded by interceding for the people: "Pardon, I pray, the iniquity of this people according to the greatness of Your lovingkindness, just as You also have forgiven this people, from Egypt even until now" (Num. 14:19).

The Lord responded to His servant Moses with a most amazing statement: "I have pardoned them according to *your* word" (v. 20, emphasis added). God Almighty acted according to Moses' words rather than His own! This is another example of godly assertion where God allowed a person in submission to humbly but confidently speak up and challenge Him.

I believe that God listened to Moses because He saw His own heart reflected in Moses' heart. Moses' humility caused him to care more about God than himself. Moses asked for mercy instead of the judgment that God had spoken. Moses' heart of mercy and compassion caused God to listen to his servant's opinion. God was testing Moses' heart in both of these situations.

What if Moses had believed that all he could say to God was, "Yes, Lord, whatever You say"? What if Moses had believed that because he was in submission to God he could only silently obey? What if Moses had believed that it was a sin to speak his own thoughts back to God? God demonstrated that even He would listen to a submissive servant who humbly but courageously stood and spoke out of a heart of love, mercy and faith.

Husbands can learn a lot about the role of headship from Moses' example. He demonstrated godly headship over the nation of Israel by faithfully serving them without dominating them. He served them and still completely followed God. He never forgot that the people in submission to him belonged to God, not to him. Moses continually encouraged the people to be faithful and to bring glory to God. Even when the people rejected God, and Moses' leadership, he still wanted God's mercy for them.

And wives can learn a lot about the role of submission from the life of Moses. He humbly obeyed God, yet he expected good things from God. Moses was not afraid to respectfully speak his opposing ideas to God, even after God had spoken clearly to him. When Moses spoke up to the Lord, he was concerned about what was best for the Lord and for the people. In his role of submission to God, he was not motivated by selfishness but by selfless service. Moses is a great example of how the roles of headship and submission can honor God in a marriage.

Godly Assertion of a Wife

In 1 Samuel 25, we find the story of Abigail and her husband, Nabal, which demonstrates that God directly supported a wife in submission who spoke up and challenged her husband. At the time of this story, David and his men were running from King Saul and the army of Israel. David was hiding in a place near the home of Nabal and Abigail. Nabal was a wealthy man who owned 3,000 sheep and 1,000 goats. David had instructed his men not to take anything from Nabal's servants and not to give them a hard time. In fact, David's men became a wall of protection to the shepherds.

One day, while Nabal was shearing his 3,000 sheep, David sent some of his men to humbly greet Nabal in his name, to bless Nabal and to request some food for David and his men. Nabal coldly refused to give David anything, and he showed no respect for David. When David heard Nabal's reply, he told his men to strap on their swords; he vowed to kill every male in Nabal's household before the next morning.

One of Nabal's servants ran to warn Nabal's wife, Abigail, and suggested that she consider what she should do. The servant added the comment that Nabal was "such a worthless man that no one can speak to him" (1 Sam. 25:17).

In response to this information, Abigail quickly loaded a large supply of food onto donkeys and instructed her servants to go before her and take the food to David and his men. When Abigail met David and his men on their way to kill Nabal and all his male servants, she humbly bowed to the ground and then she spoke. Abigail began by taking the full blame for what Nabal had done. She openly acknowledged that her husband was a foolish, worthless man. She boldly but respectfully confronted David on his intention to sin by killing Nabal and his servants. She called it shedding blood without cause and avenging himself by his own hand. She went on to bless David and affirm God's plan to make him ruler over Israel. David received the gifts she had brought. He blessed Abigail and acknowledged that the Lord had sent her to keep him from sinning.

Abigail returned home and found Nabal drunk and holding a feast of his own. She wisely waited until morning when he was sober and then she told him of David's plan to kill him and all of his male servants. When Nabal heard these things, "his heart died within him so he became as a stone." This is where the Lord directly intervened: "About ten days later, the LORD struck Nabal and he died" (1 Sam. 25:37-38). Then David sent his servants to Abigail to ask her to become his wife. Abigail became a wife of the king of Israel.

Why would God choose to judge Nabal, who had every right to do as he wished with his own possessions? Remember that Abigail said David would be sinning to kill Nabal and his servants, because he was shedding blood *without cause*. Why didn't God punish Abigail for opposing the wishes of her husband? I believe the reason God supported Abigail was because she had a high regard for David, God's anointed. Like Moses, she cared about what God cared about. She acted humbly, yet boldly, in great faith. She risked her own life when she took all the blame. She represented God and not herself.

In contrast, Nabal only cared about himself. He cared about *his* water, *his* bread, *his* sheep and *his* shearers. He had no concern for David, whom God loved and anointed. Nabal asserted *himself*, while Abigail asserted the desires and values of God. Nabal demonstrated mere self-assertion, while Abigail perfectly modeled godly assertion.

Again, God demonstrated in this story that He would support a person who boldly represented Him through godly assertion. Abigail is an example of God's willingness to bless a wife in submission who humbly follows God even when it means that she must contradict her husband who has no regard for God.

A Challenge to Jesus' Words and the Plan of the Father

The last story we are using to exemplify godly assertion by a person in submission is found in Matthew 15:21-28. This is the story of a Canaanite woman who approached Jesus, crying out, "Have mercy on me Lord, Son of David; my daughter is cruelly demon-possessed" (v. 22). Jesus totally ignored her. She brashly persisted to the point that the disciples wanted Jesus to tell her to go away. Instead, Jesus told her about God's plans for Him: "I was sent only to the lost sheep of the house of Israel" (v. 24). In other words, "Lady, you don't fit into God's plans yet. He's only interested in the Jewish people right now. Your time will come later." Completely undaunted, the woman bowed down to the ground and persevered: "Lord, help me!" (Are you beginning to see the consistent pattern of humble, godly assertion?)

Jesus now tested her heart with a painful insult: "It is not good to take the children's bread and throw it to the dogs" (v. 26). What a seemingly cold-hearted comment! Strategically and humbly, the woman ignored the offense and replied, "Yes, Lord; but even the dogs feed on the crumbs which fall from their master's table" (v. 27). Astounding! She is a woman in a male-dominated culture. She is a Gentile, despised by the Jews, and she has already been told that she does not fit into God's plan. She had been profoundly insulted by Jesus, yet she continued to engage Him.

I believe most of us would have been like the disciples. We would have thought this woman was completely out of line, disrespectful and even arrogant. What was Jesus thinking? Jesus replied, "O woman, your faith is great; it shall be done for you as you wish" (v. 28). What did Jesus call her words and behavior? He called them *great faith*, and she received exactly what *she* desired! What would have happened if she had focused on her feelings and her offense instead of unrelentingly pursuing Jesus? What would have happened if she had believed that it was inappropriate to persist for her daughter's deliverance in the face of Jesus' contradictory words? She would not be on record for eternity in the Gospels as one of only two people who are honored by Jesus as having great faith.

Can you see how this woman was not merely asserting her own fleshly wishes? She was desperate for her daughter to be freed from Satan's clutches. She was motivated by a passionate love for her daughter. No embarrassment or humiliation could stop her. She was willing to completely lay herself aside for her daughter. She saw the authority that Jesus carried and she knew that He alone possessed the help her daughter needed. She was honoring God when she completely ignored her own hurt feelings—her reputation—and relentlessly pursued her conviction to see her daughter delivered.

She had the same desire for her daughter's welfare that Jesus did for the world—He gave up His life so that we could be delivered from sin and all the powers of darkness. This is the kind of person the Lord is seeking to represent Him to the world: people who will humbly, yet boldly, stand for Him and His good, no matter what difficulties or personal insults they may face. This is godly assertion.

We are all in roles of submission. The Caananite woman is another example of how God gives people in submission more latitude than we often do. God is more concerned about the heart attitude of a wife or of any person in submission than He is about the precise way the role of submission looks like.

Conclusions About Headship, Submission and Godly Assertion

1. The primary charge to any Christian in a role of headship or authority is to lovingly represent the Father to those in subjection to them.

2. The primary characteristic that represents godly submission in a man or a woman is a humble respect for any person placed in his or her life who carries a God-given role of authority. It is not silent, passive obedience that best represents godly submission.

3. All men and women in a role of submission, who are seeking to promote God's ways rather than their own, have the right and the *obligation* to assert themselves through words and actions as long as it is done with respect and humility toward the person in authority.

4. We honor the Spirit of God within us by asserting what He has placed in our hearts to do and speak.

5. We insult the Spirit of God within us and treat Him as unimportant when we fearfully or passively keep silent about what He gives us to speak.

6. We deprive the world of experiencing what God wants to uniquely do and say through us when we keep silent out of fear and passivity and do not assert ourselves in a godly way.

7. We honor ourselves rather than God when we assert ourselves instead of asserting His truth and His righteousness.

ACTIVITY

1. Are there ways that you should be expressing yourself through words or actions, but you don't do it because of fear?

2. Are there ways that you dominate and control instead of asserting the way God wants you to?

3. What is your marriage missing out on because of your inability to do what God has put inside of you?

HOMEWORK

1. Choose one night this week to hold each other as you watch the sun go down (or watch the sunrise, if you are morning people), and share three things you love about each other.

2. Walk and pray (or whatever works for you) three times this week.

3. Utilize your tools (*Listening Exercise; Feeling Words; 1-2-3 Skidoo; Steps to Reconciliation; Rules for Working Through Conflict; When the Poop Hits the Fan*) as pertinent situations arise.

4. Do your Spirit Blessing exercises morning and evening.

5. Do your *Face-to-Face* exercise three times this week.

Notes

_____
_____
_____
_____
_____
_____
_____
_____
_____
_____
_____
_____
_____
_____
_____
_____
_____
_____
_____
_____
_____
_____

13

KEEPING FINANCES FROM BECOMING A PROBLEM IN MARRIAGE

Financial pressures and conflict over finances create division and separation in many marriages. Most statistics place conflict over finances in the top 10 reasons for divorce. We will not be offering you a budgeting program; for that you can consult a variety of good teachings that already exist. Rather, we want to focus on ways that you and your spouse can remain united in the area of finances.

When Lori and I married, there was no question in my mind that all I owned was shared equally with her. I was not wealthy, by any means, but I owned considerably more than Lori. It was my desire to share everything with her. Thirty-two years later, I still want to do that! One of the reasons this attitude has remained is because we have always been completely open and trustworthy with each other regarding our finances.

A few years ago, a middle-aged couple came to me for premarital counseling. This was a second marriage for both of them. The woman had received a sizable inheritance from her mother. She managed it well and lived from the proceeds of her investments. In contrast, the man owned almost nothing. He owned an old car and an old motorcycle. He loved to travel, and he had many ideas as to how they could spend her money. At one point in the counseling, I met with the woman alone. She asked me what I thought about the fact that she had quite a bit of money, and that he did not. She did not feel comfortable with the way he managed his money. I told her that she should not seriously consider marrying any man that she could not trust with her money. This type of trust is essential for long-term harmony in marriage.

Here's how Lori and I kept our budget: We paid the bills and saved for upcoming large expenses; if there was extra above our expenses, we would decide together what to do with it. In addition, I always kept a small savings for emergency expenses. I balanced the checkbook and did almost all of the financial management. However, Lori kept the checkbook because she did most of the shopping. Since my responsibility was to be aware of our financial status, while Lori did most of the spending, if she needed to spend more money than usual, she would ask me about it. I would check our financial situation and let her know how much extra she could spend. I could always count on her to be faithful to do whatever we had agreed upon.

The Bible teaches some important attitudes toward money. Here are Jesus' words, recorded in Luke 16:10-13: "He who is faithful in a very little thing is faithful also in much; and he who is unrighteous in a very little thing is unrighteous also in much. Therefore if you have not been faithful in the use of unrighteous wealth, who will entrust the true riches to you?" Jesus is saying that whether we have a lot of money or a little, our possessions are always a "very little thing" to God. However, our attitude about our money is not a little thing to Him. He is also saying that we must prove faithful with the "very little thing" of "unrighteous wealth" in order to be trusted with "true riches." Our attitude toward money and possessions is one of the ways that God qualifies us to be entrusted with His "true riches," which are things that are of the kingdom of God.

To prove faithful, we must not be afraid of wealth, nor be greedy. Both greed and the fear of wealth will prevent us from being faithful as God wants. Just as we cannot love money and still love God, neither can we be afraid of money and still fear God. We must be able to trust God with our possessions and our provision. Some of us, who have very little in terms of wealth or possessions, may be more controlled by greed or fear than those who have much. God is looking for people to give His power and anointing to accomplish His work on earth. These people need to be proven faithful in the use of money and possessions.

People are called to a variety of lifestyles. Some people are called to the business world to make money and use it for the Kingdom of God on earth. Others may be called to a simple lifestyle as missionaries. Whether you are called to be a financier for the Kingdom or a missionary for the Kingdom, your marriage and then your children need to take a place of priority over ministry and employment.

It has always been clear to Lori and me that our marriage and our family were more important than our employment. In the next section, we will recount several major financial decisions that significantly shaped our financial and family history.

Life Decisions Affecting Family and Income

I married Lori when I was 26 years old. I had just completed my master's degree in counseling while working at Safeway Stores. Shortly after we married, I seriously injured my lower back while working. When it did not heal quickly, and I was unable to do the heavy and constant lifting required in the stores, I was offered a job in the Los Angeles division office as an assistant buyer. After one year, I was promoted to buyer. The job was very demanding. Daily, I met with sales executives from large food manufacturers, and I was responsible for making decisions about purchasing and advertising for 200 grocery stores throughout Southern California.

The job required me to be "thick-skinned" and to become pushy and demanding in order to get good deals that would make money for Safeway Stores. I worked hard and I did a good job, but it was not rewarding or fulfilling to me. I grew to despise my work. I became depressed. For the first time in my life, I lost motivation and felt empty inside.

On top of all this, I had told my boss that I would not move my family to other locations just to get a promotion. This limited me to the job I had. Since the Los Angeles division was the largest division, they would typically send employees to a smaller division when they were promoted. This would require moving your family to another location of the company's choice. I made the decision to put my family above my work, but that put a ceiling on my ability to be promoted as long as I worked for Safeway.

During this time, I had an opportunity to take a job as the manager of a small grocery store. My father-in-law knew a man who owned five of these small grocery stores. I could have become the manager of one of the stores and immediately doubled my income. It was very enticing. However, it was one of those situations where the manager made a good income but the rest of the employees were paid minimum wage. Because of that, it would have been difficult to hire good, reliable help, and all of the responsibility would ultimately fall on me. When someone doesn't show up for work, the manager must fill in. Every way I looked at this tempting opportunity I ended up a slave to the store—always on call to solve any problem. After extensive thought, prayer and discussion, we turned down the opportunity.

During my sixth year of employment at the Safeway division office, the Lord showed me that I had developed a strongly negative attitude toward my work, and that was the primary reason for my depression. As the Lord instructed me, and as I adjusted my attitude by stopping my complaining and judging, my peace returned, although my work was still unfulfilling.

After about one year of the Lord's adjusting my attitude, I applied for a position as the Executive Director of Alpha Center, a nonprofit Christian counseling center. The job allowed me to resume my counseling career and to manage the center at the same time. I loved the work, even though it meant a 25 percent cut in my income. I worked for Alpha Center for 15 years while we were raising our four sons. I earned a modest income, but I was happy. The dread of returning to work on Monday mornings, which haunted me while working at Safeway, was gone.

In August 2000, I left Alpha Center and began my own private counseling practice. I was 47 years old with no retirement from the 15 years of work at Alpha Center. But I had been able to invest a little in a 401k retirement fund.

After only one year of working in my private counseling practice, my income almost tripled. I had an ideal situation. My office was about one mile from my home, so driving in traffic on Orange County freeways was not an issue. I had my own executive suite on the third floor, with a balcony, and I was my own boss! I thought to myself, *At last, I can do what other people do, and save some money for retirement, and live a comfortable lifestyle.* Well, that was short-lived.

My idea of living a comfortable, middle-class life in Southern California came to a screeching halt two years later. Through numerous dreams and experiences of hearing God's voice, the Lord clearly called us to move to Redding, California, to attend Bethel Church. Both Lori and I were self-employed. (As a piano instructor, Lori ran her own business as well.) Both of our jobs had taken years to build up clientele. This move to a new location meant that we would be completely starting over financially. I had never made a bold move like this in my life. We had lived in the same home for 24 years. We had both lived in Orange County for 40 years

In October 2003, we went to Redding to attend a weeklong conference at Bethel Church. During that week, I interviewed and was hired as a counselor in a nonprofit counseling center like Alpha Center. In this new job, I hoped to make half of what I was earning in private practice.

During that same week, we also bought a home in Redding. We returned to Orange County, and the following weekend we sold our home in Fullerton. It sold the first weekend that we put it on the market. At this same time, I announced to all of my clients that I would be moving in three months and ending my private practice. Everything was moving along so quickly and easily that we felt God's clear confirmation on the move.

Now the plot thickens. Three weeks after returning from Redding, selling our home and announcing the termination of my counseling practice, we discovered that a $150,000 investment we had made was a Ponzi scheme, and we had lost all, or most, of the money. (In a Ponzi scheme, money is taken from one investor and given to another, as their profit. There is no real profit being made. Eventually, the scheme collapses because more is paid out than taken in.) The money we invested had come from the equity in our home. Remember, I had almost no retirement. The only money we had was the equity in our home. We had prayed together before making this investment and felt very strongly God's leading to do so. This was another first for me. I had never taken a risk financially like this before. The one saving grace was that Lori and I were completely united in the decision.

Learning to Trust God More than Money

This began the scariest season of my life. I could have remained in Fullerton and kept my well-paying counseling practice, but I fully believed that God was leading us to Redding. We also believed that God had led us to invest in the Ponzi scheme, even though we'd lost $150,000. The decision to proceed with the move became the hardest decision of my life. Would I trust what I believed God was speaking to me and take a further risk to move, or would I take the safe route to remain in Fullerton and trust my well-paying private practice? Lori and I had to decide this together. Both of us were still utterly convinced that God had clearly told us to move to Redding.

During this time of tremendous inner turmoil, I had an encounter with the Lord. One day, while in my office, I had an hour with no client scheduled, so I lay down on my couch and began to pray. I had recently heard a preacher ask the questions, "What do you do when your faith bubble bursts? What do you do when everything seems to be going the opposite of what you believed God had said? Will you still only believe?"

I prayed in desperation, saying to God, "I want to only believe! Help me to believe!" I fell asleep and had a dream that Jesus took me by both hands and swung me around like a playful parent swings a young child until his or her entire body lifts off the ground. Next in the dream, Jesus was standing beside me like a father with a young son. His arm went behind my head, with His hand resting comfortingly on my shoulder. I awoke from the dream laughing! I felt that the Lord was saying to me, "If you can trust me like a child, this will be fun."

I wish that I could tell you that I had fun and laughed through the entire transition. I did not laugh the entire time, but we did get through the greatest challenge of trusting God that we had ever experienced. Because our financial loss created a new financial strain, I began commuting 575 miles back and forth, from Fullerton to Redding, every week. I made this commute for two-and-a-half months so that I could begin building up a clientele to have some income by the time we moved.

On December 12, 2003, we moved into our new home in Redding. Six weeks later, I completely left my private practice in Fullerton. In spite of all my traveling back and forth to build up adequate provision for our family, my income for the first month after moving to Redding was less than $1,000. I was making less than one of my sons who worked at In-N-Out Burger! For the next six months, I battled fear and anxiety like never before in my life. I did not know how long I could continue to make our house payments. I wondered if we would end up losing everything. Could we trust what we believed God had spoken to us?

God Restores

God has been good to us in Redding. We managed to survive the first six months, and then my income began covering our expenses. After nine months, my client caseload increased even more, so my income jumped up as well. After two years, I had enough personal referrals that I started a full-time private counseling practice in Redding. Not only has my practice been profitable, but my anointing for counseling has also increased. I feel God's presence and power working through my counseling more than ever before.

In addition, He has given us the Love After Marriage workshop, the Single Life workshop, and a couples' coaching ministry that we are raising up as well. We are incredibly full and blessed as we minister here to our

Bethel family and around the world to bring a message of hope and healing to marriages and singles. As Jesus said in Luke 16, quoted above, we had to be tested in the use of unrighteous wealth in order to be entrusted with the true riches of the Kingdom.

The Need for Agreement About Important Financial Decisions

Can you imagine what would have happened if I had made the decision to invest the $150,000 of equity from our home without Lori's agreement? It could have been devastating for our marriage.

Making important financial decisions without agreement is one of the ways that finances become a strong force of division between spouses. A couple must have the same openness, trust and honesty in their finances that they do in their spiritual and emotional connection. Together, as husband and wife, they must surrender their financial state to the Lord while simultaneously doing the best they can to manage their money well.

God Patiently Repeats Himself

It would take too long to relate to you the kindness of God during that time of our financial uncertainty. I have never received so many prophetic words and dreams about financial prosperity as I did during that season. The words and dreams from God sustained me through the next six months when I wasn't earning enough to pay our bills, and our financial future looked bleak, even disastrous, at times. However, true to His words to me, after about six months, I was earning enough to pay our bills; and after two years, God had restored a full and prosperous private practice to me. Not only was my counseling practice financially prosperous, but through that difficult season, God also increased my confidence and effectiveness as a counselor.

What Lori and I gained through that intense season of testing has been priceless—worth far more than the $150,000 we lost. We had to press through the fear and anxiety to the place of trusting God's words to us. Our attitude toward money and our ability to trust God with money is dramatically different than it used to be. Our money and our possessions simply do not mean as much to us. We are freer to trust and risk with money. It is also easier to be generous in our giving.

Continual Trust

Now the Lord is asking us to trust Him again with our finances. As the Love After Marriage ministry is growing, we have felt the Lord asking us to let go of our "secure" income from the counseling and trust Him to provide through Love After Marriage. In obedience to that, we have cut back the counseling and, therefore, our counseling income has been reduced by 50 percent. Still, God has continually provided through income from LAM.

Even with this reduction in the counseling work, we are still busier than we have ever been. For the past two years, we have not taken a week-long vacation. The most we have taken is a day or two here and there. However, we want to tell you a story about how good our God is to provide when we step out in faith and obey.

A few months ago, we were walking and praying on a trail in the forest near our home. I spontaneously began to pray and cry out to the Lord about how we needed help with our schedule. Our lack of discretionary time was our biggest concern. I became a little dramatic as I prayed, "God, we really need Your help with our schedules. We need time to rest! We need Your help, and I really, really mean it, God!" I was not angry, but I felt desperate for His help. We continued to talk and pray as we enjoyed our warm evening walk through the woods.

Three days later, on a Friday morning, we were talking to a couple who are friends of ours, and the husband said, "I was in the prayer chapel this morning, and the Lord told me to pay you for one session of counseling per week for the next year so that you can focus more time on LAM. And you know the way that you discount your fees for people who can't afford your regular fee? Well, God doesn't do that, so I'm going to pay you at your full rate."

Wow! They gave us an amount that was equal to more than one third of my annual income! Around the same time, two other couples came to us and told us the Lord had spoken to them about supporting us monthly so that we could pursue all that the Lord has put in our hearts for LAM. We poured out our hearts to God, and then He told three different families to give us the money to help our schedule! How can we ever doubt His goodness again? He has proven Himself to be good when it looked like everything would be lost; and He has proven Himself generous when we cried out for help.

When I was the executive director of the nonprofit Alpha Center, one of my responsibilities was to raise funds. Fundraising was not my favorite thing to do, and I wasn't really very good at it. I managed the finances well at Alpha Center, but I never raised much money. Most of our income came from our services, and not from donations. In contrast, Lori and I have been given far more money for LAM (without asking for it) during the past three years than I raised in 15 years while asking for donations for Alpha Center. From our personal experience, we can confidently say that as we trust God, He will always give more than we could ever ask.

A Wife's Perspective

In looking back on all that happened to us during that season of learning to trust God for our finances, I (Lori) can honestly say I would not have changed one single thing. For what God did in all of us, but especially in my Barry B, I would be willing to go through all the difficult times again, many times over. What we gained is invaluable! Through it all, God proved to be very good to us financially; but more than the money, we gained so much spiritually and relationally.

Throughout our married lives, Barry has been a steady and responsible provider. He has led our family well, and I have always felt peace and security in his financial leading. Most of our lives we did not have a lot of money, but the Lord gave us all that we needed; and together, we managed that well. When we felt God leading us to make the investment, and then we lost the money after we had committed to move up to Redding, He was strategically preparing us for a spiritual promotion. We thought we had surrendered everything to Him, but He wanted the control of our finances in a more complete way. If we were truly going to move in a new level of faith, we would have to let go of simply trusting in our own ability to manage our finances.

Barry had learned to be extremely self-reliant from the time he was a young boy. Living in a family of 13 children, he learned early on that if he was going to get what he needed in life, he would have to depend on himself. This sounds like a very responsible thing to do, and he learned to do it quite well in all areas of his life; but after the move to Redding, God began to introduce another perspective. Even though Barry's self-reliance had served him well in many areas, it did not represent God's economy. God wants us to trust Him and rely on Him to provide what we need.

Time to Join Together

During our first six months in Redding, Barry did all he could possibly do to provide adequately for our family. When his best efforts appeared to be insufficient, something unfamiliar set in; panic began speaking to him. One night after a couple of hours of battling the spirit of panic and still getting nowhere, he finally woke me up and asked me to pray with him. When we prayed together, the panic left and he was able to go back to sleep.

For some reason, he was unable to battle the anxiety on his own, and he needed me to join him to pray against it. We were stronger as a couple than individually. It was crucial that we stay connected emotionally and spiritually while facing those intense difficulties. It was so important for us to pray daily together regarding the financial trials.

Many couples tell us how difficult it is for them to pray together consistently. However, it is worth pressing through any obstacle so that the spiritual power for your marriage will be multiplied through united prayer. "One [could] chase a thousand, and two put ten thousand to flight" (Deut. 32:30).

God Speaks About Our Provision

God was graciously helping Barry during this time by giving him frequent dreams, visions and prophetic words; most of them were about provision, abundance and wealth. They were the opposite of what appeared to be happening to us!

The first week after we arrived at Bethel Church, three different people who did not know us came up to Barry with the same message; "If you focus on your lack, lack is what you will have." The Lord was speaking to us, and in case we didn't get it the first time, He was kind enough to repeat it two more times. Two of our boys had dreams about receiving money in the mail. I had a dream in which I saw Barry sitting down, and instantly a robe was placed upon his shoulders. He was given a scepter, and wealth was piled up all around him. A week later, a woman at church told him the Lord had given her a vision about him. As she recounted it to Barry, her vision ended up being exactly what I had seen in my dream. These dreams were, of course, symbolic, but we took them as personal confirmation of God's promises to provide for us.

When we were still not earning enough income to cover our monthly bills, Barry saw his monthly paycheck in a dream. The check was written with gold ink and was far more money than he had earned to date at the counseling center. It would more than cover our bills. He was not expecting a large check based on the number of appointments he had that month. However, when he received his paycheck a few days later, it was within $25 of the amount on the check in the dream. This was quite amazing and encouraging. We felt as though God was reiterating that He was taking care of us. It was as if He was saying, "Your checks are coming from the bank of heaven, and I'm the one who is writing them."

Hummingbirds here, hummingbirds there—during this season, we were seeing hummingbirds everywhere. While we were walking and praying one day, a hummingbird flew right up in front of us and flew backward, remaining in front of us as we walked down the street. Wherever we were in our home, we repeatedly observed hummingbirds hovering at our windows. One day, Barry and I were out talking on the deck when a hummingbird flew out from under the steps I was standing on. These tiny little birds had definitely captured our attention.

One night, Barry had a dream that hundreds and hundreds of bright orange hummingbirds were flying around his head, tickling him with their wings as they fluttered. He was laughing in the dream and actually woke up laughing. Finally, Barry asked, "What is the deal with all these hummingbirds?" After six months of exceptionally frequent hummingbird sightings, Barry decided to search out their meaning. In a dream interpretation workshop we had attended, the teacher mentioned that hummingbirds stand for the "prophetic promise of fruitfulness." Wow! God was speaking to us again about our finances and His promise to be good to us. God graciously continued to send Barry this message until he received it and was operating from a place of peace and joy.

I love what the Lord has done in all of us through this time, but especially in my precious husband. God had us fully covered financially even when it looked like everything was falling apart. As Barry continued to work through this financial test, he became victorious over the spirit of self-reliance. His faith increased, and his ability to risk and trust Jesus grew exponentially. It was a crucial step to prepare him for the next leg of our journey with the LAM ministry where the Lord is now asking for complete trust again.

The Lord wants to take us deeper and farther and higher, if we will let Him. Letting Him have complete control over our finances is a necessary part of taking us to the next level with Him. Thank You, Jesus, for gently and faithfully leading us in every area of our life.

⟨⟩⟨⟩⟨⟩⟨⟩⟨⟩ ACTIVITY ⟨⟩⟨⟩⟨⟩⟨⟩⟨⟩

(Put on some soaking music.) Take some time to listen to the Holy Spirit as you answer the questions below. Share your answers with each other. Spend time praying together regarding the areas in your finances where you need help. When you are done praying, recommit your finances to the Lord. As you follow through with this commitment, watch what He will do!

1. Have finances been a source of tension and/or conflict in your marriage? Explain.

2. Do you need to manage your money better? If yes, what changes do you need to make?

3. What does trusting God with your money and possessions look like for you? How well are you doing at this?

4. What is the most important lesson God has taught you regarding finances?

⟨⟩⟨⟩⟨⟩⟨⟩⟨⟩ HOMEWORK ⟨⟩⟨⟩⟨⟩⟨⟩⟨⟩

1. During your prayer times together this week, pray for any financial breakthrough or increase you may need.

2. Do the *Spirit Blessing for Couples* morning and evening.

3. Put on some soaking music and dream with the Lord as you consider the following question: "What would we like to do as a couple if money were not an issue?" Share your answers with each other.

4. As pertinent situations arise, use your tools (*Listening Exercise; Feeling Words; 1-2-3 Skidoo; Steps to Reconciliation; Rules for Working Through Conflict; When the Poop Hits the Fan*).

Notes

14

OUR SEXUAL ONENESS

In preparation for this chapter's focus on sexual oneness, we strongly recommend that you set aside at least four to five hours, plus an overnight time to be alone. Don't plan this at a time when you will be exhausted from work. If you have children, you will need to get away to a hotel. If that is not possible, have a friend or family member pick your kids up early, keep them overnight and return them no sooner than noon the next day. It would be nice if you could go out to dinner together. An entire weekend would actually be the best, if you can do it.

You need to read the next three sections together as a couple. We will lead you through stories, testimonies, prayers, activities and homework—and yes, there is homework! All of this is for the purpose of bringing God's best from heaven to earth on behalf of your sexual oneness. Be prepared for God to be a part of this weekend with you. He created sexuality, and He is very interested in making this a good time for you.

Part 1: Releasing Sexual Freedom

After the Lord gave us the "Flatbed Truck Dream" (you can review the details in the Preface), He has been highlighting to us through revelations, spiritual experiences and dreams that He wants the sexual relationship of marriage to be nurtured, healed and transformed throughout the Church. It is important to understand that out of the spiritual, emotional and sexual aspects of a married relationship, sex certainly is not the most important part; but right now it is a priority on the Lord's heart! In fact, as we look back at all He has taught us about marriage, God has given us the most direct revelations in the area of sexual intimacy.

The Church has not done a very good job of stewarding this amazing gift, while the world has twisted and subverted sex. In response, we, the Church, have taken our hands off and labeled it as something shameful and, therefore, something we do not speak of. As Barry and I have shared our stories and the things that God has shown us in the area of sexuality, we have seen hundreds of couples gain tremendous hope, freedom, creativity and joy in their sexual relationship. Hallelujah! The Lord has shown us very clearly through a recent dream that He wants to bring about the same breakthrough in your life as He has in the lives of the couples that have attended the LAM workshops.

Achieving Breakthrough

You may be experiencing fear as we open up this subject. Your heart might even be beating a little faster. Some of you may feel hopelessness speaking: "We've been like this far too long . . . our sexual relationship is not going to change . . . nothing is going to help." You may even be feeling anger and do not want to discuss this subject at all. It is quite normal to feel these things, but don't stay in that place. The Enemy, who has robbed and bound you in these areas, is lying to you. He is intentionally bringing these thoughts to keep you from getting breakthrough. If you are feeling or hearing negative thoughts (lies) coming into your mind regarding this subject of sex, please walk through these next steps as a couple.

Activity

1. Get some paper and a pen.

2. Wives, jot down the negative thoughts and lies that are coming into your mind right now and speak them out loud; then have your husband lead you through the prayer below. Repeat after him as he leads you through the prayer.

3. Husbands, do the same thing and then have your wife lead you through the following prayer and repeat after her.

> *I nail to the cross all thoughts and lies [say the specific thoughts and lies out loud] that are raised up against the purposes of Jesus regarding the truth of who I am called to be sexually and who we are called to be sexually as a couple.*
>
> *These thoughts are coming to stop me, and us, from pursuing freedom in this area.*
>
> *I break all agreements I've made with these thoughts and lies, known or unknown.*
>
> *I turn away from listening to them, in the name of Jesus.*

I ask You, Father, to send these lies and thoughts away from me.
As You send these thoughts and lies away from me, what do You want to
show me or say to me instead?

4. Take your time; listen for what the Holy Spirit is giving you, and be sure to write it down.

5. Now, wives, lead your husband through the same process of naming out loud the lies that are coming against him about your sexual relationship and repeat the prayer out loud. When finished, continue reading together.

A Little Piece of History

Before I (Lori) launch into my story, I need to give you a little family background. My grandmother Thelma Amabelle was 30 years old as she sat on the bed talking to her brand-new husband, Charles Arthur, on their wedding night. She was telling him where she thought babies came from. I'm sure that Charles Arthur was quite surprised to hear from Thelma Amabelle that she believed babies came supernaturally by simply praying for them. I'm also quite sure that Thelma Amabelle was very surprised herself when Charles Arthur very lovingly and patiently explained that there was "a lot more to it than that."

Now, I don't really know what my grandparents' sex life was like, but I do know that my parents, Grace Amabelle and John Frederick, have experienced a very healthy and enjoyable sexual relationship throughout their married life and are still very much enjoying each other today, in their upper 70s. As for Barry Joseph and me, Lori Lynn, when we got married, everything worked the way it was supposed to. We enjoyed having sex on an average of three to four times a week and both of us would have described our times of lovemaking as enjoyable and satisfying.

So there you have a little bit of my family's sexual history (whether you wanted it or not). Now fast-forward 15 years into our marriage as I share with you an encounter the Lord gave me that began a process of changing me (and Barry). I thought we were doing fine sexually, but God wanted more for us, just like He does for you. Whatever state your sexual relationship is in with your spouse, He has more for you!

A Big Surprise

I was settling down in my bedroom loft to have a quiet time with the Lord. It was morning, and I had just gotten the boys off to school and Barry off to work. All of a sudden, right in the middle of reading my Bible, I began seeing images in my mind of Barry and me making love, doing all kinds of different things I'd never thought of doing in 15 years of marriage! I saw new ways of moving and using my body to bring Barry pleasure. As these images continued to flash through my mind, it suddenly felt very hot up in my little loft. I was definitely aroused and excited by seeing this very stirring "movie" of me and my Barry B. I had never been in a trance before, but what seemed like the passage of a few minutes had actually been a whole hour when I checked my watch.

In coming out of this experience, I knew two things: First, this was definitely from God, for I would not have thought up the things I was seeing. Second, I knew that God wanted me not just to view these things, but to do them. Yikes! This did not feel like me. It was way outside of the box. But I knew it was from God. I also knew this was something I had to do *that day*.

As the day progressed, I started planning how I would go about doing what I had seen. I knew I needed to strip in a way I hadn't before; I also knew I needed to dance freely and express myself in a way I hadn't fully done before (a little scary). So I went into the bathroom and started practicing moving in ways that I thought would be arousing to Barry. After my time of dance practice in the bathroom, I thought, *Okay, I think I can do this,* and I went on with my day.

Later that afternoon, Barry called to see how my day was going—something he often does when he has a break. As we were talking, I thought, *I had better say something that will commit me, so that I don't chicken out, but still doesn't reveal my plan.* Halfway into the conversation with my Barry B, as casually as possible, I hinted that I had something I'd like to show him when he got home. How do men pick up on these things? His answer to my comment was, "REALLY?"

It is difficult to describe what I felt coming from him over the phone, but he totally knew the surprise was sexual. Then he asked me what it was, and I calmly said that I'd show him later when he got home.

I continued on with my day, and an hour later (you are not going to believe this) I started my period. It *always* lasts five to seven days. The only time I ever missed a period was when I was pregnant; otherwise my cycle has been very regular my entire life. "Oh, Jesus," I said, "if all of this is really You, and if You want me to do those things for Barry, I won't be able to follow through if I have to wait. This is already stretching me, and if I'm going to do this, I need to do this tonight, or I'm afraid I'll lose my nerve and maybe never do it at all. Lord, You're just going to have to stop my period."

I was in my late thirties at the time, and that had never happened . . . ever. But you know what? Jesus did it. He completely, miraculously stopped my cycle right then and there. Wow! He really did want me to do this.

When my Barry B arrived home, he flung open the door with great joy and expectation. "Not yet," I calmly said. "After the boys are in bed." When it came to helping take care of our boys, Barry has always been amazing; but that night (maybe I imagined it) he seemed extra helpful and extraordinarily engaged.

Finally, the boys were in bed, and I led Barry down the hallway to our bedroom. We have a little sitting room in our bedroom, and I nervously told him, "Here . . . umm . . . you sit here in the rocking chair." Most of what happened that night was planned, but this next part was not. I blame it on the Holy Spirit. I went over and sat on Barry's lap, put my arms around him and out of my mouth came the (unplanned) words, "Tonight I want to give you a gift you didn't get to completely unwrap on our wedding night."

Then I did my little thing, and afterward, Barry said, "Wow! Where did you learn to dance like that?" I smiled as I told him it was the Holy Spirit who taught me in the bathroom earlier that day.

My story may sound normal to you, or it may sound very scary. Honestly, I'd have to say it was a little scary for me, too, but I really knew it was from the Lord. We all simply need to be ready to listen to Him and then to do what He tells us.

Barry and I are still experiencing the benefits of my choice to obey, step out of my comfort zone and do something that didn't feel natural. God wants to invade every area of our lives. He wants to be involved in the most intimate details. Yes, if He calls you to risk, it could feel unnerving or even frightening, but your gain will far outweigh any risk. The benefits, when following His voice, last for a lifetime!

A Very Sacred and Holy Gift

Do you want to hear something amazing that my Barry B told me as I gave myself so freely to him? He looked me straight in the eyes and said, "I have never felt so loved by God through you."

As I share this in workshops, it's not uncommon for me to cry as I say those words and think of what this experience meant to Barry. What I had done by fully and unreservedly giving my body, my emotions and my spirit to my husband not only ministered to his body and soul, but also lifted up his spirit to feel God's love in a way he had not experienced before. Not only was the Lord letting me give this incredible gift of love to Barry, but God had also created me with the capacity to raise Barry up to experience and feel God's love. No one on the face of the earth could do this for him like I could.

Until this time, my spirit, soul and body had not been completely free to do this in the way the Lord intended it to be done. The Lord was helping me see there was a lot more "clean" than "unclean" about the precious gift of sexual intimacy He had given us in a covenant marriage relationship.

The Holy Spirit had given me such an amazing experience. Maybe it was similar to what Paul described in Acts 10:10, during a trance, when all the "unclean" things he was forbidden to eat were laid before him on a sheet. "Everything is clean," the Lord said.

The truth that the Holy Spirit showed me through this is how the world has taken His gift of sexuality and made it selfish so that pleasure has become the main priority and goal. Our church culture has been afraid of truly embracing and exploring the beauty, pleasure, freedom and holiness of sex. We have been deceived into feeling that it is inappropriate to talk openly about it in the church, even in the perfect context among married couples. We need to be free to talk together about God's design for our sexual relationship. In our marriages, we need to be free to express ourselves with our bodies and bring ecstasy and enjoyment to our spouses.

The Lord was tearing down the walls of the box of what I had accepted as "clean." He was telling me that even though what I thought I had was good, there was far more for me and my Barry B than what I'd settled for.

God is reclaiming this very precious gift from Him, reigniting it in His people and re-presenting it to the world. Yahoo! Thank You, God!

Part 2: Sex Is Sacred and God Is in It!

Can you imagine having God as your personal sex teacher? Whoa! But that's what happened. God was teaching us about sex and what He desired for it to look like. He began visiting Barry and me with such intensity that we could literally feel His presence in our sexual relationship. Every time we made love, the Lord would physically manifest in our bodies. (Barry will share more about this later.)

The Lord began giving us sexual dreams about each other. Do you know what happens when you wake up from one of those dreams? Your heart is sexually and emotionally turned toward your spouse. We had these dreams fairly often, especially when we'd get too busy with life and had not taken time to be intimate. Again, the Lord was speaking to us; He didn't want us to go too long without coming together physically/ sexually. I think this relates to 1 Corinthians 7 in the Bible, where God instructs Paul to write about not depriving each other of sexual relations.

I recall one night when we'd had a very slight disagreement before going to bed. I thought, *Oh, this is such a silly thing. I don't even need to say anything; I can work through this on my own.* I wanted to avoid making a big deal out of something I felt was insignificant. (Some of you have heard that voice before.) I wasn't mad; I simply wasn't as "toward" Barry as I would usually be. When we went to bed, we kissed each other goodnight and said, "I love you," but I still felt a very slight disconnect. We both fell asleep.

In the middle of the night, I had a whopping sexual dream about my Barry B. I knew immediately that the Lord hadn't been okay with my little disconnect, however insignificant I thought it was. He wanted me to set things right by surprising my husband with some "middle of the night delight." In case you're wondering, God didn't tell me to surprise Barry; it was simply something I knew when I woke up. Besides, after the dream He'd just given me, I was ready to go!

By that time, I was fully awake, sitting there watching Barry sleep while planning my "attack" when suddenly Barry woke up. He looked over at me and said, "I just had this amazing dream." He then proceeded to tell me about it. It had nothing to do with my "attack" plan, but instead was about one of my women's ministry groups. So, he told me the dream, went to the bathroom, we talked a bit more and right in the middle of talking, he fell back asleep.

There I sat, watching him sleep again, still not having carried out the plan. A few minutes later, he woke up again, looked at me and said, "I just had the funniest dream. I was walking downtown in front of the Cascade Theater, and written on the marquee were the words, 'the show is about ready to start.' Then a car drove by, honked its horn and woke me up!"

I could hardly believe the Lord had given him a dream in order to help me with my "mission." What a great set-up! Needless to say, "the show" did start. It ended with Barry Joseph and Lori Lynn having enjoyed a surprise encounter, in the middle of the night, that restored our connection. Isn't God good?

Yes, Jesus Loves Me

When Lori tells her story in our workshops about what God showed her to do for me, I usually joke and say, "Yes, Jesus loves me." And He does! But more than that, He loves for us to enjoy His gift of sexuality within marriage. He loves for us to demonstrate love for one another with our bodies, as well as with our words and actions.

Earlier, Lori mentioned that the Lord manifested His presence during our times of intimacy. Here's what she meant. The Holy Spirit began manifesting Himself in our physical bodies after we were filled anew with the Holy Spirit in 1994. One of the ways He revealed Himself to me is through involuntary contractions of my stomach muscles. This is often accompanied by an involuntary sound (*hmmmph!*) coming out of my mouth because the muscle contractions force air from my lungs. This manifestation began happening to both of us while we were making love. At first it was confusing, and we would ask, "Lord, what are You trying to say to us?"

Eventually, we concluded that the main thing He must be trying to communicate to us was that He was right there in the midst of our lovemaking! God wasn't embarrassed. He didn't leave the room while we were being intimate and wait to come later. He didn't tell His angels, "Close your eyes and don't look. They're naked and making love." He was saying to us, "I created sex, and I want to be in it, just like I want to be in the midst of all that you do. I am not ashamed of your passionate lovemaking. This is my special gift reserved for marriage."

A Revelation from God

I had the following experience with the Lord at the time of our first Love After Marriage workshop. Lori and I had been talking to couples about releasing sexual freedom. One morning, we were lying in bed together, and while I was kissing Lori, the thought went through my mind, *Sex is sacred and God is in it.* Immediately as those words went through my mind, my stomach muscles involuntarily contracted and the *hmmmph* sound came out of my mouth. Lori was instantly alert, knowing that God was trying to communicate something to us, and she asked me what I was thinking about. So I told her.

A few minutes later, she reached for her journal to record what had happened. She asked me again, "What were you thinking when your stomach crunched?" I repeated, "Sex is sacred and God is in it." Again my stomach muscles involuntarily contracted as I repeated the phrase.

As Lori began to write in her journal, I was watching her, and I began to think about making love. My stomach muscles crunched again! She asked, with a smirk on her face, "Now what are you thinking about?" Busted! But I had an excuse. I jokingly told her, "It's not me! *God* wants me to have sex!"

God has consistently and clearly manifested Himself during our love-making for the past 15 years. The area of sexuality in marriage is very strong on His heart right now. He wants to restore sexuality to its proper place—an expression of the holy, passionate, powerful union between a husband and wife. Sex is not merely physical; it is an exceedingly spiritual experience. With the Holy Spirit in the midst of our marriage and in the midst of our sexual relationship, God wants to give us a sexual love that will greatly supersede any temporary pleasure that carnality or lustful indulgence can offer.

Lori's Unusual Prophetic Dream

We were experiencing a sexual awakening during that season of our lives, and the Lord was expanding our understanding of all He had intended our lovemaking to be. God gave us His perspective of sexual oneness by revealing that sex is worship to Him. He opened our eyes to this truth through a dream.

In the previous chapter, we discussed that dreams are often symbolic. This dream was no exception. In the dream, Barry and I were making a sex video (you can go ahead and laugh, everyone else does). However, I never saw us naked.

The people producing the video were a team of worship leaders. There was such an atmosphere of purity about this "project" that it caused the members of the production crew to share with us how beautifully pure it made them feel and how honored they were to be involved with it.

I knew the video was going all over the world, and the Lord let me see the places it was being shown. I remember being taken into a house (flying in through the roof unseen and undetected) where I found a father and his 13-year-old son sitting down in the living room to watch and discuss the video in a purposeful way. This was not pornography to them, but a pure and godly perspective on sex. God wants us to take hold of the responsibility to bring a true, clear example of sex, without shame, to our children. It is His desire for parents to teach their children how He created us to function as sexual beings in this sacred and beautiful act of worship.

The dream revealed a profound truth in regard to how God viewed sex. First, it confirmed what He spoke to Barry: *Sex is sacred and God is in it.* The Lord is saying that sex is just as much a spiritual experience as it is sexual and emotional. Second, the producers of the sex video were all worship leaders because God was saying that *sex is worship!* This pure, holy, pleasurable act of love, when expressed openly and freely between a man and woman in covenant before God, is an act of worship!

The amazing truth that "sex is worship" explains why Barry and I have felt the Lord's presence every time we've made love throughout the past 17 years. When we come together as He created our bodies to, it is another way we worship Him. It expresses our love through one another to Him . . . as unto Him. It is His desire to be smack in the middle of this holy act of worship. He strongly desires to unveil and release this perspective all over the earth. It is time!

We've seen this truth manifest in so many couples during our workshops. It occurs when we go through the sexual material and then give them homework. The act of making love is so significant and powerful that God chooses to manifest His tangible presence during it. He has done this with countless couples, and we are fully confident that He wants to come into your sexual relationship as well.

For some, this has seemed like a very strange and even sacrilegious concept until they have felt His presence themselves. If you are willing, He will bless you in ways you have needed and desired. Sex is sacred, and God is in it.

Wow, Jesus! Don't let us stop until our perspective has become Your perspective. Keep us moving toward You until we receive all You have for us!

Johanna's Story

A few years ago, a pastor and his wife came to me (Barry) for counseling. Their marriage was in serious trouble. The husband had lost almost all desire for his wife, and he had become rather bitter and critical toward his bride of 30 years. He explained that she was like a machine to him, always doing the right thing and doing things very well, but there was no passion toward him. He went on to say that she would make love, but she lacked sexual desire and was even uncomfortable being naked in front of him.

Johanna quietly confirmed these statements but expressed a desire to change. With very little digging, I found that she had grown up in a very strict, austere home, where the terror of crossing the father's wishes permeated the atmosphere.

Near the end of one of our sessions, I felt prompted by the Holy Spirit to tell Johanna about Lori's "trance" and what God had done for her. When I finished, Johanna quite nervously replied, "Oh, I could never do that!" I reinforced that I was not suggesting that she do what Lori did; I simply felt it important to share the story.

The next week, Johanna's husband began the session by stating, "It really scared Johanna last week when you told the story about your wife." I could tell that he was reinforcing his stand that she was unable to risk being passionate and sexual.

Well, one of the very wonderful things about Johanna was her willingness to hear and obey God's voice. A few weeks later, while alone with the Lord, He spoke to Johanna and asked, "Will you let Me change you sexually?"

Again, Johanna was very frightened. However, she seriously considered what the Lord had asked her and she cautiously but willingly answered, "Yes."

Weeks later, Johanna told me of her encounter with God that night and her decision to say yes. She then told me that something began happening to her. Night after night, she would be awakened from her sleep. She told me, "I don't know what is happening, but every night I am being awakened and I can feel things literally being drawn out of me."

Soon things began to change for her. Her husband excitedly reported that he had never seen this side of his wife. She was becoming a very sexual woman. She reminded him of himself when they were first married. He would be undressing for bed and find her just staring at him as he used to stare at her. He said, "I don't know this woman!"

As Johanna's sexual desire increased, the Lord asked her, "Will you initiate sexual intimacy with your husband?"

This again was very frightening because her husband's heart was still somewhat cold and indifferent toward her. However, because of Johanna's willingness to be changed and to obey, she said, "Yes."

Though their marriage still needed healing in many areas, Johanna was totally healed from her fear of being sexual. After a few months, Johanna reported that she felt completely normal sexually. She was always ready to be sexual when the opportunity arose. In fact, she mentioned to me that she was procrastinating on some minor "female surgery" because she would have to refrain from sex for six weeks afterward! She did not like the idea of going six weeks without sex. God wants us whole sexually, just as He wants us healthy and whole in every other area of our lives.

An interesting side note to Johanna's story: After the sexual healing took place, Johanna disclosed that she had been sexually abused as a child. With God's help, we worked through that abuse rather quickly. It struck me as very interesting how God first had her risk and step out sexually *before* the sexual abuse was addressed. I don't know why He worked in that order. As a counselor, I would first deal with the sexual abuse before expecting a person to be made whole sexually. It is obvious that God's ways cannot be put into a box or formula. We simply know that He loves to heal His people.

Will You Allow God to Change You Sexually?

Perhaps you and your spouse have a very satisfying sexual relationship. Is the Holy Spirit invited and welcomed into your lovemaking? It is His desire to make it even more satisfying.

Perhaps you have been mistreated or abused sexually, as Johanna was. Will you let God change you sexually? I cannot promise that your experience of healing will be exactly like hers, but I can promise that God cares about your pain and trauma, and He wants you to be whole sexually. Will you trust Him to lead you through your own unique healing process?

Perhaps you have had very poor parental examples of sexuality. Sadly, during this last year, two different men shared with me how their fathers "taught" them about sexuality by masturbating in front of them. Recently, we ministered to a man who was given pornography at a young age in an attempt to "teach" him about sexuality. In each case, these approaches created extremely distorted views of sex. If your introduction to sexuality was perverted and far from the truth God wanted for you, will you let God change your mindset about sexuality?

Maybe your parents never demonstrated physical affection to each other or to you. Maybe you were left with the attitude that sex is dirty or sex is just for men. Maybe you got the idea that you are not a man until you can get women to have sex with you.

God is waiting to hear your response. Can you say yes to Him and then be ready to follow however He leads?

Activity
1. Stop right now and ask the Lord to reveal to you any wrong concepts the Enemy may have brought to you about sexuality through negative sexual experiences, poor family models, fear from abuse, and the like.
2. Write them down. Now take turns leading each other though the *1-2-3 Skidoo* tool regarding these lies about sexuality.

Take time with this. Ask the Holy Spirit to direct you and speak to you.

Part 3: Breaking Free

It is our Enemy's great desire to prevent and destroy intimacy within marriage. Let's focus on two of the lies he employs to prevent us from experiencing the freedom of fully enjoying each other's bodies during lovemaking. We will also present a model that will help you overcome these lies, and that you can apply to any other lies the Holy Spirit exposes for you.

The two lies are, "I hate my body" and "I don't want my spouse to see me naked." We constantly meet people all over this planet who have listened to and agreed with these destructive lies. The great news is that we are witnessing, over and over, the power of the Lord setting couples free from these lies!

This issue of body image disorder has nothing to do with weight or appearance. During our workshops, we deal with this topic very openly. Again and again, we see tall, thin, perfectly formed women and strong, fit men stand up when we give the call for those who want to get free in this area. It cuts to the core of who they are, telling them they should be ashamed and they are not desirable. They believe a lie and, in turn, they hate their bodies. Let me repeat, this goes deeper than weight and deeper than appearance.

Recently, we offered this call to stand at one of our Single Life workshops. Surprisingly, almost as many men as women stood for ministry. What a far-reaching lie body image is! And it has greatly affected both sexes.

Hatred of our bodies is like a widely spreading cancer in our society. If not identified and dealt with, those who are living under its stranglehold will continue to see significant negative effects within their marriage, including a serious lack of freedom within physical intimacy.

We are done with seeing intimacy and the enjoyment of each other's body being annihilated within marriages. And that's why we've answered God's call to help others courageously attack this lie, take the necessary risks and push forward for breakthrough. Those who do will find the Lord moving mightily on their behalf.

This self-hatred has a deep root, which some say came out of Hollywood. However, if the truth be told, I believe it goes much deeper. It may be connected with identity issues, sexual abuse, poor role models . . . but no matter what the root, the lies of the Enemy are behind this epidemic, and the Lord desires to deal with it. He wants to walk into your world right now, and through the power of the testimony, set you free.

To those of you who live under the power of the lie of self-hatred—the lie that your body is ugly and undesirable, and that it is shameful to be seen naked—it is time to receive heaven's perspective. It is time to stand against the disorder of seeing yourself through the Enemy's lies. It is time to see yourself as God sees you!

As you read the next story about one woman's victory over the lies "I hate my body" and "I don't want to be naked in front of my spouse," our desire is that you receive God's power and experience His ability to heal and restore your mind, will and emotions. Receive it for yourself!

Seeing Through New Eyes

At one of our workshops, there was an absolutely beautiful, perfectly proportioned, drop-dead gorgeous woman. Devastating attacks had come against her throughout her life, especially the loss of her mother and brother to suicide. Most of her life, when she stood in front of the mirror, she would think, *You're a fat pig* or *Your legs are so ugly.* Such thoughts perpetually surfaced to accuse, curse and condemn her every time she looked at her reflection.

During the workshop, the Lord directed us to pray for spiritual encounters over all the participants. The next day, this precious woman returned and shared the following story with us: That night, the Lord woke her up at 4:00 A.M. At first, she fought it, simply because 4:00 A.M. was horribly early; but the Lord persisted, and she finally pushed herself out of bed. On the way to the living room couch, she managed to pick up her journal and somehow found herself completely awake. She then had the thought, *This is my encounter with the Lord*, and became quite excited about what the Lord had in store for her.

She sat there, pen in hand, ready to record whatever revelation the Lord was about to bring. Just as she began to wonder how long she might be waiting, it began. Heaviness settled over her and she quietly sank down into the couch in a state of utter relaxation, leaning over and resting her head on the couch pillow. Surprisingly, she didn't fall asleep, but instead immediately found herself in a vision.

In the vision, she watched as Jesus came walking up to the couch and stood right in front of her. He reached down and painlessly popped out her eyeballs. As if that wasn't unusual enough, He then popped out His eyeballs. He proceeded to place His eyeballs into her eyes sockets and said, "There, now you will see yourself as I see you," and the vision ended. She rose from the couch, went back to her bedroom and fell fast asleep.

The next morning, as she walked by the mirror, she stopped, stared at herself with great surprise and thought, *That's me? Wow! I look really hot!* She continued to look at her reflection in the mirror and thought again, *Those are really nice legs! I think I'll keep them!*

Through one encounter with the Lord, He dramatically changed how she perceived her body. For the first time, she was seeing herself as He did. The Lord truly did what He had shown her in the dream. From that point forward, she was finally able to see herself as the beautiful woman He had created her to be. After 40 years, the lie had been broken!

Her husband stood up and testified that between the Lord having brought heaven's perspective to her body image and their invitation to the Holy Spirit to come into their time of intimacy, it was the best sex ever! Yippee, God! You care about us so much. You care about how we see ourselves, and You remove the "hurtful way" so that we can freely give ourselves—our bodies and our love—to one another! "See if there be any hurtful way in me, and lead me in the everlasting way" (Ps. 139:24).

Breaking the Power of Lies

Now it's *your* opportunity to get rid of the debilitating lies "I hate my body" and "I don't want to be naked in front of my spouse." We have watched so many people receive freedom as we've led them through the following prayer. If you and your spouse desire to remove these false perspectives, take turns leading each other through this prayer:

> *Heavenly Father, I nail this lie to the cross of Jesus that says, "I hate the body You have given me" and "I don't want to be naked in front of my spouse." I break all agreements I've made with these lies, known or unknown, in the name of Jesus. I turn away from listening to these lies. Lord Jesus, bring to my mind any vows I have made in connection with these lies.*

Vows

A vow is something you have not only come into agreement with, but it has also become a binding code in your life. You may have come into agreement with a vow knowingly or unknowingly; ask the Holy Spirit to bring any vows to mind.

Here is an example of a vow. I know a woman who stood in the middle of her kitchen when she was 15 years old and, for various reasons, said, "I never want to have kids!" She grew up, married and began trying to conceive a child; but for years she was unable to get pregnant. As she sought the Lord about this problem, He reminded her of what she had spoken out when she was 15. Armed with this revelation, she broke the power of the vow (just like you are going to do with the "hatred of your body" lies), and she got pregnant!

Our words can be binding: "Death and life are in the power of the tongue" (Prov. 18:21).

If the Lord shows you any vows you have come into agreement with, pray the following:

I nail the vow of_____ to the cross of Jesus.

I break all agreements I made with this vow, in the name of Jesus.

Father, send this vow and all its effects in my life away from me now, in Jesus' name.

(You may need to do this several times if the Lord reveals to you more than one vow. Don't rush this; it's important.) When you are finished with the vows, you can proceed with the lies.

Father, I also ask that You send the lies "I hate my body" and "I don't want to be naked in front of my spouse" away from me now.

As You send this lie away from me, what do You want me to know about how You see my body? (Stop and listen; this is a very important step.)

Write down whatever the Lord gives you (He may speak in the form of a picture, a thought or a feeling):

Thank You, Jesus. I receive Your word about me.

Activity

(Put on some soaking music.) Take some time right now to write down your answers to the following two questions and share your answers with each other.

1. What things do you like best about your sexual relationship?

2. What areas of your sexual relationship would you like the Lord to help you grow in? (Be sure to answer only for you, and not for your spouse.)

3. Spend some time right now praying through the areas in your sexual relationship that you would like the Lord to help you grow in.

Reminder: If you struggle with praying out loud with your spouse, keep it simple. Take turns speaking short sentences out loud to God concerning what you want help with. Then declare out loud (a few short sentences) the things He wants to do in order to help you. Take time to allow the Holy Spirit to bring God's thoughts to your mind. You will be amazed at what will come forth as you partner in prayer with Him. Praying is simply talking to God.

Lord, give them noticeable freedom and encouragement as they make the effort to do this together!

A Call to Activation

Ever since the Lord showed us so much in the area of sexual oneness, we knew beyond a shadow of a doubt that we needed to step out, activate our faith and give the Lord an opportunity to reveal all that He intends for us in this area. James 2:17 tells us that "faith, if it has no works, is dead," so I started asking Him what activating all of this new understanding should look like. Something that caught my attention at that time was an article concerning a recently written book titled *Just Do It.*[1] It was the story of a couple who decided to have sex for 101 days in a row. Yes, they really did it; they lived to write their book and are still alive, as far as we know!

We thought it would be a great challenge for the LAM workshop. So now we want you to do 101 days of . . . just kidding. Here are a few quotes from the article about Doug and Annie Brown's experiment in sexual intimacy: "They stopped feeling like roommates, parents, or partners, and felt more like lovers." Annie said, "Having so much sex made me feel affirmed and wanted, and feeling physically confident extended into my emotional and mental well-being." Doug said, "This experiment left me feeling closer to my wife . . . I didn't feel as much anxiety to 'perform' during sex. Plus, I felt more open, excited *and* we fought less."

Quite interesting results, eh?

While I was pondering their story, the Lord opened the door for me to speak with a woman I knew. She was working hard at strengthening her sexual relationship with her husband. One day, the Lord said to her, "I want you to have sex with your husband seven days in a row. I want you to initiate it, and I don't want you to tell him it was Me who told you to do this."

She did what the Lord told her and, in turn, received some wonderful results. She felt closer to her husband and they were more aware of each other and enjoyed one another more. *Hmmm, very interesting,* I thought.

As I continued to ponder what the Lord desired for us to do, He brought me another example through an Internet clip on Fox News. A church in Texas had been interviewed because of a seven-day sex challenge they had recently completed (seven is the number representing "completion" in the Bible). As I watched the interviews, I heard a most interesting fact. *Every person* interviewed felt closer as a couple, enjoyed being with each other more, were more considerate and kinder to one another, and thought more about their spouse. One gentleman from the church in Texas shared his testimony on the news. Many years prior to this he had had an affair and, fortunately, he and his wife chose to stay together. They worked through much of the damage but he had never been able to forgive himself. Every day of the sex challenge he felt the shame weakening, and by the seventh day, he was completely free of shame!

Your Sex Challenge

"That's it!" we said. "We are going to do a seven-day sex challenge for our workshop!" And so, dear couple, that's exactly the opportunity we want to present to you. Within a seven-day period, we want the two of you and the Holy Spirit to decide exactly what your sex challenge will look like. Perhaps you haven't had sex together in five years (this is not uncommon to hear in our workshops), so one time in that seven days is going to be your challenge. Maybe the Lord will lead you to make love three, six or all seven days. We had one couple who hadn't had sex for quite a while; their sex challenge was simply to come together and cuddle for seven days in a row. I have to tell you they ended up doing a lot more than just cuddling! Their full written testimony is on our website if you'd like to read it.[2] It's so beautiful!

Activity

1. We want you to take some time right now to talk together and listen to the Holy Spirit after asking Him what your sex challenge should be.

2. Decide what your sex challenge will look like. Any amount of time is okay as long as you both are in agreement with each other and listening to the Holy Spirit.

Testimonies from the Sex Challenge and Beyond

Earlier in the book, I shared a prophetic word given to Barry and me by one of our intercessors. We were told that LAM would not just give good information, but we would also *impart* to couples through our ministry. Well, He started releasing amazing sexual experiences to other couples after we shared our story with them. I have to say, many have reported the Holy Spirit manifesting in stomach crunches during lovemaking, and much, much more! The manifestations simply show us that the Holy Spirit is present and validating the importance of sexual oneness. Many couples who are not experiencing physical manifestations of the Holy Spirit are still enjoying greater fulfillment and intimacy when they invite His presence into their sexual connection.

There are so many testimonies from couples who have taken the seven-day challenge that we cannot share them all, but I will share with you a few.

A young wife had always had heart palpitations while making love. The doctor said her heart was fine and there was no physical reason for her response. This wonderful young lady had recently begun to deal with fear in many different areas. The heart palpitations were caused by fear. When she faced the fear head-on during the sex challenge, all heart palpitations ceased! To this day she has not had a recurrence.

Several couples reported having visions and revelation during orgasm.

Many women have come forward for prayer, asking for the Lord to stop their periods just like He did for me so they could begin the sex challenge that night. Time and time again, I would tell them (oh, me of little faith) to wait until after their periods to start the sex challenge. "No!" was their adamant reply. "We strongly feel the Lord wants this for us now, tonight." How could I disagree? I half-heartedly, with less than a mustard seed of faith, prayed, "Lord, bless them and stop their periods, in the name of Jesus. Amen." Every single one of them came back the next morning with the same astonishing report. The Lord had *completely stopped* their periods! What their hearts were longing for in the sex challenge was so important to the Lord that it moved Him to disrupt their menstrual cycles.

One man, throughout his entire married life, had experienced pain with sexual intercourse. At the workshop, he and his wife received breakthrough in many areas but not in this sexual/physical one. Regardless, they were so impacted by their time in the workshop that they decided to bring LAM home to their church. They began leading the 18-week workshop. During that season, the Lord gave this man dreams, letting him know that he was going to be healed. When it came to the seven-day sex challenge, he, his wife and the Holy Spirit made the choice to have sex seven times. The Lord miraculously healed him and he experienced seven days of sex with absolutely no pain.

Couples who had been trying desperately for several years to become pregnant finally conceived during the sex challenge. In one of our 18-week workshops at Bethel, we had several pregnant women in the class. Four of those women traced the point of conception back to their seven-day sex challenge.

We had one man who was taking medication for erectile disorder but found he could function well, without medication, during the sex challenge.

Another man desired the gift of tongues but had never received it. During the sex challenge, right in the middle of orgasm, "at the moment of truth," as he refers to it, the Lord gave him his prayer language.

Some of the greatest testimonies we have received are those from hundreds of couples who continue to experience emotional, spiritual and sexual oneness in the bedroom—things they *never* had before. All of it resulted from a willingness to participate with what the Holy Spirit is doing. Lord, You are *so* good!

We have many other wonderful and inspiring testimonies of what the Lord is doing for couples in the midst of their spiritual, emotional and sexual relationship. You can read them or hear them live on our website.

Praise You, Father! Bless You, Jesus! Holy Spirit, thank You for being here!

Last-minute Instructions

1. For those of you who just got rid of the "body image disorder," and in preparation for your sex challenge, we want you to go into the bathroom by yourself and stand naked before the mirror. We bless your spirit to be in a prominent place and we ask your soul and body to step aside. As you do this, ask the Holy Spirit to come be with you and guide you as you bless all the sexual parts of your body that the Lord highlights to you, as well as any parts that you have felt negatively about. Rededicate all these wonderful, God-fashioned parts back to the Lord and to your spouse.

2. This next exercise is for *all* couples, whether you had the body image disorder or not. Stand naked before one another. Take turns blessing each other's bodies, sexual and nonsexual parts, as the Lord leads. There is something in this exercise that has the power to break shame! Try to look into each other's eyes as you bless each other's body parts. "_____, in the name of Jesus, I bless your thighs, I bless your face, I bless your breasts, . . . or, I bless your penis, I bless your stomach, I bless your eyes . . ." Let the Lord lead you; listen to Him for the things that need to be mentioned. You may be surprised!

3. During the times that you have committed to come together sexually this week for your sex challenge, put aside any past history, past patterns or mindsets you have operated under that are not what God has for you. (You may even need to *1-2-3 Skidoo* some things.) Invite the Holy Spirit to come and be with you in this time, as unto the Lord. Remember, this is worship, and He loves to be in your midst!

Prayer

*We bless your spirits to remain in a prominent position,
leading your bodies and souls throughout your time of
lovemaking. We impart to you whatever the Lord has given us
in the areas of vulnerability, freedom, creativity and enjoyment.
Jesus, release the fullness of all You have for them in this area,
in Your precious name. Amen.*

HOMEWORK

1. Honor your agreement and complete your sex challenge for this week. Be sure to invite the Holy Spirit into your lovemaking each time.

2. Do the Sprit Blessing morning and night.

3. Do the *Face-to-Face* blessing daily.

4. Be prepared to use the tools to overcome anything that comes against you this week.

5. Read and discuss the following Healthy Attitudes Toward Sex:

   • Learn to be okay with enjoying each other sexually.
   • Don't worry about whether or not you come to climax (orgasm) every time.
   • Just enjoy each other's body.
   • Think about giving more than receiving. Talk to each other about what feels good so that you will know how to give to each other.
   • Think about sex as a way to communicate love to your spouse.
   • Prepare for sex by keeping all anger, resentment, bitterness, offense and any other like emotion out of your life and out of your marriage.
   • Don't allow discouragement or fear of performance to steal your intimacy. Keep talking, praying and inviting the Holy Spirit to help you overcome any obstacles.
   • Prepare for sex by having quality time together.

Notes

_____

_____

_____

_____

_____

_____

_____

Notes

1. Douglas Brown, *Just Do It: How One Couple Turned off the TV and Turned on Their Sex Lives for 101 Days (No Excuses!)* (New York: Crown Books, 2008).

2. See www.loveaftermarriage.org.

15

GOD IS SPEAKING TO US ABOUT SEX

An urgent matter on God's heart today is that we reclaim the area of sexuality for His kingdom. Sexuality is displayed in ungodly ways on TV, the Internet, commercials, magazines, billboards, newspaper ads and movies. More than any time in history, immoral sexual materials are readily available. We even need special programs on our computers to prevent unwanted pornographic images from "popping up" unexpectedly. God does not want us to be afraid of our sexuality or deny it. Instead, His desire is that we understand our sexuality. And by understanding, we will honor Him in a way that will allow us to enjoy all the powerful blessings He has intended for us in this God-ordained sacred act.

God has surprised Lori and me with the dramatic amount of times He has spoken to us through dreams and spiritual experiences in regard to sexuality. In 1995, Lori and I made a covenant together before God. The covenant was a consecration of all we were and all we possessed to be used for His purposes. The first thing we consecrated was our "bodies, a holy and living sacrifice." We had no idea of the impact God intended that statement to bring about. He continually reshaped our sexual relationship and then asked us to share those very personal experiences with the world. Even though we have strongly emphasized vulnerability in the LAM workshops, sexuality has been one of the most vulnerable areas for us to expose. However, there's no better way to encourage vulnerability than to model it.

As we completed our first LAM workshop in 2008, the Lord gave me four dreams/experiences related to sexuality over a period of five weeks. Each of those experiences is described below, accompanied with an explanation of what the Lord was communicating to us. We take these experiences seriously, as communication directly from the Lord. When the Lord speaks, He also releases power to accomplish His words.

First Journal Entry

The first experience occurred on the Sunday morning of our last session of LAM. This is what I entered in my journal that morning:

> This morning, 12/14/2008, when Lori and I awoke, we were lying in bed together, and I felt no sexual desire. I was not angry or irritated at Lori. I was not worried or distracted. I just had no sexual desire, which is not unusual in and of itself. Now comes the strange part. Lori began to touch me sexually, and I felt absolutely nothing. For the first time in years, I didn't have the "stomach crunches" as was typical; and for the first time in my life, my body did not respond with sexual excitement. I began to feel scared, like something was broken in me. Then, after a few minutes, I suddenly felt two small "crunches" in my stomach, and a wave of sexual feeling flooded over me. I said aloud, "Wow!" surprised by what was happening to me. Then Lori told me that immediately before my stomach crunched, she had silently asked, "Holy Spirit, where are You?" It was as though a switch had been turned off and then turned back on when she asked the Holy Spirit, where are You. We ended up making love. The Holy Spirit was present and everything worked as usual.

We discovered several important messages from the Lord in this experience:

1. God wants to be invited into our sexual relationship. He wants to be intimately involved in every area of our lives. It is our responsibility to welcome Him in so that our intimate physical connection can be blessed by His presence with us.

2. God is not ashamed of our nakedness or our passion. It was His design to give us desire for sexual pleasure.

3. Sexual pleasure is a gift from God for all marriages.

4. Even though our body may function well sexually, we are still dependent on God for it to continue to function, just as we are dependent on Him for our next breath or for our ability to see or walk. It is important to be grateful and acknowledge what a blessing it is to have healthy sexual functioning.

Second Journal Entry

This journal entry was from the first week of January 2009.

I dreamed that I was touching Lori sexually and caused her to have
an orgasm. In the dream, I wanted her to do the same to me, i.e.,
bring me to orgasm manually. But I was uncertain whether or not
this would be something God would approve. Next in the dream,
I was kissing Lori and touching her all over her body, and she was
saying how God had made all of this sexual activity "clean" inside
of marriage.

I awoke and told Lori the dream. At the time, she had a urinary tract
infection, and we were unable to have normal sexual intercourse; so she
made my dream come true.

From this dream, we concluded that God was saying He gives us freedom to be creative in the ways we pleasure each other inside of the marriage covenant. He loves creativity and wants us to be creative in the ways
we love each other with our bodies.

I am not going to list what is "clean" and what is not. We must all make
these decisions together before the Lord. We all have an internal "meter"
that tells us what crosses over the line of clean and not clean. For example,
there is no place for using pornography or fantasizing about other people
as a way of creating sexual stimulation in marriage. As you give to each
other and love your spouse physically, you need to trust that God will help
you find spiritual, emotional and sexual fulfillment within your marriage.

Third Journal Entry

My third journal entry is from a dream I had about one week later, on
1/13/2009.

I dreamed that I was being sexual with Lori in bed. I was kissing
her breasts and she told me they were sore and I had to be very
gentle. Next, I turned around and saw that our bedroom door was
open and a young child, in his pajamas and wearing a white sleep
mask, was walking into our room. The child could not see because
of the sleep mask. In the dream, I began to think of the passage
in Proverbs 5:18-20: "Let your fountain be blessed, and rejoice in

the wife of your youth. As a loving hind and a graceful doe, let her breasts satisfy you at all times; be exhilarated always with her love. For why should you, my son, be exhilarated with an adulteress and embrace the bosom of a foreigner?"

The first part of the dream seemed to be a message to us men about being sexual in a tender, caring way with our wives. There is a difference between passion and being aggressive or forceful. Men must learn to be passionate while remaining gentle and loving.

Second, the small grandchild coming into the bedroom seemed to represent the importance of parents passing down godly attitudes about sexuality to their children and grandchildren. The child wearing a "white" sleep mask, white as a symbol of purity, was a picture of the importance of providing protection and purity for our children and grandchildren. The child's eyes were protected by not being exposed to sexuality in an inappropriate way.

Children must be protected from impure attitudes about sexuality. Impure attitudes can come from unrestrained sexual license, but they can also come from religious attitudes that associate shame and guilt with sexual feelings. When talking to our children, we must honor sexual feelings as from God while teaching godly self-control to direct their behaviors. Finally, the verses I thought about from Proverbs 5 illustrate how God wants parents to pass on His own words and attitudes about pure and passionate sexuality in marriage, without shame or embarrassment.

· Fourth Journal Entry

The most significant of these encounters with the Lord occurred on the Saturday night and Sunday morning in January before we began our second LAM workshop. Here is what I wrote:

On Saturday night, 1/17/2009, the night before we began our LAM workshop at Bethel Church for the second time, Lori and I were watching one of my favorite movies, *Prince of Egypt*. Soon after the movie began, Lori fell asleep (as she often does during movies). Throughout the movie, I was talking to the Lord in awe of what He had done through one man, Moses, and what He had done by delivering an entire nation through signs and wonders.

During the dramatic scene where God speaks to Moses through the burning bush and says, "With this staff you will do my wonders!" all of a sudden my stomach muscles "crunched." This completely surprised me because the Holy Spirit usually does this when Lori and I are being sexual or when the Lord awakens me from a dream. Surprised, I asked the Lord, "What are You trying to say to me? What do You want me to see?"

I did not hear anything from the Lord, so I began to pray and tell the Lord that I wanted to be as clear about my life's calling "as Moses was of his when You spoke to him." I also repeatedly told the Lord that I wanted to be positioned to do all of the "wonders" that God planned for my life. I continued praying and enjoying the presence and awe of God throughout the movie. When Lori awoke near the end of the movie, her first comment after waking was, "Wow! I can sure feel the presence of God in this room!"

We went to bed and I fell asleep praying the same prayer over and over: "Lord, I want to know that I am in my calling, just as Moses knew, and I want to do whatever wonders You have planned for my life."

At 5:38 A.M., my stomach "crunched" and woke me from a dream. In the dream, I was making love to Lori. Puzzled, I once again asked the Lord, "What are You trying to say to me?" I felt the Lord say, "I am answering your prayers that you prayed last night." Still mystified, I thought and I listened, and I felt the Lord say, "That's what I was saying to you when I crunched your stomach during the movie."

The Lord continued speaking to me, "Your calling is to bring My love, and all that I have taught you and Lori, to heal marriages. Healing a marriage is as wonderful to Me as healing a blind eye or even parting the Red Sea. After all, I am the one who does it all. I simply need willing servants to do what I ask. Moses followed my call and I used him to deliver a nation with signs and wonders. If you are faithful to follow Me, I will equip you to heal marriages. As long as you are doing what I have called you to do, you are doing the most *wonderful* thing possible with your life."

This was such a great word from the Lord for Lori and me! He was confirming our calling and validating the worth of it. We approach this ministry with bold confidence in the Lord's deep desire to heal marriages. The Love After Marriage ministry is His. He has placed His desire to restore marriage in our hearts. We must remain His willing servants, obedient to His word over us.

In my journal, I recorded the time I was wakened from the dream, 5:38 A.M. I felt there was something significant about the number, but I couldn't figure it out. About one year later, during a LAM workshop, a woman heard me teach this lesson on DVD. When I mentioned the time, 5:38, she immediately heard in her mind, *Luke 5:38*. That verse records the words of Jesus: "But new wine must be put into fresh wineskins." I feel that the Lord is saying that the "new wineskin" is a marriage movement of vulnerability and transparency in love—truth in love. This is not a new concept, but God is calling husbands and wives to a higher level of operating in this Kingdom concept. He is ready to respond to any couple who will risk trusting His ways with the empowering presence of His Holy Spirit.

God Is Speaking

Sex is intended by God to be a profound physical act of love, transparency and vulnerability that reflects an even deeper spiritual mystery of two persons becoming one flesh. Living in truth and grace within our marriages is what God is challenging us to do. He desires for us to be true in love—spiritually, emotionally and sexually. God is speaking to us about sex—and since He is not being silent, we will not be silent either.

HOMEWORK

1. Give each other a really good neck and back rub. While you are massaging your spouse, bless his/her spirit with as many blessings as the Holy Spirit brings to mind. For example, I bless you to know the Father's affection for you; I bless you to walk in confidence; I bless you to have peace in the storm, and so on.

2. Walk together and pray.

3. Do the Listen Exercise twice each.

4. Intentionally spend time being physically close three times this week.

   • Sit close and touch each other.
   • Hug each other.
   • Sit close with legs intertwined.
   • Spoon and cuddle in bed.
   • Hold hands while talking.

5. Remember to use the tools presented in earlier chapters to deal with any issues that arise.

Notes

16

GOD-GIVEN DIFFERENCES
IN SEXUALITY

Since the 1960s, our culture has been reacting to a society built around dominant men. In 1966, at the age of 13, I (Barry) watched as free love, free sex and free drug use was widely advocated by the youth of our nation. Women burned their bras as a symbol of their determination to be free of the oppressive restraints they had lived under for so long. Anti-war demonstrations were a common reflection of the anti-authority atmosphere of the day. The feminist movement emerged as a result of the oppression and dishonor women had experienced from men for decades. It was absolutely true that an adjustment to the attitude and value toward women was definitely needed, but an aggressive reaction motivated out of hurt and bitterness was not the answer. The pendulum had swung again, and in some ways, we have shifted to a female-dominated culture.

One of the lasting results of the feminist movement is license to judge male sexuality. The female values of connection through communicating and being sensitive are now generally considered of much higher value than the more typically male value of connecting through sexuality. The male sexual desire is looked on as base and carnal in comparison to the woman's "superior" desire for emotional connection. Generalizations such as "Sex is all that men ever think about" or "That's all that men really want" reflect the freedom to label all men as having no control over their sexual passions and no desire for emotional connection. Men are portrayed as lacking the capacity to be sensitive and caring. Sadly, there are many men who fit these labels and generalizations, but there are more men who are deeply caring despite being unskilled at verbally expressing their feelings. Any kind of rating of our gender differences creates division and competition.

Equally damaging are the disparaging remarks that men make about women, such as mocking women for their emotional sensitivity or their need to process their thoughts by talking. Any such judgments undermine the God-intended harmony between the sexes. We *must honor the differences* in each gender. As we have clearly emphasized in this book, a man must learn to honor his wife's need for connection by being an attentive listener and being quick to understand. Similarly, a woman must honor a man's need for bonding through sex. I am sure the Enemy has been strategically attempting to divide husbands and wives—male and female—since the beginning of time. However, if we can honor the God-given differences of each gender, we will find that our deep-seated needs for bonding, connection and love will be satisfied.

Common Differences Between Men and Women

As we have talked about the sexual distinctions of bonding in men and women, we must pull back and evaluate all the dissimilarities from a broader perspective.

Men and women are vastly different in so many ways: physically, emotionally, relationally and sexually. As I (Lori) was contemplating this one day, I jotted down a number of differences that quickly came to mind:

1. Men are physically stronger/women are physically weaker.

2. Male sperm (Y chromosome) swim fast and die quicker/female sperm (X chromosome) swim slower and survive longer.

3. Men release 10,000 words in a day/women release 25,000 words in a day. (As some have so aptly pointed out, men have usually used up their 10,000 words before they even get home; and women, if they are at home with little ones all day, have barely gotten started.)

4. Men enjoy talking about external details (sports, guns, work and tools)/women enjoy talking about relational details (people, relationships, family, children, and so on).

5. Men are aroused visually and are ready to go/women are aroused by emotional engagement, affection, nonsexual touch; and they take more time to get ready for sexual intercourse.

6. Men usually reach orgasm quickly/women usually reach orgasm more slowly.

7. Men achieve emotional connection through sex/women achieve emotional connection through communication.

8. Men primarily have a singular focus at any given time and are often irritated by interruptions/women are usually able to multitask and more easily handle interruptions.

Why did God make us so different? Was it a cruel joke intended to keep us from truly connecting? The way we think, the way we relate, the way our brains are wired, the way we function sexually; it is all so incredibly different! I am sure that when I arrive in heaven, I will fully know the answer to this question; but this side of heaven, I have only one theory. The Lord was pleased to create us so completely and utterly different because He desired for us to learn how to give to one another.

It would have been so much easier had He created everyone alike. But He knew the strength that would come from honoring our diversity. It is His plan for tremendous power to be released as we put forth the effort and sacrifice necessary to honor our differences, which give us the strength to remain one. What a stroke of genius! God designed a perfect plan to keep us from the snares of selfishness and self-centeredness . . . if we follow it.

Imagine husbands intentionally pursuing their wives through emotional connection when, most of the time, their greatest needs are met by sexual interaction. Consider wives truly pursuing their husbands through the initiation of lovemaking, when their love tanks are most often filled by emotional connection and nonsexual touch. We would constantly be thinking less about self and more about our spouse, and, in the process, we would be truly loving and become more like Jesus.

Jesus gave so completely in His relationships that He literally gave everything He had! Jesus, the Bridegroom, lay down His life and gave all of Himself to us, His Bride. We're called to give everything back to Him as living sacrifices. We learn to love Him more completely as we fully give and love one another. As a benefit, our children will see us loving and giving to one another just as Jesus modeled. In turn, they will catch it as well. In addition to all that, the world will see the incomprehensible love we have for one another and will want it.

It is impossible to carry out real giving and real love without His Spirit in us; but when real giving and real love are present, what a powerful sign and wonder that points the world to Jesus! In these last days, this is exactly what the King of kings is establishing in His Bride, the Church.

The Process of Bonding Is Different for Men and Women

When we do not honor the gender differences, especially in relation to how God designed us to bond, the marriage union suffers from misunderstanding, loneliness and separation. As a result, resentment, bitterness and judgments are built toward each other. Honoring the gender differences is vital for a couple to feel and experience true connection in their marriage.

In his book *What Could He Be Thinking?: How a Man's Mind Really Works,* Dr. Michael Gurian sheds some light on the differences in male and female chemistry, helping us understand the contrasting bonding processes of men and of women.

> Female hormones make the woman's brain better wired for long-term romantic activity than the man's. Nowhere do we see this more clearly than in oxytocin activity in the hypothalamus. Male oxytocin (bonding chemical) levels are lower than in females. In many men, they can be ten times lower. Just as testosterone levels are much higher in males, oxytocin levels are generally higher in females.
>
> However, there is one time of the day when the male oxytocin levels approach the normal female levels—during sexual orgasm. When a man ejaculates, his oxytocin level shoots up to the levels that females experience during other times of the day. When a man ejaculates, he bonds utterly with her.
>
> Soon his oxytocin level will go back down to its normal level . . . During orgasm, the female-dominant chemical became his dominant chemical. Testosterone and vasopressin, which got him to the point where he could successfully achieve coitus, receded in dominance—their job complete—and oxytocin, the bonding chemical, took over. But then testosterone and vasopressin begin their journey back to dominance, while oxytocin recedes.
>
> One of the primary reasons that men want sex more than women (on average) is because it feels so good to them to have the high oxytocin—it feels so great to be bonded with someone.[1]

Our God-given physiology makes the bonding experience vastly different for men and women. On average, women have considerably more oxytocin available, enabling them to experience bonding on a far more frequent basis than men. As a result, many different social interchanges become a source of bonding—a tender moment with their children or a friend, a brief connection with the check-out lady at the grocery store, a story about someone's life, a good conversation with their husband . . . the list is long. For men it is very different. There is very little that compares to the deep experience of bonding through sex. I think of it as women having a buffet before them that they can snack on frequently to enjoy an experience of bonding, while men must wait for the occasional gourmet meal that powerfully satisfies their need for bonding through sexual intercourse. These patterns are not choices; they are simply a result of the chemical differences between men and women.

God Is Responsible

Men, if you don't like the fact that your wife loves to connect with you in a multitude of ways, especially emotionally, then you need to talk to God about it. It is how He designed women. So many men say or think, "All my wife wants to do is talk." It is precisely how she was designed to bond with you.

Women, if you don't like the fact that your husband desires to have sex more often than you, well, you need to do your complaining before God. It was God who designed men with this desire. It is precisely how he was designed to bond with you.

Doesn't this explain a few things about men and sex? For a man who genuinely loves his wife, sex is not just a desire for physical pleasure. It is his desire to feel emotionally connected with his wife. Understanding the depth of bonding men experience through sex has brought amazing clarity to many couples.

Last year, we conducted a five-day LAM workshop for a church. After sharing this information about oxytocin, two different couples approached us and said, "That explains something that never made sense to us before." Both men talked about a similar experience they encountered while grieving the death of a close family member. One man had lost his mother while the other had recently lost his sister. While both men were walking through their painful ordeal, each told his wife of a strong desire to have sex. Both wives struggled to understand, thinking, *Why would you want to have sex at a time like this?* After hearing about oxytocin's role in bonding, they understood. The husbands had a need to feel emotionally connected with someone during their time of grief and loss. Sexual intercourse was the most natural way to accomplish that. Their desire for sexual connection finally made sense to them and to their wives.

We were teaching this lesson at one of our five-day workshops when a wife in the class recalled this relevant story from the Bible. In Genesis 24:67, Isaac's servant brought Rebekah to him to be his wife, and it says, "Isaac brought her into his mother Sarah's tent, and he took Rebekah, and she became his wife, and he loved her; thus Isaac was comforted after his mother's death." The bonding he had had with his mother was now transferred to his wife. It would appear that there was a void in Isaac during this time of loss that only a deep emotional connection with his wife could fulfill.

Sex can be, and has been, used in selfish, destructive ways by both men and women, but we cannot allow men who have abused sex to determine our attitude toward the male desire for sex. As long as we honor the gender differences that God created, these differences will bring us closer together rather than separate us.

SIDE NOTE: Sometimes it is the wife who has the stronger sexual desire, and the husband has a deeper need for emotional connection. And for other couples the need for sexual intercourse may be very similar for both husband and wife. The most important factor is that a couple is ready to give to each other to meet valid needs, no matter which end of the spectrum a spouse is coming from.

The Power of Giving

The kind of giving that a good sexual relationship requires doesn't always come naturally. We must be intentional and fueled by His love; and this needs to become a way of life. Next, we will give you an example and a simple suggestion to help you do this.

Quite a long while ago, we had a couple in a LAM workshop that, on the last day, came up to talk with us. They had gone through the whole course and not received any breakthrough in the area they'd hoped for. We only had about 10 minutes with them, but here is what we discovered.

Jack had never been able to truly connect with his wife emotionally. He came from a family background where he had endured so much accusation, criticism and condemnation that it was very scary for him to risk emotional connection. Because of this, he relationally shielded himself most of his life, living in a survival mode he had adopted as a little boy.

Sherri, his wife, had also been relationally deprived while growing up and had hoped that when she got married her husband would fill some of those deep needs and longings. Whenever she specifically asked Jack for what she needed, he would hear it as the same old criticism he had grown up with, especially when it was spoken out of hurt and frustration. Moving into protection mode once again, he would shut down. On top of this, he didn't know how to connect and be emotionally intimate, which constantly made him feel insecure and uncertain. For Sherri, his withdrawal felt like a knife being twisted into an already infected wound.

Think about what we previously stated concerning men. They have their strongest emotional connection at the point of orgasm. Jack definitely wanted and needed a healthy dose of oxytocin. Sherri, on the other hand, did not feel pursued in a manner that even scratched the surface of her ongoing emotional deficit. And, since women (most of the time) need to feel cherished, pursued and wooed emotionally, she was unwilling to give him any sexual response at this point.

Jack felt that what she wanted was exactly what he did not know how to give, so he threw himself into ministry and work, desiring to feel good about something he could do well. Of all the places in his life, Jack felt most like a failure when he was at home. In order to avoid repeatedly facing his blaring inadequacies, Jack unconsciously found himself avoiding home.

The 4-2 Plan

We didn't have time at that point to do any reconciliation with Jack and Sherri, but we did give them homework. We told Jack that every week for a month we wanted him to pursue his wife emotionally. As a rule, men need to have a plan; they need to have structure. When we saw the "deer in the headlights" look on his face, we realized he needed some very concrete instructions. So here is what we recommended. For 20 minutes a day, 4 times a week, we told him to initiate a time to meet and talk with his wife. We gave Jack the questions following this paragraph (you can use them too if they are helpful to your situation) and told him to start the conversation and then be sure to listen well and respond with interest and understanding.

- How was your day?
- How are you doing emotionally?
- How are you doing spiritually?
- What is one good thing that happened today?
- Was there anything difficult that happened today?
- Did you make a significant connection with anyone today?
- What ways did you think about, feel or connect with God today?
- If you could plan the perfect date for us, considering our resources and time commitments, what would it look like?

We told Jack that a wife really wants to know what's inside of her husband, so he needed to share with her as well. Here are some suggested topics:

- What are some things you're really excited about in your life right now that you simply haven't shared with her?
- What are some hard things you're going through?
- Share how you see yourself doing emotionally.
- Share how you feel you are doing spiritually.
- What are some things you'd like God to do for her, for you, for your kids, for your marriage?
- Tell her something that you would really like to do with her on a date.
- Tell her things about your day that you think she would enjoy hearing about.

With a noticeable amount of hope, Jack communicated that he would willingly do it. Then we turned to Sherri and gave her homework as well. For one month, twice a week, she was to pursue her husband sexually. Here are some suggestions we gave her:

- Initiate having sex.
- Make him feel wanted and desired.
- Create a romantic atmosphere with candles or lighting.
- Consider wearing something visually arousing and pleasing to him.
- Plan ahead; early in the day let him know you have something "special" for him later on that you think he will really like.

• During the day, at a time when he least expects it, touch him sexually in a way that lets him know you want to give him more.
• Be creative and think of ways to pleasure him with your body, which is your gift to him.
• Invite the Holy Spirit to be with you in your lovemaking.

With a touch of apprehension and a smile of resolve on her face, Sherri responded that she would do it.

We had no idea what the outcome would be, but we could clearly see that the Enemy had them stuck in a cycle that kept them from giving to each other, and it needed to be broken. This narrative represents one couple's account, but we have heard similar stories from numerous couples that have experienced this same type of problem. During the last three years, many couples that attended LAM with similar backgrounds and similar issues have given themselves in obedience to this exercise, and the Lord has met them in some very significant ways.

The coolest part of this story came from an email Sherri sent us about two weeks later. In the email she asked us, "Would it be okay if we wanted to have sex *more than* two times a week?" Ha! We could only assume they were doing really well at executing their assignment. Thank You, Jesus!

We have told many couples that if they find themselves retreating into old patterns of blame, disappointment and offence, to simply keep the *4-2 Plan* (our nickname for it), as a maintenance plan while they continue working on their relationship. And do it until it becomes a part of their lifestyle.

You may be having similar struggles. We highly recommend that you try the *4-2 Plan* that Jack, Sherri and countless other couples have used because of their desire to bring a beautiful emotional and sexual balance into their marriages. Whatever attempt you make to move toward God's highest for your marriage, the Lord will meet you. He cares more about your sexual and emotional oneness than you do.

The Addictive Power of Sex

Here's another thought about the strong bonding that occurs when a man ejaculates. What do you think happens when a man looks at pornography or fantasizes about another woman and then masturbates? Who or what is he bonding with? I believe, in these situations, a man is actually bonding with a spirit of seduction, perversion and lust. It is not a connection with an imaginary person, but with a spirit. If a man looks at pornography and masturbates, and then he has sex with his wife, he opens up his wife's spirit to all of the spiritual darkness he joined with.

From God's perspective, sex is more sacred and spiritual than it is physical. Over the years, we have had many women confide in us about how they felt dirty while in bed with their husband, or they had demonic dreams about snakes and reptiles, only later to discover that their husband had been actively involved in pornography. The wife's spirit was sensing and perceiving what was going on in the spirit realm. Her spiritual gift of discernment was revealing the truth before she knew the facts.

The intense bonding experience connected with a man's orgasm can partly explain why it is so easy for men to become addicted to sex. When we look into the deeper issues behind a man's sexual addiction, we almost always discover that he is trying to deal with pain, identity issues or a longing for connection. This does not make the addiction any less destructive, but it does expose the issues that must be dealt with in addition to stopping the behavior.

Husbands, we must be very careful to guard our hearts from pornography, which is so easily accessible, and its destructive spirit of lust. We, as men, are chemically wired to easily and quickly become addicted to the feelings experienced when we use fantasy or pornography to masturbate. As I already mentioned, pornography and masturbation are not typically the root issues, but the spiritual realm of darkness cares little about this fact. The Enemy will happily use anything at his disposal to lure us into a lifestyle of temporary pleasure, which then brings crushing, debilitating thoughts of shame. If he can persuade us to buy into the shameful thoughts and feelings, he has succeeded in destroying meaningful intimacy in our marriage.

As long as we continue in a sinful, immoral connection to pornography and lust, the Enemy will be relentless at smothering us with shame. It is a sad fact that giving in to the pleasures of pornography and lust will prohibit the deep gratification of bonding and connection God desires us to have with our wives.

God Has Designed Sex to Promote Physical Health

Medical studies have confirmed a strong correlation between frequent sex and health. A study from the *American Journal of Cardiology,* involving more than 1,000 men, documented that men who have sex at least twice each week can reduce their risk of developing life-threatening heart conditions by 45 percent—almost in half!

Dr. Joseph Mercola comments on the benefits of frequent sex: "If you are fortunate enough to be in a mutually monogamous relationship, frequent sex is an excellent way to improve your health and even prevent future disease."

The health benefits of regular sexual activity extend to women as well.

"'Frequent' is all relative, of course, and although the above studies counted twice a week as frequent, other studies have found that having sex even once a week can benefit your health in the following ways":

1. Fewer colds because of an increase in Immunoglobulin A, an antibody that fights infection
2. Women can get more predictable periods because of exposure to male pheromones
3. A better physical response to stress
4. Lower blood pressure, which lowers your risk of heart disease
5. Lower your bad cholesterol and increase your good cholesterol
6. Help tone your abs, glutes and pretty much any muscle in your body
7. Natural increases in estrogen improve the appearance of your hair, skin and nails
8. Improve your memory because blood flow increases to your brain
9. Increased feelings of motivation because of the release of endorphins.[2]

During one of our workshops in Europe, a woman who had recently completed her degree in sports medicine shared the following information with us. In her studies, she was taught that having sex two times a week is better for your cardiovascular system than three periods of prolonged cardiovascular exercise. Of course, regular exercise is needed to keep our muscles and other parts working properly. Isn't it amazing that God has put within us a means to keep our hearts healthy by making love on a regular basis?

Obviously, we need to do much more than have sex to be healthy, but there is a strong correlation between frequent sex and "heart health" in men. This is hardly surprising if we consider the fact that sex is one of the principal ways God designed men to feel bonded and connected to their wives in a deep emotional way. A man's physical heart is nourished through sexually connecting. If deprived of regular sexual intimacy, it has been shown that a man's heart becomes more susceptible to disease.

Although this phenomenon has been observed and measured scientifically, I believe the real source of the health benefits is spiritual. When sin came into the world, so did pain, sickness and death. They are the results of sin, not God. I cannot explain all of the relationships between sin and disease, but I believe that when we "make love" with our wives, and not just have sex, we are not only bringing God's love to our wives, but we are also warring against disease and other divisive schemes of the Enemy. The result is not only greater health, but also a stronger and more intimate connection.

When you use sex as a way to bring God's love to your spouse, and you both give to each other, God's presence is released to do His healing work within you. The health-promoting benefits of frequent sex in marriage stand in sharp contrast to the many serious and even fatal diseases that promiscuous, illicit sex exposes a person to. Some sexually transmitted diseases are incurable, and AIDS can be fatal. You do not have to worry about these diseases in a mutually monogamous relationship. Rather, you experience the health-promoting benefits of your lovemaking.

ACTIVITY

(*Put on some soaking music as you do this next activity.*)

1. What can I give? Write down what you desire to give your spouse in order to take your spiritual, emotional and sexual relationship to the next level.

   • spiritual
   • emotional
   • sexual

2. Take turns blessing your spouse's spirit with the things you have just written down by using the following format:

[Spouse's name], I call your spirit to attention and bless you to receive (Now read the things that you wrote down) . . . In the name of Jesus.

༄ HOMEWORK ༄

1. Make time this week to do something restful, relaxing and enjoyable for both of you.

2. Call forth your spirits to be present and engaged as you make love . . . invite the Holy Spirit to come.

3. Do the *Spirit Blessing* each morning and evening.

4. Do the *Face-to-Face* exercise two times this week.

5. Do the *4-2 Maintenance Plan* as needed.

6. Use the other tools as needed.

Notes

_____

_____

_____

_____

_____

_____

_____

_____

_____

_____

_____

_____

_____

_____

_____

Notes
1. Michael Gurian. *What Could He Be Thinking? How a Man's Mind Really Works* (New York: St Martin's Press, 2003).
2. Statistics and comments from Dr. Joseph Mercola are taken from the article "Having Sex Twice a Week 'Reduces Chance of Heart Attack by Half,'" cited in *The Telegraph*, January 8, 2010, and in the *American Journal of Cardiology*, January 15, 2010, vol. 105, no. 2, pp. 192-197. http://www.telegraph.co.uk/health/healthnews/6950548/Having-sex-twice-a-week-reduces-chance-of-heart-attack-by-half.html.

1 7

DREAMS, VISIONS AND
SPIRITUAL EXPERIENCES

The Lord loves to give us spiritual experiences. As a married couple, you are no longer two, but one flesh. Because you are one flesh, your spiritual experiences with God take on a different dynamic than when you were single. When one of you prays for a dream, your spouse may receive it. When one of you prays for direction, the answer may be given to the other. When one spouse receives direction in a dream, vision or prophetic word about the future, the revelation is for both of you since you are one flesh. When the Holy Spirit breathes on the Word, bringing revelation, it's not only for the one who is reading, but for the other spouse as well.

Rejoice in whatever dreams, visions, spiritual experiences, revelation, prophetic words and anointing God releases to your spouse. Receiving them for yourself affords you twice as much blessing from Him. Blessing the revelation God is giving your spouse takes away the temptation to compare or compete. Not only are you on the same team, but *you are one flesh!* (See Gen. 2:23-24.) "One flesh" couples receive from each other's blessings.

I (Lori) have always been a dreamer, but recently I have been in a season where I have had fewer significant dreams. Barry's dream life, however, has been quite prolific. I get really excited when he wakes up and has had a dream, because I know the Lord is speaking to both of us. Since we are one flesh, what is mine is his, and what is his is mine. Even if the dream is only about one of us, both of us are strengthened when either of us is receiving and being strengthened. "Two are better than one" (Eccles. 4:9).

You have heard very clearly through our writings and the exercises in this book that we place a high value on listening for God's specific words to us. If we are not hearing God's voice through the Holy Spirit, we are missing out on one of the greatest gifts God has for us. Part of what Jesus gained for us on the cross was the right to send us the promise of the Father—the Holy Spirit (see Acts 2:33). Jesus stated clearly that living with the Holy Spirit would be better for us than having Jesus present with us (see John 16:7). Jesus further stated that the Spirit of Truth would lead and guide us into all truth by revealing to us what Jesus and the Father are saying (see John 16:13-15).

In Acts 2, Peter, while filled with the Holy Spirit, spoke of God pouring out His Spirit on all mankind, with these results: speaking in tongues, prophesying, dreams, visions and salvations. Over and over, we have witnessed God's power released as we hear and believe the words of the Holy Spirit, instead of trusting our own thoughts. We pray that as you have journeyed with us through this book, you are becoming more and more skilled at hearing His voice for your marriage, your family and your ministry.

Learning to hear God's voice and distinguish it from your own thoughts, or the Enemy's voice, is a skill you develop over time. He speaks in different ways to different people. Some people see mental pictures. Some people see things in the spirit realm with their eyes wide open. Some people hear through internal feelings; while others sense impressions that are from God. We want to bless you to be free to find your own journey and learn your own way to hear God's voice.

As you read the following accounts of a few of our dreams, visions, prophetic words and spiritual experiences, know this: The Lord has specifically shown us that what He has given us, He will give to you as well. We will be extremely excited to hear reports and testimonies about your experiences as you encounter the Lord together.

It's Going to Snow

God has led us very specifically through dreams. We have written down dreams that we felt were from God and then completely forgotten about them, only to discover months or years later that God definitely had been speaking. It is a pure step of faith to follow God as He leads us through dreams.

In 2003, when Lori and I took the biggest step of our lives by moving from Southern California to Redding, in the far north of the state, it was only because of dreams and visions that the Lord had given us. Two years prior to our move, Lori asked me one morning, "If we could choose to have our boys raised in any spiritual environment that we know of, where would it be?" I thought about it for a while, considering several pastors and ministries that I respect, and then said, "I would want to go to Bethel Church, Bill Johnson's church in Redding."

Lori replied, "That's where I would want to go too."

As we continued on our prayer walk, we told God that we would be willing to leave Orange County, but we would not take a step toward Redding until He confirmed that He wanted us there. It would take hours for us to relate all of the dreams and spiritual experiences that we and our sons had during the next two years about our moving to Redding. (By "spiritual experiences," I mean things like praying and asking God for direction and then seeing pictures of Redding in my mind; or praying for direction and then feeling the Holy Spirit manifest physically in my body; or having someone who doesn't even know us declare things prophetically that confirmed God was leading us to Redding.) God was very patient with us. He confirmed the direction over and over and over again. However, if we had not been accustomed to paying attention to our dreams and spiritual experiences, we would have missed God's leading.

One week before we actually packed up all of our belongings, left our jobs and our home of 24 years to move to Redding, I (Barry) had the following simple dream. In the dream, an unknown, unseen voice spoke, declaring, "It's going to snow in Redding at Christmas time." Then, in the dream, I saw the city of Redding covered with snow.

We moved into our home in Redding on December 12, 2003. The average annual snowfall, including sleet and ice pellets, is four inches. We typically have one to three light snows per year. Snowfall very rarely affects travel on the roads. However, on Sunday evening, December 28, 2003, three days after Christmas, and 14 days after moving to Redding, we were sent home from the evening church service due to heavy snow covering the roads. Large snowflakes fell all night long. A thick white blanket of snow, approximately 20 inches deep, covered the ground in the morning. It was the single largest snowstorm Redding had seen for more than 100 years!

I remembered my dream from the week before we moved when someone declared it would snow in Redding at Christmas time. The dream had accurately prophesied snow at Christmas time, and the dream was fulfilled in an extravagant way. It was as though the Lord was saying, "See, I *am* speaking to you in your dreams. Trust Me!"

We Dream of a New Home

God actually showed us our current Redding home in two different dreams before we ever planned to move. In early 2002, we decided that we had to either add on more bedrooms to our existing home in Orange County or buy a new home. Our little house was bursting at the seams. We had three young adults, our four boys and the two of us crowded into a three-bedroom home. On April 18, 2002, I (Barry) dreamed that we moved into a much larger home. In the dream, Lori commented how much she liked the natural wood floors and doors. Lori was about to show me our bedroom upstairs when I awoke from the dream.

I recorded the dream in my journal because I "felt" it was from the Lord; but I had no idea what it meant. The home in the dream did not resemble our home in Southern California at all. We lived in a single-story home that did not have natural wood floors or doors. For an entire year, we discussed plans to add on to our existing home or purchase a new home in Orange County, but nothing worked out.

Exactly one year later, on April 20, 2003, I prayed silently in bed while Lori slept, "Lord, it seemed very clear to us that You wanted us to have a larger home to accommodate people living with us. We thought you were calling us to use our home to parent young people who have been fatherless and motherless. We will add on to our house or buy a new home; but we just need to hear what You want. Would You please give us a dream to show us what we should do?"

When I awoke the next morning, I immediately recalled my prayer from the previous night, but I could not recall any dreams. Soon, Lori woke up and said, "I just dreamed that we went out looking for our new home again and found the perfect house. It had everything we were looking for and it had a basement with two bedrooms; but where are there any houses with basements in Southern California?"

At the time of the dream, we had no plans to look for a home outside of Orange County, but those two dreams described details on each floor of a home in Redding we had never seen, 575 miles away! When we purchased our home, we remembered the dreams recorded in our journals. If we had not recorded those dreams, we probably would not have remembered them. The dreams dramatically confirmed that we were in the exact home God had chosen for us.

When our financial condition became frighteningly uncertain during our first six months in Redding, we could stand firm and encourage each other on the fact that God had undoubtedly spoken to us through dreams and spiritual experiences. The many confirmations that God had given us became an anchor for us while we waited for His provision. In Redding,

God has blessed us financially through Barry's counseling practice, and now He has blessed us with the Love After Marriage ministry.

God wants to direct you and instruct you through your dreams. If it hasn't happened already, we pray that God will open up your exciting journey of learning from Him and being directed through your dreams.

Bethel

One sunny Sunday afternoon, while we were still looking for a new home in Orange County, we decided to walk up a hill near our home and ask God to show us if He had a home for us in that area. The homes in that neighborhood were much larger and were priced at least double what our home was worth, putting them way out of our price range. But just for fun, as we walked, we started dreaming about the house the Lord had for us. As we strolled up the steep sidewalk, a woman practically ran right into us while chasing a runaway Ping-Pong ball. We caught the ball and gave it to the lady. After talking for a short while, we discovered that her name was Bethel. We went looking for the house God had for us and ran smack into *Bethel,* which means *house of God.* We were merely looking for a home to move into, but the Lord was not only showing us where we would live, but also the church home He had chosen for us. We did not realize it at the moment (sometimes we're a little dense), but He had so beautifully confirmed the answers to our prayers.

We could look at that event as merely coincidence; however, while we were walking, we were praying and talking with God the entire time about where He wanted us to live. Up to that point, our thoughts had still been on a new home in Orange County, but we believe that by running into the woman named Bethel, God was indicating where our new home would be. This was not a coincidence; it was a spiritual experience from God. It was one of the many confirmations that would eventually lead us to conclude that God was indeed leading us to Redding, California, and Bethel Church.

A Transition Dream

In the spring of 1994, we were living in Orange County with our four sons, attending my parent's church, Calvary Church of Placentia. I (Lori) had been there since I was nine years old. Barry and I were deeply committed to this precious church family and we were both extensively involved in leadership.

One day, while driving to the grocery store, the Lord reminded me of a dream I had seven years earlier, but it was so vivid it was as though I'd just had it. In the dream, my dad was hanging on a cross in my backyard, and I was kneeling at the foot of the cross, weeping. After I awoke, I felt sad but had no awareness that God might be trying to communicate to me. At that time, we had not yet learned to recognize and value the dreams given to us from God.

In the car, as the Lord replayed the dream in my mind, I heard the following inaudible but clear words. The Lord said, "You have put your father in a place that only I belong." This thought pierced me deeply, but I knew it was true. I loved and respected my father very much. I had been guided by him, learned from him and emulated him in many ways throughout my life. Both of my parents had loved us well, and I was grateful for the godly foundation they had laid for me and for my siblings. But through this dream, the Lord was letting me know I had stepped over some boundaries, and I needed to adjust. God wanted me to make Him the highest influence in my life, especially above my dad. I knew the Lord wanted me to make some changes.

The next morning, as I lay on my bedroom floor imploring the Lord for direction, He confirmed what I already knew from the moment He spoke to me about the dream. He was asking us to leave my parents' church. God was calling us to pack up all the good instruction we had received from them and follow Him on a journey without really knowing what it would look like.

I burst into tears as the reality of what God was asking hit me. I told the Lord it was too hard to think of leaving my family, and I needed Him to make this very clear. I needed another sign. I picked up my Bible, and out of desperation said, "If You are really asking us to leave our family and church, I need to hear from You right now!" Hoping the Lord would answer, I randomly opened my Bible and landed in the book of Psalms. It was as though I had never read this psalm before when my eyes fell upon these words: "Listen, O daughter, give attention and incline your ear: forget your people and your father's house; then the King will desire your beauty. Because He is your Lord, bow down to Him" (Ps. 45:10-11). I gasped in sheer amazement and wonder; it was as if the Lord had personally sent me a message from heaven and answered my prayer.

The time had come to leave my people and my father's house. I needed to honor God by keeping Him in first place and following His direction. To say no to this request from the Lord would have kept my desire for family in a place above Him. That would have been idolatry. Seven years prior to this, when I first had the dream, I missed what the Lord was saying because I never imagined that He could speak to me in this way. He was so faithful to continue to grow me spiritually and then bring the dream to mind at a time when I could receive it and act upon it. He was so patient with me, waiting for just the right moment to speak. It was like the time when Jesus said to His disciples, "I have many more things to say to you, but you cannot bear them now" (John 16:12).

This dream and the miraculous way He met me in His Word that day helped launch us into an amazing 17-year adventure with Him! The Lord knew I would need these experiences with Him to help me leave my dear parents for the journey He wanted to take us on. We are now at Bethel Church in Redding, California, living out the destiny God had for us—the destiny He knew long before we did.

We both stood before the entire congregation on our last Sunday at Calvary Church Placentia and shared about the journey God had us on, and that we would be leaving. That same afternoon my parents went for a long drive. They revisited all the places where we had lived together as I was growing up—from the first house to the last. Choosing to let go completely, they entrusted me, and my family, to the one they had trusted all their lives. My mom and dad continue to be a wonderful blessing and support to us, and to our boys, for which we are so grateful.

Called to the Nations

When we began writing this chapter on hearing from God, we read through some of our journals and discovered the following prophetic words that we had forgotten. Seventeen years ago, in the fall of 1994, we were in a home group where an internationally known pastor was ministering prophetically to us. (By ministering prophetically, we mean that the person was speaking and praying about specific words he heard from the Lord concerning our lives.) When we returned home that night, we wrote down all the words spoken about us that we could remember.

In the middle of the night, the Lord awakened me. As I listened, waiting to hear from the Lord, He reminded me that the prophetic minister had stated that we were called to the nations—to an international ministry. It was easy to forget about this because neither of us had any aspirations or plans for an international ministry; but the Lord woke me and specifically reminded me of the words. He wanted me to record them.

In 1998, a lady from our church approached us and said that the Lord had been speaking to her about us. She felt the Lord said that I (Barry) would be a father to thousands. She spoke further that I had the heart of a pastor, and I would have an international pastoral ministry. We had actually forgotten about this prophetic word from 13 years ago until we began writing this chapter and reviewed the entries from our past journals.

In June 2004, I was at a pastor's prayer meeting at Bethel Church when a woman I had never met began to prophesy and say to me (Barry), "When I first saw you, I saw you at an airport coming and going, coming and going on airplanes. God is training you, and you will be training others. You will be going all over the United States, and beyond. I see a huge network of people around you. God is changing your thinking that says you will only have a small ministry." Then she said, "Ephesians 3:20 is for you," and she quoted, "Now to Him who is able to do far more abundantly beyond all that we ask or think, according to the power that works within us."

I had no idea what those words could possibly end up looking like, but I wrote the words in my journal. That prophetic word was spoken to us in 2004. In 2010, we went to Germany to conduct our first LAM workshop outside of the United States. It was the first time in our lives that either of us had traveled outside the U.S.

We did nothing to try to create an international ministry except follow God the best we could. Even when we began LAM, we had no plans beyond Bethel Church; but God had a different plan. Although our greatest desire and the majority of our time and effort have been focused on strengthening the marriages here at Bethel, by the end of this year, LAM will have been taken to Germany, Switzerland, Scotland, England, Finland, China and Australia, as well as numerous churches in the U.S. We never sought out an international ministry, but God spoke to us through His modern-day prophets to let us know the plans He had for us.

God Talks About Our Boys

Our first encounters with the gift of prophecy and impartation through the laying on of hands occurred in the spring of 1994. Often our bodies, especially our limbs, would involuntarily shake as we received prayer and listened to the prophecies. We did not know what this meant, except that the Holy Spirit was touching us. After one of these prayer times, we went home so excited and aware of the Holy Spirit's presence that we hardly slept that night. We spent hours excitedly talking, praying and praising God, until we finally fell asleep in the early hours of the morning.

At 3:00 A.M., I (Barry) was awakened by a bright white light, which shot through the wall of our bedroom and the headboard of our bed. Startled out of a sound sleep, I was wide-awake again, wondering what God was up to. After a while of waiting and listening for the Lord, a picture like a dream was going on in my head, but I was still awake! I believe this was a vision from the Lord.

In the vision, I saw a translucent figure made of light standing at my left side, and somehow I knew He was the Lord. He spoke to my mind: "You will hear My words through your son Justin." I waited a few seconds and then responded in my mind (it was as though the conversation happened through my thoughts rather than with words), "What about my other boys?" Next I heard, "People will know my love through Caleb," and "Brendon will be a bright light for Me."

I waited to hear about my fourth son, Jeremy. As the image of the translucent figure seemed to be fading away, I held on in my mind, waiting a short while for a word about Jeremy. Then I saw a picture of Jeremy playing basketball when he was eight years old. He had a big smile on his face, as he always did when he played, because he absolutely loved basketball. It did not matter whether he won or lost, he just loved playing. As I saw the picture in my mind, I heard the words, "I have much work for Jeremy to do, and he will love it, just as he has loved basketball." Then the image faded away and was gone.

How precious it was to hear what God thought about our four boys, and what He would do through them! As they have journeyed though different stages of their lives, we have held on to those words, believing that God will use our boys exactly as He said. We have already seen these words coming to pass in their lives.

Lord, I Want That!

Barry was up reading in bed one night while I was already sawing logs in dreamland. He was reading an autobiography by Mahesh Chavda, a man the Lord used to raise a six-year-old boy from the dead.[1] As a young man, Mahesh had a supernatural experience while praying. As soon as he spoke the name Jesus, a strong gust of wind blew open the door to his room. For a moment, it took his breath away, but as he opened his mouth to continue praying, he started singing in tongues for the first time. At this point in the story, Barry was overcome with a desire to be touched by God's Spirit as well. He stopped reading and began praying, "Lord, I want that; I want the baptism of Your Spirit in my life." As he silently prayed, my hand started shaking underneath the covers and woke me up. "Hey, what's happening? My hand is shaking . . ." I said sleepily. Barry looked over at me and smiled, then looked up to heaven and playfully commented, "Lord, You missed!" This was the beginning of many common spiritual experiences we would share.

What in the World Did We Do Last Night?

While in the midst of a sound sleep, I (Lori) bolted upright in bed, and out of my mouth came the words, "We must leave what lies behind!" I was still sitting there, not quite awake, but fully aware of what I had just spoken, when Barry sat up in bed as well. He said, "And reaching forward to what lies ahead!" (Phil. 3:13). With a dazed glance, we briefly made eye contact, lay down and fell back to sleep.

In the morning, we woke up thinking, "What in the world did we do last night?" As we pieced it together, we couldn't believe we sat up, right on cue, recited the first and second part of the same verse and fell back asleep. It was so fun to realize that the Lord spoke these words to our spirits while we were still asleep and had us speak them out loud at the same time. That verse we both recited out of a dead sleep was a prophetic declaration of what was actually happening in our lives. We had left so much behind, and we were certainly reaching forward to what was coming. We guess the Lord wanted us to declare that word together in the middle of the night. We don't always know the reason why He does things; we definitely know that this experience was a result of His increased presence in our lives.

Barry B, Where Did You Go?

The Lord woke Barry up one night, as He often did, to get up and pray. On this particular night, he was praying for me. I was still asleep in bed. While he was praying, my right arm and hand started shaking, and it woke me. Noticing that Barry was not in bed, I got up and hunted for him. I found him in the family room, praying for me, just as I suspected. I still don't understand why God makes our bodies shake, but in this instance it gave us physical evidence that we affect each other by our prayers. Whether you shake or not isn't important. What's important is that you know God has given you authority and power to pray effectively for your spouse in a way that nobody else can.

Why Can't I Make this Decision?

Whoa! I sat up in bed so fast it made my head spin. Just a second ago I had been sound asleep. It was early morning, and I noticed Barry wasn't in bed. As my sleepy eyes scanned the room, I found him facedown on the bedroom floor. Unbeknownst to me, he had slipped out of bed way before dawn to pray and seek the Lord regarding a bothersome battle that was taking place in his mind.

As soon as I saw him, out of my mouth came, "What was it James had on his back? Remember the sermon he spoke a long time ago about the spirit that was holding on to his back? What did he call that spirit, what was it, what was it . . . ? It was 'indecision'! The name of the spirit on his back was 'indecision,' and that is the spirit that is affecting you!"

Barry was looking at me like he couldn't believe what I was saying. He had been wrestling with a decision that seemed clear in his mind and heart, but he still didn't have the peace to act on it. It had never been hard for Barry to make decisions. In fact, he had been making clear, thoughtful and godly decisions all his life. But here he was, at 5:30 in the morning, imploring the Lord, "Why can't I make this decision?" and the Lord woke me up with this seemingly silly soliloquy. I was not even fully aware of what I was saying, but Barry heard me, and realized the Lord was answering him through his crazy wife. When he understood that his inability to confidently decide was nothing more than an annoying spirit of indecision, the battle was over. He prayed right then and there, and the spirit of indecision left. Immediately, he was free to think clearly, and he quickly made his decision.

Barry had been asking God for specific direction, and the Lord answered him through me. It was astonishing that right out of a dead sleep, He brought to mind a sermon I heard 10 years earlier, had me speak it out and declare what was coming against Barry!

I think the Lord gets quite a kick out of the creative ways in which He answers our prayers . . . and so do we.

Prayer

We bless your spirits to receive and treasure all that the Lord wants to give you in dreams, visions, spiritual experiences and prophetic words. We impart to you grace and anointing to use these encounters with God for the further growth and maturing of your connection with Him. We bless you with the joy of encountering God together, during the day and as you sleep. Lord, enlarge their capacity to hear and see in the spirit realm as never before.

ACTIVITY

1. Put on some soaking music and get two pillows. Find a comfortable place to lie next to each other. As you listen to the music, dream with the Lord about what destiny He has for you as a couple.

2. Take a few minutes to write down the things the Lord is showing you.

3. Share them with each other.

4. Begin praying about the things the Lord has shown you during your prayer time together this week.

HOMEWORK

1. Talk about starting the 4-2 Maintenance Plan if needed.

2. Purchase a journal to record your dreams. When you receive dreams from the Lord, value them by writing them down. Pray about them. Discuss them and ask the Lord to give the interpretation.

3. Continue using all the tools as needed for your life and your marriage.

4. Take a leisurely walk, hold hands and pray prayers of thankfulness.

5. Surprise your spouse by doing something special he/she would enjoy.

Notes

Note

1. Mahesh Chavda, *Only Love Can Make a Miracle* (Ann Arbor, MI: Servant Publications, 1990). *Play some soaking music while you read the commitment out loud to each other.*

CEREMONY OF LOVING COMMITMENT
TO GOD AND MY SPOUSE

In the middle there is a separate section for husband and wife to read.

My dear (spouse's name), as I stand before God and these witnesses, I recommit myself to fulfill my marriage vows to you. I promise to devote myself to knowing, understanding and loving you more.

I purpose to pursue knowing God's love and affection for me, walking obediently with Him and loving Him above anything or anyone else so that I can become the person God desires me to be for you.

[Husband] I purpose anew to cherish and love you and lay down my life for you as Christ lay down His life for the church. I commit myself to joining with the Holy Spirit on your behalf to encourage you into a place of maturity and wholeness in Christ that will allow us to walk in the destiny God has planned for us.

[Wife] I purpose anew to respect and honor you as the protector and covering that God has called you to be over this home. I commit myself to joining with the Holy Spirit to affirm, support and lovingly encourage you toward your godly role as the spiritual head of our home.

I choose to make you and our marriage relationship a priority over any other human relationship.

I promise to continue to move toward living with you in a truthful, honest and vulnerable way, withholding nothing of significance, concealing nothing of importance. I will honor you by taking the initiative to share things with you about my life and about us that would be important to you, to God and to the wellbeing of our family.

I commit to not settling but consistently going farther, deeper and higher in our relationship to one another so that my heart will be fully turned toward you, so that the world will see Jesus' love in us and in our family.

Now hold hands while facing each other. Look into each other's eyes, remembering all of the good things the Lord has shown you about your spouse.

APPENDIX 1

A WORD FROM OUR BOYS

Caleb Michael

People will know My love through Caleb.

When I think of my parent's relationship with each other, I see one common thread woven through every part of their lives. They make the choice to place God first, every day. Having just been recently married, I now have an even deeper appreciation for my parents and how they love each other.

Even though the following example is about my father, it typifies my mom as well. During our birthday celebrations, we share what we appreciate about the person who is having the birthday. I have heard my mom make this same statement numerous times with tears in her eyes: "Barry B, I'm so thankful that I can trust you to follow God above anything or anyone else, including me and the boys."

It is this mindset in both of them that has enabled them to get through any difficult situation and still continue to grow in their own personal health and love for each other. Because this is a lifestyle for them, when pain, misunderstandings or disconnections come, their first instinct is to turn to God to work things out with Him and each other. By trusting God individually and in each other, He has become the driving force that keeps them growing.

Even the way they give and sacrifice for each other is God-focused. They are not enslaved to meeting each other's every need or taking responsibility for each other's happiness. They know very clearly that if they focus on loving with God's love, they will be far better spouses than they could ever be with their own love apart from God.

My parents are fully human and so they have not trusted God or loved each other perfectly. They just keep returning to the place of looking to the Lord and trusting Him to show them how to love each other.

This seemingly simple life principle requires consistent honesty about themselves and a strong sensitivity to the voice of the Holy Spirit. It has required that they check the motives behind their words and regularly ask, "Am I speaking and acting in a way that puts God first, or is it my own selfish desires leading me?"

Watching my parents continually strive to put God first through their commitment to truthfulness and their sensitivity to His voice shaped me for marriage long before I met my wife. When people asked me how I was preparing for marriage, I would tell them that I am trying to be the best version of me that I can become by following God first. If I can do this, God will take care of all the other unknowns I will face in my own marriage, just as He has done for my parents.

Jeremy Joseph

I have much work for him to do, and he will love
it like he loved basketball.

In a world and a generation that desires things quicker, easier and more efficiently, I have realized a sad truth: This prevailing paradigm has filtered into our relationships. This is made evident in the somewhat dismal statistics of marital and relational monogamy, fidelity and qualitative success. I find myself extremely blessed, however, as a young man, for the example I am given in my parents' marriage and lives.

Marriage is a beautiful bond and a blessing. Not only do I believe that the holy institution of marriage is one of the primary, if not *the* primary, relational arenas with which we can truly cultivate a courageous, wholehearted environment for growth, but I also believe that it is in this God-like union that we begin our legacy to live on the earth. From the love that is grown and gestated in a marriage comes life—both spiritual and physical. And that life enters a world where the relational dynamics of the parents who conceived and bore it will create the norm for how he or she relates with the rest of the world.

A marriage is the most intimate form of community between humans. It affords the opportunity, if we desire it, to become the most genuine, powerful, lovable and loving "us" that we can be. I do believe this to be a true principle of most investments though; we will reap what we sow. If honesty, genuineness and deep, intimate love are what you seek, then the amazing design and permission God has given us in marriage can be just that—the most rewarding earthly investment you will ever be offered. When I look at the intricate and intentional design of a man and a woman, I can't help but be reminded of the great value God has for intending one for the other.

We can see the beauty and goodness of God in everything if we are looking for it. In the same way, I choose to see marriage as an extravagant gift from our extravagant Father. And by aligning my value system with His in regard to this issue, I can live with a joyful and hopeful expectation of all that He has for me and for my wife in marriage. That's not to say there won't be trials and tests along the way, but when seen from His perspective, trials and tests tend to become tales of victory and success.

There is a movement happening in marriages. God is reclaiming what has been lost and redeeming what has deteriorated the family system, as we know it. When there is a generation of passionate husbands and wives, inevitably there will also be true fathers and mothers. And when there are mothers and fathers instilling an identity of love, acceptance and vision to a generation of children, the tares of destruction from the enemy will become the spoils of victory for the family of God.

Justin John

People will hear My words through Justin.

As I get a little older, I realize more and more the value of what was modeled to me through my parents' marriage. Friends have come to me, asking, "How do you make a marriage last and not end up in divorce?" I had to stop and think about it because I had never thought like that before. Divorce was never on my radar and, therefore, I never feared it. It was not on my radar because it was never an option for my parents. When difficult situations arose that might cause other couples to consider divorce, my parents would talk through their pain or pride until there was understanding.

Our family was known for our open communication. Friends and family were welcome and often present during family arguments and heavy discussions. Being honest and open was treated as much more important than just keeping the peace. Many believe the opposite; but to find unshakable peace you must be willing to face the pain. As we faced our own painful situations, *countless times*, we learned that intense emotions are just as important to acknowledge as love and joy. We learned that a key to successfully facing relationships head-on is the willingness to look at the problems, especially when you're the one creating them.

My parents displayed what I would call *inner strength*. It was this inner strength that allowed them to face and overcome the pain, disappointment, hurt and all the powerful things that happen in relationships. They drew this inner strength directly from God's leading, not from what they saw or felt. It was the possessing of and the accessing of that kind of strength in their marriage that taught them to be humble, to be quiet, to take responsibility or to confront as needed. My parents drew their own personal strength from God, and they brought that same strength into their marriage.

I am incredibly grateful to have been exposed to these "secrets" over and over throughout my life. I have seen them proven, tried and true. Now all I want to do is share them with others who may be struggling. I am blessed to have parents who have fought and sacrificed for truth and love to be first.

Brendon Paul

Brendon will be a bright light for Me.

All families have their strengths and weaknesses, and ours was no exception. Just like any other family, we had our conflicts and problems to work through; but oddly enough, these conflicts became one of the greatest gifts my parents have given me. My parents created an environment in our household where it was not okay to leave issues unfinished or to stay angry with one another. The lingering harm of being disconnected from the family was much greater than any issues caused by confronting. So as one could imagine in a household of six very opinionated individuals, there was plenty of confrontation to be had. In fact, most of our friends knew this about our family and it wasn't uncommon or even uncomfortable (after the first few times) for them to come over and see two people in a heated discussion, trying to work through a conflict.

I am so thankful my parents set the standard of connection and relationship higher than avoidance of conflict. Because of this, I have deep and meaningful relationships with both my brothers and my parents. I also see conflicts as opportunity rather than something bad. It is a chance to let someone know that he or she can trust me and be understood, or to give someone else the opportunity to do the same with me.

Our family has grown and gotten better at handling conflict over the years; and as with anything else, practice makes perfect. Even though it's still a work in progress, these values to prioritize relationship and truthfulness over the fear of conflict have now become core to who I am. Any significant relationship we have will experience problems, but because of the effort and experiences I have gained through my upbringing, I am able to face those conflicts with hope and God's perspective rather than fear and anxiety.

Thank you, Mom and Dad, for setting the standard for our family. Having had much practice at an early age in working through the pain and hardship of conflict has shown me, without a doubt, the closeness and love that come from resolution; and understanding is so worth going through the hardships of working through conflict itself. Both of you have given me, my brothers and all your other spiritual children a gift. We will go through life with a new standard of connection and trust to those we love, and we are ruined for anything less.

Mom and Dad

In spite of our shortcomings and blunders as parents, the grace of God has always covered the times when we failed or misunderstood our boys. From the time our first son was just an infant, we began praying, *Lord, please make up for the things that we lack.* He has been more than faithful to answer our prayer.

In this season of our lives, we have come to realize that the greatest gift we could give our children while they were growing up, and even now as young adults, was a loving, vibrant marriage. This book is not just about healing and strengthening your marriage; it is about positioning you and your family to reach their God-ordained spiritual and relational destinies in these last days.

APPENDIX 2

STORIES FROM LOVE AFTER MARRIAGE COUPLES

The power of the testimony will be released to you as you read through these stories. Just as we wrote at the beginning of the book, we encourage you to grab hold of any miracle, breakthrough or victory you read and claim it for your own marriage. If God has done it once, He will do it again.

Desmond and Elaine

We came for LAM after trying numerous marriage counseling sessions. We were both very drained, and Elaine wanted to leave for another guy. LAM was going to be the last try before signing the divorce papers. We couldn't see how our marriage could be restored, but God performed a miracle! LAM equipped us with many practical marriage tools, but what really saved our marriage was the work of the Holy Spirit. Throughout LAM, Barry and Lori were so sensitive to the Holy Spirit's leading that LAM seemed tailor-made for every couple. The Holy Spirit spoke to Elaine directly through a vision and the scales that blinded her eyes fell off immediately. She sobbed uncontrollably and instantly knew she had to stay in the marriage. She also experienced holy laughter during couples coaching! We had never enjoyed sex in our marriage because Elaine had had bad sexual experiences and Desmond was influenced by pornography. During LAM, we were delivered from past bondages that manifested in our marriage, causing the breakdown. We've been having good sex ever since. We couldn't talk to each other before, but we've been communicating nonstop ever since. The love is back and God is in charge!

Wade and Annette

Marriage is good if you know what marriage really is. Love After Marriage helped to define our marriage covenant, to value one another and to deepen our emotional intimacy. We gained a wealth of courage, strength and understanding in seeing each other from another perspective through the use of LAM tools, interactive homework in the workbook, group discussions and examples of other couples' struggles. The first lesson, called "Nothing Hidden," gave me something to stand upon and helped in our communication. I finally felt free to share everything I was feeling, hiding and thinking (the good, the bad and the ugly). The change I wanted in my relationship with my wife finally felt tangible and hopeful. We went from a lukewarm marriage to passionate true love. My wife and I struggled for almost 20 years of not really hearing what the other was saying, because we perceived things through our own lenses. Barry and Lori make it very easy to understand how to use the LAM tools effectively and remind us of the key role of the Holy Spirit. I now am emotionally connected with my wife instead of with pornography, and we are able to fight the good fight together, thanks to LAM. Thanks, LAM, and Lori and Barry, for sharing truth and nothing hidden! We love you all so much, and LAM really did make a significant change in our marriage, and Wade loves to share it.

Thomas and Barbara

My wife, Barbara, and I have been married for seven years and have one daughter. People thought of us as the happy Christian family. But in reality, Barbara was overwhelmed with being a mom and pursuing a career. Due to her anger issue, she wasn't a safe place for me to talk about my inner pain and struggles with sexual purity. The 18-week LAM course created an environment to finally open up our hearts to each other. One evening, I confessed to her that I was unfaithful for the last two years. To my surprise, she didn't freak out or run away but was so committed to forgive and still love me. We both felt God's supernatural peace in our home for the next few days—hope surpassed our sadness. The reconciliation tool and couples' coaching helped us work through our broken past and receive restoration. After years of hiding from my wife, I felt emotionally connected again because there were no walls or secrets between us anymore. I always doubted her love since she didn't know the real me—this changed completely, and I could finally receive her true love. We were ready for new beginnings!

Mark and Marla

We were teenage sweethearts, running from abusive childhoods, when we found each other. We were 18 and 19 when Marla became pregnant with our first child. We married in 1969, and began many struggling years with counseling giving us just brief signs of improvement. Hope had faded and divorce seemed like the best option. When we separated, I was involved with another woman. Two months after leaving my family, I was involved in a deadly head-on collision that left me emotionally and physically broken. During our separation, my wife ran to God for healing in her life. Seeing changes in her, God began showing me that I needed to return home. Two years ago, we attended a five-day LAM workshop that brought major breakthrough. God has completely transformed our lives as we began to review lessons daily and apply the tools diligently. After several months of amazing change, we knew we wanted to bring LAM to our church. We have now facilitated two LAM I workshops this year and are overseeing another couple that is facilitating LAM II. We know God has placed LAM in our hearts as a ministry, and we believe it is our calling and destiny in the Body of Christ!

Peter and Karen

While we have a very strong foundation in our marriage, one area that was a tremendous struggle for us was my fear of leadership and godly confrontation. We prayed together for God's breakthrough and the opportunity opened up for a LAM couples' coaching.

Through the Holy Spirit, the root of the fear was identified from when I was a young boy. In my parents' innocence they made me take a girl's part in a play. I was forced to wear a dress on the day, and while the whole crowd laughed at me, I was forced to continue with the play. As we prayed, we realized this had shut me down from standing up for justice and my manhood; and throughout my childhood, my dad's loving yet dominant personality meant I became very fearful of all confrontation.

The breakthrough was significant; and though I used to shrink in fear with even small decisions or confrontations, I now lead confidently. In all areas, from making financial decisions to confronting Karen lovingly, and even in our sex life, I am now secure in my manhood and we are both flourishing in the freedom this has brought us into. Thank You, God!

Eric and Evelyn

LAM week in Switzerland was just fantastic. My wife and I didn't have any big problems in our marriage. There was only one point, and we really wanted to get rid of that. I didn't recognize my son as my son, and we always were quarrelling with each other. It even came to a point where I didn't really want him anymore.

We heard about the couples' coaching, and when we saw how that was going on with the people up front, I thought, *Oh no, I don't want to be vulnerable like that.* But deep inside I knew we had to do it.

We were the last couple to do the couples' coaching. The Holy Spirit really opened the door that evening and He carried the whole thing through. At the end, my problem that I had about my son was solved. My wife said she never saw me crying and sobbing like that evening. The greatest thing about that coaching was that the Byrnes hardly had to say anything because every step was shown to me in the Spirit. I even had the glimpse of Jesus who came and reconciled my son and me. Since that evening, my relationship with my son has become deeper and closer. I even had the chance to have a good reconciliation with him. He is 10 years old, but he understood me very well. Thanks to the Holy Spirit.

Since that week, we are always recommending all the couples we know to go and participate at such a LAM conference. It changes life.

The Holy Spirit has become our closest friend and coach. In all our decisions, we ask Him, What would You do? That's what we learned in that week.

Great thanks to Lori and Barry for the work they are doing. This book will be a great blessing to a lot of people all over the world.

Michael and Deborah

Though we are missionary pastors, we battled each other for years. We attended seminars and counseling. They were all good, but we didn't get a breakthrough. We wanted a miracle marriage; we didn't want to settle for less.

The LAM classes guided us through our private life in an honoring way. We received love and support. By using the *1-2-3 Skidoo* and doing all the homework, we got breakthrough. Now we don't blame each other or suffer in silence. I received complete freedom from bad mental images from sexual abuse for the first time in 35 years. I am truly free! We are able to resolve issues and feel loved by each other. And our communication and intimacy are growing. God is in our marriage! Wow! What a change. Thank you, Barry and Lori.

Dave and Hope

We laid before Barry and Lori our impasse. Within a minute they identified the spirit of accusation. We nailed it to the cross, broke all agreements with it and sent it away from us. Our relief was immediate. For the first time in years there was an easy, light feeling between us. That was just the beginning of the breakthroughs for us and for other couples. God didn't bring us back to the state of love we were in when we were first married. It went way beyond that. This is a completely new work—the foundation we've never had.

Barry and Lori identified a spirit of accusation at the root of our significant, marriage-long struggle. We took authority, nailed it to the cross, broke all agreements and sent it away. The spiritual relief was immediate and foundational. This was the beginning of many breakthroughs for us, and in turn we are helping other couples overcome. The victory is won as we stay diligent to keep our spiritual ears open and to take captive the thoughts coming against our marriage. God continues to bring us to new heights where affirmation is now our standard of success.

A Grateful Couple

We've been so impacted by Barry and Lori's Love After Marriage ministry. If our marriage can be saved, ANYONE'S can! In a nutshell, we've been married almost six years, have two kids, and until we started LAM three months ago, we've been hanging on by a thread to our rocky marriage and had zero breakthrough until now. Led by the Holy Spirit, Barry and Lori found the root to all my husband's anger, shame, pornography, anxiety and desire to divorce. They led him through a memory that he'd kept private his whole life of being raped by a man at the age of six. Then Jesus came and took the shame. Doing this in front of all the other couples in LAM was so powerful, because when my husband confessed all these things publicly, he thought he would feel nothing but shame and embarrassment; instead he felt acceptance and received a standing ovation.

The next morning, my husband woke up a completely different man. The spirit of shame was gone. We can see now that when a fight starts brewing it is an actual spirit, not who we really are. And we are looking forward to a lifetime of marital bliss.

Chad and Angie

From the very start, Chad and I made a conscious choice to really pour ourselves into LAM. As we did our homework every night, we began very quickly to see fruit. We learned that on the spiritual battlefield we were on the same team. As we fought the lies and pain that had snuck into our marriage, we experienced freedom in ways we never thought we would. God was showing us what His idea of marriage looked like.

Chad, although experiencing these things with me, had not broken through a silence that had always held him back from living in all God had for him. After being silent for so long, it was hard for him to recognize it.

During the teaching on "Honoring God Through Godly Assertion," something changed dramatically. Chad began to choose faith and courage to overcome the silence, and the miraculous happened. My husband came alive right before my eyes. He began to share feelings and ideas and hopes and dreams. There were times that it was hard and awkward for him (we kept the *Feeling Words* sheet on the fridge for a year!). But he pressed through and persevered . . . and the silence left!

Now my husband has the freedom to love unashamedly, share courageously, teach fearlessly and speak confidently. When I don't have words for a couple or know how to help, he is right there with his gentle boldness and anointing. We have really become a team. Chad persevered to get to this place. I am so overwhelmed that I can experience the Chad I always knew was there, the Chad I longed to see set free.

Erik and Jen

At LAM, we experienced the Holy Spirit in a way we never had before—together.

Before LAM, we felt alone when it came to the deepest hurts and challenges in our marriage. We thought surely few Christian couples experienced challenges like we did, and we didn't know where to go for help. We were committed followers of Jesus, but it was like sex seemed to be a topic only the world really dealt with—as if God couldn't be the CREATOR and the HEALER of our sexuality. At LAM, we experienced something far beyond a typical conference—we encountered the Holy Spirit in the area of our marriage and sexuality in an atmosphere supernaturally charged with grace, safety, loving relationships and healing power.

It was like heaven invading our marriage.

That week, God began to heal Jen and me from wounds in our hearts and in our marriage. God gently revealed significant areas of abuse Jen had experienced as a little girl, which she had never remembered before. He gently and powerfully brought love and healing to these places. God revealed and transformed areas where I'd sinfully substituted fascination with my work for fascination with my wife. My strength and power as a husband were charged.

As Jen and I became more intimate in spirit and body, the power of the Holy Spirit began flowing through us *together*. Something started in our marriage during LAM that permeated every area of our lives . . . and continues to this day.

Phil and Ginny

Phil and I have been married for 17 years. This is a second marriage for me, and a first for him. I knew in my heart and soul that I wanted to do it right this time. God gave me a clear picture of what marriage and love under His covering were supposed to look like, and I expected to live that. Phil and I had what I would classify as a great relationship and a pretty darn good marriage. In my heart, I knew there was "more" that God wanted for us to have together . . . to be experiencing and to be living. In May 2009, we attended the first weeklong Love After Marriage Conference with Barry and Lori. What we experienced during this week was life-changing, to say the least! Barry and Lori set a stage for vulnerability and truth with God in ways we had never experienced. With our small group designed by the Holy Spirit, we were able to work through the lessons and achieve breakthrough in every area of our marriage—even ones we didn't know needed it. The simple tools learned in LAM have become a way of life for us. We are living life and our marriage at a whole new level.

Anthony and Jenney

When we started LAM, we went into the workshop hoping to get some tools for our marriage. We never expected to get something for our kids as well.

Our son Noah was seven when LAM started. He had been throwing massive screaming fits since he was a toddler. These were not everyday tantrums. These were screaming rages. Sometimes it would go on for over an hour. It was terrible for us, for Noah and for his three younger brothers. Over the years, we tried parenting classes, reading books, praying for Noah, worship music, rewards and consequences, but nothing changed.

During the workshop, we decided to try to meet with Lori. We met with her for about 45 minutes, spending most of the time breaking off generational strongholds, which is a tool in one of the LAM workshop lessons. It was a simple prayer breaking off lies such as manipulation, control, anger and other things. Since that meeting where Noah *wasn't even present*, he has not had one screaming fit. *Not one!* After years of screaming, in 45 minutes it was *gone!* When we choose to go after God's highest for our marriage relationship, not only does it affect our marriage, but it also affects the whole family!

Mario and Marit

Love After Marriage gave us understanding, healing and tools for our marriage of 13 years. Before LAM, we wanted to connect, but we did not know how. And we had problems to work through conflict. Our communication was poor. Instead, we had constant patterns of reacting toward each other, using blame and accusation. This led to disconnection, self-protection and being closed up, because often we hurt each other.

I withdrew, manipulated and grew cold in my emotions toward my husband. I often stayed offended for hours and even longer. Through a revelation of the love of my heavenly Father—He healed my heart from loneliness, rejection and father wounds in this workshop. He gave me deep acceptance, affirmation, love and freedom in my life. I received personal ministry during the couples' coaching and God's presence was so powerful.

A key moment for me as a husband was when we were up for couples' coaching. I had a very strong anger issue. When I had to wait for my wife, I was so angry and punished her for making me wait. Then, in that couples' coaching, the Holy Spirit was invited to show me what the root of that anger was. He gave me a picture of when I was a lonely four-year-old boy and my parents were not there—they left me alone. Suddenly, big pain came up and a big scream came out, and I cried a lot. But later on, that turned into laughter. God ministered to me in the deepest places of my heart. He healed the deep wounds and loneliness, which I felt as a boy. He took away those trigger points my wife was pressing. I am so very thankful that I can now be patient and not react out of hurt anymore. I am now able to decide to react in a godly way to my wife. Now, after she has changed so much as well, I know and feel that she is a safe place for me. I can just be myself before her.

We are able to communicate deeply and can be vulnerable with each other. We learned to work through disagreements and stay connected. The workshop empowered us to make the right decisions and true reconciliation enabled us to get to know the deepest places of each other's heart.

Jordan and Sarah

My husband and I recently attended a five-day Love After Marriage workshop. On day four, Barry and Lori gave our class the 4-2 sex challenge for seven days (unless the Holy Spirit gave a different number). I heard nothing, and my husband heard 40 days. My first response was, "Are you serious?" I thought he was taking advantage of the assignment! He said he felt the Holy Spirit was saying it would be a fast from separation.

That evening, we went home feeling discouraged and annoyed with each other, but Jordan took the lead in suggesting we ask the Holy Spirit if there was anything we needed to reconcile. There were of course some hurts that still needed to be healed before I could be physical. We got our workbooks out, went through the *Steps to Reconciliation*, asked the Holy Spirit to reveal anything spiritual coming against our marriage and then got rid of it using the *1-2-3 Skidoo* tool. It was amazing to finally feel emotionally connected!

We prayed before making love, inviting the Holy Spirit, and we definitely felt His presence. He even woke us up individually the next morning, suggesting we do it again! When I shared with Jordan that I had been secretly on a seven-month fast for breakthrough in our marriage, we discovered that mine would end the same time as our sex challenge "fast." We knew there was something significant about the correlation—the number 7 represents completion, and we felt like we would come into a new measure of authority and power in our marriage after the 40 days.

We found that once we got back to a very busy routine with work and kids, it was incredibly hard to come together every day sexually. We took a trip to visit Jordan's parents 10 days into our fast and ended up having a big fight and not making love. Again, Jordan took the lead in using the tools we had learned, and we talked things out. We also remembered that we had made love twice in one day at the start of the fast, so we continued on without feeling bad about missing a day. It has been fantastic—every argument we have had since then we have been able to resolve within five minutes. No raised voices—we are able to communicate and it is done. We don't feel like arguing, but talking through and recognizing when things are coming against us. You cannot trust feelings, so you have to look at what is true and bypass the feelings.

Around day 20, Jordan had become so sensitive to any emotional disconnect that he literally couldn't perform sexually until we reconciled something or had spent enough time connecting—not just emotionally, but spiritually too. As I was giving the Holy Spirit permission to change me sexually, I realized that I had really slacked off in pursuing my husband and making him feel wanted and desired. During this time, the Holy Spirit uncovered some hurts from before we were even married that were being acted out in our sexual relationship, which led to more reconciliation. As we continued to pray and invite the Holy Spirit to be with us every time, He was giving us new creativity and passion in the bedroom, even giving us energy when we were exhausted from the day.

Another interesting side effect was that when we'd pray together or worship together we'd sometimes get aroused and want to be together sexually. When our spiritual and emotional connection is good, then our physical connection is good. We've also become pretty bold about sharing this testimony and truths about healthy, godly sexuality with friends, co-workers and even strangers. We've discovered that people are so hungry to hear what God really thinks about sex! The Lord has been rebuilding our foundation and we are feeling stronger than ever. We've had numerous people comment on how different we are and even the positive effect on our kids! We're really excited (and expecting) to see more fruit and continued breakthrough because of this fast.

APPENDIX 3

THE LOVE AFTER MARRIAGE TOOLS

For easy access, we have compiled all of the tools taught throughout this book into one place. If you have an iPhone, you can download all of our LAM Tools as an app. Search for: Love After Marriage Tools.

Rules for Sharing as a Couple

1. When your spouse is talking, really listen.
2. When your spouse is sharing, questions need to be limited to:
   a. Clarification: "I didn't understand that. Could you repeat that?"
   —or—
   b. More information: "Could you explain why? How did you feel when that happened?"
3. When asked to give feedback:
   a. Always start with what you can affirm and agree with; then share other questions or opposing thoughts.
   b. In all your responses, think about how to build up your spouse and encourage him/her toward what God has for him or her.
4. Respect the vulnerability and the trust given to you by the open and honest sharing of your spouse. Do not share that information with other people inappropriately and do not use the information to hurt him or her.

Listening Exercise

The purpose of this exercise is simply to connect with each other by understanding your spouse's words and feelings. When responding to your spouse, try to use individual feeling words as much as possible rather than long, wordy explanations. No fixing problems or giving advice is allowed. There is a time for problem-solving, but this is not it! A husband will go first and then repeat the exercise with his wife sharing an issue.

1. Husband: briefly describe one part of an issue, 10-20 seconds maximum—only three or four sentences. Talk about anything going on inside of you. It could be about your relationship or any other situation or issue of significance to you. (If needed, use the list of *Feeling Words* below to describe how you are feeling.)

2. Wife: listen for what your husband is *saying and feeling.*

   • After your husband talks, your job is to respond with words that let him know you understand him, what he is feeling and why this is important to him.
   • Once you have responded, ask for feedback to find out how closely you understood your husband.
   • If you did well, your husband should let you know that he felt understood by you.
   • If you did not understand him well, ask for more explanation (max 10-20 sec.) and try responding again.
   • Continue this process until your husband can say, "Yes, you understand me and know how I'm feeling."

3. Ask your husband to let you know how it felt to be listened to and understood.

When done correctly, this exercise will lay a solid foundation for self-lessly understanding one another with the capacity to deeply touch the person sharing.

Feeling Words

What follows is a short list of feeling words to help if you have difficulty putting your feelings into words:

Affection

close	loving	passionate	sexy
tender			

Anger

annoyed	bitter	enraged	frustrated
furious	hateful	indignant	
infuriated	irate	irritated	
livid	offended	ticked off	

Doubt

defeated	distrustful	dubious	helpless
hesitant	hopeless	powerless	skeptical
unsettled			

Eagerness

anxious	enthusiastic	excited

Fear

apprehensive	fearful	frightened	horrified
nervous	petrified	scared	terrified
threatened			

Fearless

bold	brave	courageous	daring
determined			

Hurt

aching	afflicted	betrayed	crushed
distressed			

Happy

amused	carefree	cheerful	delighted
ecstatic	elated	excited	exhilarated
joyful	playful		

Interested

curious	excited	fascinated	intrigued

Sad

choked up	disappointed	discouraged	heavy-hearted
low	sorrowful	unhappy	

Ideas for Going Deeper

Listed below are ideas to help you get to more personal, intimate communication as you move forward in strengthening your marriage.

1. Talk about your dreams and hopes.
2. Talk about your purpose and destiny as a couple in these last days.
3. Talk about revelations the Lord is speaking to you. *What He's speaking about you. What He's speaking to you about your spouse or your family.*
4. Talk about things you're learning.
5. Share your dreams from the night before and talk about the possible interpretation.
6. Review and discuss prophetic words you both have had.
7. Talk about your children, family and friends in a meaningful way. *Who are they? What do they need? How are they affecting you and you them? What is God doing in them? Discern how the Enemy may be coming against them and how you can help them overcome.*
8. Talk about how you are feeling—good or bad.
9. Talk about how you are doing spiritually.
10. Talk about what you appreciate about each other.
11. Pray together.

1-2-3 Skidoo

First, bless your spirit to be prominent over your soul and body as you answer these questions and follow the instructions.

1. What is coming against you spiritually?
2. How is it affecting you and what is it trying to steal from you? Remember "anger" trying to get Barry mad at Lori for throwing away *The Recycler*?
3. Take yourself through the *1-2-3 Skidoo* tool with each thing you've mentioned that has come against you.

1-2-3 Skidoo Tool

1. In the name of Jesus, I nail _____ to the cross. (The thoughts could come as a feeling [anger, depression, hopeless-

ness, rejection, self-protection, etc.]. They could also come as words or thoughts you're hearing like, "Nothing is going to change" or "This is impossible" or "Nothing really happened." Insert the feeling or thought that is coming against you. There may be more than one.)

2. I break all agreements I have made with _____, known or unknown, and I repent of joining with _____.

3. I ask You, Father, to send _____ away from me.

4. Father, what do You want to give me in place of _____? It will be critical to remember the Father's words and use them to win your spiritual battle.

Steps to Reconciliation

Respond to the following with clear, concise statements and without any explanation or justification for your behavior.

1. This is what I did wrong, or this is what I did that hurt you.

2. This is the pain that I believe I put you through because of what I did; this is what you felt because of what I did. (Ask for feedback to verify that you have accurately identified your spouse's pain.)

3. This is how I feel about putting you through that pain.

4. Express your sincere desire and your intention to change this behavior and not bring this pain into the relationship in the future.

5. Look at the other person and ask, "Can you forgive me for this pain I have brought to you, or this wrong I have done to you?"

SIDE NOTE: If you go through this exercise with empty words and do not follow through with sincere and diligent effort to change, you will only succeed in disappointing the other person again and betraying his or her trust in you.

Rules for Working Through Conflict

The following will work well when both parties are actively and willingly working toward understanding each other in a mutually respectful and honest relationship.

Begin with Prayer

Pray together and ask the Holy Spirit to empower you to keep the following attitudes as you discuss your conflict:

1. We bless our spirits to lead us and remain prominent as we:

   - Approach the discussion with the attitude "I don't have to win this argument, and I don't have to be the one who is right."
   - Make whatever is best for everyone concerned of paramount importance.
   - Present an honest accurate picture of the conflict.
   - Fully own up to our part in the conflict.
   - Follow these principles above anything that we fear or desire.
   - Humbly listen and learn from my spouse.
   - Validate any good ideas coming from my spouse.

2. The first person talks.

   - Only one person speaks at a time and the other person listens.
   - Stay focused and be concise.
   - Don't try to cover every aspect of the issue in one communication.
   - Don't try to do a "sales job" on the other person.
   - Do give reasons why you believe that your ideas or opinions would be the best choice for everyone affected by them.
   - The longer you talk, the more complicated the discussion becomes. When many issues are raised at the same time, it can become confusing and overwhelming for the other person to choose which issues to respond to.

- Also, the longer you talk without a chance to hear from the other person when in conflict, the more likely you are to hit sensitive issues and stir up the hurt, resentment and the like.

3. The second person listens:

- Try to pay more attention to what the other person is saying than to what you are going to say in rebuttal.
- Try to hear not only the words, but also the heart attitudes of the person talking.

4. The second person responds:

- The first response should be questions or statements to clarify what you heard, just to be sure you understand correctly before responding.
- The next step is to state the things you can agree with that the first person has said, and why you agree with them.
- Only after these two steps are completed is it okay to give your contrasting or opposing views and the reasons for them. When giving your opposing views, be sure to follow all of the guidelines listed in #2 above.

5. Resolution:

- Repeat the three steps until a mutual agreement is reached.
- Be patient. Give time to the process even though it may feel tense and seem tedious.
- Do not agree to decisions or conclusions that you don't really believe in just to end the conflict or to make the other person feel better or to try to prevent anger.
- Continue talking and listening respectfully until you come to the place where each can honestly say, "I can live with that" or "I think that would be the best choice for us all."
- Honor your agreements by keeping them until you make a new agreement.
- If you do this process well and still cannot come to a consensus, you may need a third-party mediator. There may be individual issues that need attention before you can resolve conflict well.

When the Poop Hits the Fan

*A godly option to deal with your disagreements
in the heat of the moment*

1. *Choose not to leave.* If you must leave to cool down or get control of your tongue, tell your spouse what you are doing and that you will be back. If it is longer than five minutes, give your spouse a time when you will come back to talk. Stay in the battle, even when you are tempted to physically leave or emotionally withdraw/shut down . . . don't do it!

2. *Stand back to back.* Ask Jesus to come as the Wonderful Counselor, and pray in English, or in tongues, for a few minutes until you feel a slight shift in your spirit or emotions.

3. *Remain standing.* Take turns nailing to the cross whatever you're feeling that is not from God. Break agreements with it and ask the Father to send it away. *Out loud.* Example:

   a. In the name of Jesus, I nail _____ (anger, frustration, separation, accusation, fear, rejection) to the cross of Jesus.

   b. I break all agreements I have made with _____, known or unknown.

   c. I ask You, Father, to send _____ away from me.

   d. Father, what do You want to give me in place of _____?

4. *Now turn and face one another, taking hands.* Discuss the issues respectfully, not joining with accusation and anger and the like.

5. *If discussion is going well, finish.* But if not, stop and declare the truth about what you are dealing with. Start with overall truths about yourself and your marriage. Then get specific. Don't rush this.

6. *If either spouse needs to ask forgiveness, do so.*

The 4-2 Plan

A great plan for maintaining emotional and sexual intimacy

Husband

Twenty minutes a day, four times a week, the husband is to initiate a time to meet and talk with his wife. Here are some questions to start with. Be sure to listen well and respond with interest and understanding.

- How was your day?
- How are you doing emotionally?
- How are you doing spiritually?
- What is one good thing that happened today?
- Was there anything difficult that happened today?
- Did you make a significant connection with anyone today?
- What ways did you think about, feel or connect with God today?
- If you could plan the perfect date for us, considering our resources and time commitments, what would it look like?

Your wife really wants to know what's inside of you, so share with her as well Here are some topics to talk with her about:

- What are some things you're really excited about in your life right now that you simply haven't shared with her?
- What are some hard things you're going through?
- Share how you see yourself doing emotionally.
- Share how you feel you are doing spiritually.
- What are some things you'd like God to do for her, for you, for your kids, for your marriage?
- Tell her something you would really like to do with her on a date.
- Tell her things about your day that you think she would enjoy hearing about.

Wife

Two times a week the wife is to pursue her husband sexually. Here are some suggestions:

- Initiate having sex.
- Make him feel wanted and desired.

- Create a romantic atmosphere with candles or lighting.
- Consider wearing something that would be visually arousing and pleasing to him.
- Plan ahead, and early in the day let him know you have something "special" for him later on that you think he will really like.
- During the day, at a time when he least expects it, touch him sexually in a way that lets him know you want to give him more.
- Be creative and think of ways to pleasure him with your body, which is your gift to him.
- Invite the Holy Spirit to be with you in your lovemaking.

Spirit Blessing for Couples

1. Before you go to sleep each night, take turns saying the following to each other: "_____, I call your spirit to come forth and be prominent over your soul and body so that you may receive all the rest and revelation the Holy Spirit brings to you through the night. 'He gives to His beloved even in his sleep' " (Ps. 127:2).

2. Every morning when you wake up, take turns saying the following to each other: "_____, I call your spirit to attention to operate in a leadership role over your soul and body. And, _____, I call your spirit into alignment with the purposes of Jesus for your life today."

Your spirit blessing will develop over time as you gain greater confidence and authority to bless your spouse. Partner with the Holy Spirit to discover what is on His heart to release over each other. We also recommend the book *Blessing Your Spirit* by Arthur Burk and Sylvia Gunter for more in-depth examples of spirit blessing.

Face-to-Face

1. Looking face to face into each other's eyes, call your spouse's spirit to attention and tell his/her soul and body to follow his or her spirit.

2. Begin speaking positive truths about what you see in him/her.

3. Go back and forth 5 to 10 times, speaking positive truths over each other.

Allow these two exercises to be a starting point for nurturing your emotional and spiritual connection. Be creative in the ways you bless each other.

LOVE AFTER MARRIAGE
WORKSHOPS

For more information about Love After Marriage workshops, visit our website at www.loveaftermarriage.org. You will find:

- General information about Love After Marriage workshops
- Information about hosting a 5-day or 3-day LAM workshop in your church or area
- A *Pastor's Packet* to describe to your pastor what the 30-week workshop would look like in your church
- Many written and video testimonies of couples who have completed a workshop
- Our calendar and itinerary

If you feel called to marriage ministry as a couple and would like to facilitate a LAM workshop in your area, we have a certification process. You are required to attend one of our 5-day or 3-day workshops and also have the approval of your pastor. The Lord is building an army of couples who will come alongside us to strengthen marriages. We would love to have you on board with us!

If you have an iPhone, you can download all of our LAM Tools as an app. Search for: Love After Marriage Tools.

Single Life Workshops

As a result of the testimonies about marriages being healed, singles have been asking to attend LAM. In response to these requests, we have developed a singles version of LAM called Single Life Workshops.

Contact us if you are interested in having our team put on a weekend Single Life Workshop in your area, or if you are interested in becoming equipped to reproduce the 12-week workshop at your church.

God wants to give singles a great start on a healthy marriage relationship before they are married.

For more information, see our website: **www.singlelifeworkshop.org**. You can also email us at: info@singlelifeworkshop.org.

Heartbreak Makes Room for God's Power

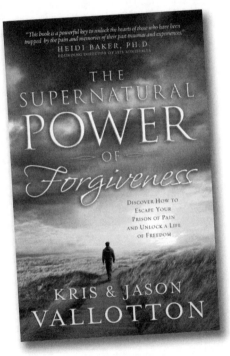

The Supernatural Power of Forgiveness

Jason Vallotton thought his world was burning down around him when he found out that his wife, Heather, was having an affair and planned to leave him. Using his own story as a poignant, evocative illustration of God's grace and healing, Jason, along with his dad, Kris Vallotton, invites you to reframe your understanding of redemption. Together, they show you how to steward the hardest times and deepest pain of your life so that God can lay a foundation for complete restoration and empowerment for your future. Although it may be hard to see emotional wounds as gifts when they still hurt so deeply, *The Supernatural Power of Forgiveness* will help you discover that God can not only heal your wounds, but He can also use the healing process to equip you for a whole, fulfilled and powerful life!